HIDDEN *Miracles*

*Dear Wanda,
   Be the miracle for someone today!
   Abigail Turner*

by
ABIGAIL
SCHRIER
TURNER

Hidden Miracles
by Abigail Schrier Turner

Copyright © 2017

All rights reserved.

Library of Congress Number: 2017913242
International Standard Book Number: 978-1-60126-547-0

Masthof Press
219 Mill Road | Morgantown, PA 19543-9516
www.Masthof.com

DEDICATION

Hidden Miracles is dedicated unequivocally to the memory of my dear brother, Andy Schrier. Andy, in life, you filled hearts with laughter and encouragement and never hesitated to point people to the God you loved and served wholeheartedly. I pray that this book creates a platform for your humor, love, wisdom, and faithfulness to continue to change lives. If, by God's grace, I achieve that, I have succeeded!

ACKNOWLEDGMENTS

I can't possibly list here all the people I need to thank. It takes a village to raise a child, and apparently, also to write a book. I could not have done this without the support, understanding, encouragement, and criticism of so many friends and family members. Thank you all!

First, to Shaun and our two amazing children, thank you for putting up with the time and emotion I've poured into this book. Your patience has made this possible.

Mom, you are the strongest, most faithful person I know. Thank you for your encouragement throughout this process—and sometimes, the kick in the pants I needed to just get it done! I'm so blessed to have walked this journey with you.

Terry, you've played an imperative role in the writing of this book, from our first meeting when I told you God was asking me to write it, to all the times I felt it was just too difficult a task. Thank you for standing beside me, praying for me, and supporting me through.

Shelly, Lynn, and Emily, thank you for offering your critiques and believing in this story when it was still such a mess!

And finally, Michael and Tom, thank you for giving me the final push to write, edit, and publish! I'm not sure it would ever have gotten finished had it not been for you!

A BRIEF EXPLANATION

Everyone faces pain to one degree or another in this life. This is my story of the most painful time of my life to date. It is a true story, at least as well as I can remember it. I'm sure my family may remember some details or conversations differently. My hope in telling this story is that those who read it can find normalcy and comfort in any pain they may be experiencing. It is also my humble attempt at tackling the problem of evil.

Hidden Miracles is unique in that, scattered throughout are the writings of my brother. His thoughtfulness touched many lives, including my own. My family and I hope that in publishing these writings of his, they will touch many more lives. Within the story, some of his writings are broken up as I interact and wrestle with his words. Some of the less pertinent information I removed for the sake of moving the story along. All of his writings we have from this time period are included in Appendix A in the back of the book. With the exception of removing some names and changing the formatting to make it uniform, I have attempted to preserve them in their original state, typos and all. His original emails also contain more of the medical updates, for those readers who appreciate a more technical description.

Enjoy!

FOREWORD

Laughter Farm

There is an indescribable emotion of exhilaration—something akin to a child waking to discover the first snowfall of the winter—which overcomes me each time I drive toward the great brick farmhouse of Laughter Farm. As an adult I instinctively want to squash that feeling. Is it because it makes my fingers and toes tingle so intensely I want to jump and shout for joy? Surely that would be too pure a display of emotion for a grown woman! Nevertheless, I am quite sure I breathe a great sigh of contentment every time my car tires crunch on the gravel at the top of the hill where the house first becomes visible. I am home.

Tall stalks of corn and tight rows of wheat stretch across the fields like a patchwork quilt. Black and white cattle dotted across the pastures create contrasting squares, and the farmhouse rises as the artful centerpiece. Its red bricks, grey stone foundation, black shutters and roof, and white front porch are the perfect counterpoint to the fresh green all around. Inevitably my memory is flooded with images of the past.

The empty land next to the two long unused silos transports me back to the early age of six. It was just after dusk on a spring evening and a storm raged outside. Daddy was picking Pete up from a friend's house on his way back from taking Dave to the doctor. Jen was still at college, working as a Residence Assistant. Katie was in her bedroom. The little ones—Andy, Tim and I—were safely nestled close to Mom in the big bed she and Daddy shared, the fluffy down comforter tucked protectively around us. Mom read out loud to us from *The Little House on the Prairie*. When her voice trailed off and her head began its tell-tale nod, one of us prodded her with an elbow and she began to read again, unaware that she was repeating what she'd already read before she'd succumbed to the world of sleep.

Suddenly, there was a loud CRACK. The house shook ominously and the room went dark. A moment later, sixteen-year-old Katie walked purposefully in. "Mom, I think the barn is on fire," she almost whispered, in an attempt not to alarm us. Always the steady one, her calm face was a contradiction to the serious nature of her statement. Mom's head was no longer bobbing with the exhaustion brought on by caring for the sheep, cows, horses, goats, and her seven children. Without a hint of panic, she quickly helped us all into the well-used ten-passenger van, counting each child several times, just to be sure. She didn't seem to lose control for a moment.

"Mom, Dad has Dave and Pete. Jen's at college. Everyone else is here, in the van," Katie encouraged Mom.

From the front circle of the driveway where we sought shelter in the giant conversion van, we could see exactly what was happening. Fire had spread from a transformer, apparently struck by lightning, to the more than 180-year-old barn, original to the 1806 farmhouse. I watched in horror as flames played peek-a-boo through shattered windows. Smoke seemed to pour out of every crevasse of the great building and its biting smell filled the air, even inside the van.

An anonymous neighbor had already called the fire department and they arrived more quickly than it seemed possible. They lost no time assessing the situation. They quickly discerned that the barn could not be saved and began to remove anything connecting the barn to the small cinder block enclosure adjacent to it in order to keep the fire contained.

Meanwhile, unbeknownst to us, Daddy had stopped at the only gas station in New Windsor before returning home. There he happened to meet Barb, a dear family friend, who was also gassing up.

"Howdy friend," he greeted her with plenty of gusto but no southwestern drawl. He thrust a husky hand towards her just as several firetrucks zoomed past, sirens blazing.

"Shall we pray for whichever of our unfortunate neighbors is in need of those trucks?" Barb agreed and bowed her head with Daddy. "Dear Lord, we ask for your hand of protection upon whoever is in danger right now. May they know your peace and comfort. We pray your mighty hand be upon the situation and bring good from it, whatever it may be. Amen."

"Amen." Barb echoed. Then they parted ways and Daddy turned his truck towards home, Dave and Pete buckled in next to him. Daddy's concern quickly turned to fear as he headed towards home. The closer he came, the clearer it became that the trucks had gone to Laughter Farm. When he reached the end of the driveway, the firemen stopped him, saying it was too dangerous to go closer. A stoic man, he had an uncharacteristically difficult time keeping his composure for the sake of his two sons who were with him.

From his vantage point, he could soon deduce that it was the barn and not the house that was ablaze. Fear for the other family members quickly subsided, but was replaced with concern for the animals trapped in the barn.

"Sir," a fireman finally approached Daddy's truck. "The fire is contained to the barn. We've told your wife it's safe to go back into the house. Why don't you go ahead and take these two home as well." The quarter mile driveway must have seemed like a hundred miles to Daddy, but he found everyone safe once he arrived. After putting Katie in charge of Dave, Andy, Tim, and me, he and Mom went back outside to see how they could help the firemen. Katie distracted us with a game and eventually got us into bed.

Outside, Daddy and Mom rushed to save the animals. Dave's goats and Pete's rabbits had been penned inside the lower level when the fire had started. Mom's sheep had been in the pasture, but sensed there was danger and crowded through the open gate and into their pens in the lower level. The stupid animals were huddled together in the inferno, in danger of being overcome by the heat of burning hay and wood all around them or crushed by the tractors which Daddy stored in the upper level.

"The floor is stable for now!" one of the firemen shouted, after what seemed to Daddy and Mom to be a very long time. "Let's form a human chain to that cinder block shed and get those sheep out." So they passed each sheep, one at a time, down the line to Daddy and Mom at the end. Then Mom placed each one safely in the shed. As the shed began to fill with frightened, bleating sheep, seventeen-year-old Pete strode in, leading Dave's goats, pleased with his reckless bravery.

"Pete, what are you doing?" Daddy was not impressed.

"I had to get the goats. I'm going back to get my rabbits," Pete answered, seemingly oblivious to the danger. Before he could follow through, however, the firemen came streaming out of the barn. "It's too dangerous. That floor is gonna go any minute. It's not worth risking human lives."

They had saved most of the sheep and Pete had gotten the goats. His rabbits were not so fortunate. Neither was Daddy's farm equipment. By morning the beautiful old barn with the decorative brick sides was demolished, no more than a smoldering heap of rubble.

The fire had been so hot we had to wait three weeks for the remains to cool down before beginning the cleanup process. In the meantime, Daddy and Mom calculated their losses. They thanked God that most of the sheep were rescued and the farm was a secondary source of income for our family—more of a hobby, really. Daddy's full-time job in medical research at the National Institutes of Health would take care of our needs for the time being. They prayed this tragedy would bring the family closer together and cause us all to depend on God for our strength and sustenance.

Slowly, the ground was cleared and we found new homes for the displaced animals. Two new barns were erected, built mostly of metal rather than wood and brick. They lacked the aesthetic appeal of the former barn, but they were functional and they would not burn. As the land recovered from the dark scars of the fire, we drew together to overcome its horrors. We all worked together, shoulder to shoulder to clean up the mess. It was exponentially more difficult to overcome the nightmares that lingered after the horrific event. Daddy's gas station prayer became our mantra in the next months. "May we know your peace and comfort. We pray your mighty hand be upon the situation and bring good from it." God alone knew how important this strengthened bond would be in the coming years and how fervently we would pray the same words over a very different situation.

Chapter 1

"IT'S SO HARD TO TELL people my dad has cancer," Katie confided in Mom and me. It was summer, thirteen years after the barn fire. The three of us sat quietly at the dining room table in a vacation home in the Outer Banks, sipping iced tea and lemonade. It was late in the evening and Katie's two young children were in bed. The crashing of the waves could be heard in the distance, a peaceful rhythm which seemed inappropriate given the current conversation.

"It just doesn't seem real. How can a man who has worked so hard to find a cure, get sick with the same disease he's been fighting for years?" Katie's words so accurately summarized how we all felt. Daddy had moved the family to Ohio a couple of years after the fire to take a job in a laboratory owned by his college friend. Later, he and two other colleagues had opened a lab of their own. He had worked on other projects as well, but his passions were rooted in cancer research. He'd spent countless hours perfecting delivery methods of various drugs and had written professional journal articles in an attempt to recruit the help of other medical researchers.

"Well, at least this type of cancer is quite treatable," I chimed in. I'd done some research on the internet, which was a rather new thing at the time. "His prognosis is really good. A really high percentage of people with bladder cancer recover completely with no recurrence of the disease."

"What will his treatment involve?" Katie asked Mom. I had heard Mom tell so many people, it had practically become a commonplace conversation.

"Well, he'll have six outpatient treatments over the next two months. The treatments are called BCG and basically they inject a live shot of the tuberculosis virus into the bladder wall. That makes the bladder shed its lining, getting rid of the cancer. They just have to make sure he doesn't have any kind of infection in the bladder first or it won't work and could make him really sick."

I went to bed that night thinking Daddy invincible. The same waves that seemed to mock me before lulled me into a deep, calm sleep. Afterall, Grandpa had been diagnosed with cancer a couple of years ago, and the worst it had done to him was make him sleep a lot.

UPON RETURNING HOME from vacation, I busied myself with getting ready to leave for my first year of college. Classes started in just a week and a half and I was so excited. I made lists of what I needed and what I still had left to do, checking off each item meticulously as I completed it. The process helped to keep my mind occupied. When the day arrived, Daddy, Mom and I loaded up Grandma and Grandpa's minivan and drove six hours to my new home. After setting up my room, securing my books, and attending the candlelight service designed for parents to say goodbye to their kids, we lingered in a grassy area outside the campus center building. I was anxious to say goodbye, and particularly to skip the uncomfortable talk of Daddy's upcoming treatments.

"Well, I've got to go meet my Peer Group!" I announced, hugging them tenderly, but much too quickly, and then rushed off to find my assigned location. I knew I'd likely hurt their feelings, but I couldn't bear to face the reality that, under the circumstances, dropping off their youngest child was an unusually painful experience.

Once alone, there was too much to do to worry about anything except what was right in front of me. There were new friends to be made, classes to find, auditions to nail, and quite a rigorous schedule to keep. I loved every minute of it. The scholar in me loved my classes, the musician thrived in all the rehearsals and lessons, and the socialite reveled in the hundreds of new people to meet. I made a point to call home every Sunday afternoon, but for the most part, kept conversations focused on me—my classes, my friends, my extra-curricular activities. I rationalized that this would serve as a welcome distraction from the trials Mom and Daddy were facing.

When I came home for Thanksgiving break, my positive outlook was tested. I was only home for a few days, but the time which would normally be dedicated solely to family was riddled with calls to one doctor or another. Had I already been told some of the details? Did Mom wait until I was home to tell me, or did I pick up on what was said in those phone conversations? I don't really remember. Mom and Daddy were angry though.

"I sustained five out of six treatments," I heard Daddy explain to one doctor or another on the other end of the line. "Yes, the nurse took the culture each time. They did not look clean to me, but she insisted it was fine and proceeded with the treatments. When Dr. K. returned, he was furious. He agreed with me that I'd had an infection all along."

He went on in doctor speak to explain that, instead of the bladder shedding its cancerous lining as intended, it festered. He was given antibiotics and told he would have to wait until after Christmas for the bladder to calm down to resume the treatments. In the meantime, the evil cells were given a horrible gift—time.

"Yes, I'll need to schedule a CT scan of the bladder and surrounding area as soon after Christmas as possible . . . Yes, I'll be researching whether or not this qualifies as medical malpractice. It certainly is not how I would have expected the hospital where I completed my residency to conduct business." I was shocked to hear Daddy speak this way. He believed in turning the other cheek and did not approve of lawsuits. Was he beginning to fear that this mistake would cost him more than just some wasted time and money?

At first I was angry too, but I lay in bed each night and prayed harder, more certain than ever that God was going to heal Daddy. *God, I know you can heal him. You are more powerful than medicine. You can use this to show your power. Maybe you even allowed this mistake so only you could get the credit for healing him.*

There were three more weeks of classes between Thanksgiving break and Christmas break. When I returned to school, I immediately immersed myself in my end-of-semester projects and studying for finals. The thought that God would choose not to heal my father did not even cross my mind. It was what a good, loving, God would do for a man who'd taught his family to be faithful to Him, largely by his own example.

Christmas break arrived quickly and my family engaged in the usual activities. There was an aura of gloom, however, particularly coming from Mom and Daddy. No one said anything about it, but powered through the holiday as though nothing was amiss. When everyone departed for their own homes and lives, it was just Tim and I left in the awkward silence. Even he retreated to work and school most days and I had to muddle through on my own.

After a few days of this, each of which seemed an eternity, it came time for Daddy's CT scan. He and Mom left for the hospital early that morning and returned late in the afternoon, their slouched shoulders, hanging heads, and quiet demeanor clearly communicating how it had gone.

"The tests showed an angry area on the bladder wall that wasn't there before," Mom summarized as she met my questioning expression. "He'll have to have it biopsied in January." Suddenly, I felt my false blanket of invincibility begin to fray a bit at the edges. *Does God really care about us enough to intervene like I've been assuming he would?* I had never questioned God's good intentions for me or my family before, but the thoughts came unbidden and I struggled to shake them off. *Is He really even capable of healing Daddy?* Try as I might, I could not rationalize away these doubts, so I tucked them quickly into a back corner of my mind. *God is in control. He works all things for our good. That must mean He is still going to take care of this.* These thoughts seemed like nothing more than clichés at the moment, but they were all I had to cling to.

Once again, I looked to school as a very welcome distraction. I had to return to school for January term—which everyone called J-term—a three-week period during which most students enrolled in an intensive course or two. I took a math class that didn't do much more for me other than fill an academic requirement. As I sat down in the sterile classroom on the first day, a tall, athletic-looking young man confidently took the open seat next to me.

"I'm Darrell," he extended a hand in greeting and smiled an *I think you're really cute* smile.

"Abby," I replied, firmly returning the handshake and the smile before asking the expected, "what year are you?" He informed me he was also a first-year student and we plunged into conversation until the professor started the class. At the end of class, Darrell turned to address me again, "Are you getting lunch at the dining hall?"

I was in fact planning to eat at the dining hall and didn't have plans to meet anyone. "I'm meeting some of my friends there if you'd like to join us." I admired Darrell's confidence and charm, so I gladly accepted the company. After a short walk through the cold to the dining hall, Darrell introduced me to his friends. We all plunged into boisterous conversation, my worries for Daddy and doubts in the God I'd blindly trusted seeming immeasurably far off.

"We're all going to play some board games tonight if you want to come," Darrell suggested, after his friends started dispersing one at a time. "I could walk you over since we live in the same dorm."

"Okay," I agreed, hoping I didn't seem too eager.

"I'll meet you in the first floor lounge at 7:45."

7:45 came and there was no Darrell. Butterflies were causing an awful lot of fluttering in my stomach and the longer I waited, the worse they got. Finally, at 7:55, he came bouncing down the stairs, seemingly oblivious to the fact that he was ten minutes later than he'd promised. *Should I tease him about it? It's kinda rude to be late on a first date. Is this a date?* I decided to pretend nothing had happened.

A group of ten or so had gathered by the time Darrell and I arrived. They welcomed me as though I'd been a part of their group for the entire year. After a few rousing games of Phase 10, I had forgotten all about Darrell's tardiness.

"Want to take a walk?" Darrell asked me, making no attempt to hide his interest in me. I happily accepted. It was past 10:00, and the temperature was in the single digits. I barely noticed. What seemed like just a few minutes quickly turned into a couple of hours. As we walked, talked, and laughed, our gloved hands found each other and held fast.

This became a typical day for me that January. I went to math class and sat next to Darrell. Then we met his friends for lunch at the dining hall, went our separate ways to do homework, then met again for dinner, played games with his friends, and braved the cold dark evenings to get to know each other better. I could not get enough of him. We talked only vaguely of Daddy's illness. He must have sensed that I didn't want to discuss it.

One night in late January, Darrell and I were walking through the dimly-lit campus as had become our habit. It was very cold—the kind of cold that made your nose hairs freeze together—and Darrell had taken my gloved hand and put it in his coat pocket in order to hold it and keep it warm at the same time. We began to walk across the covered bridge and stopped halfway to look out over the frozen water. We had been chatting comfortably, but grew quiet as the beauty of the evening enveloped us. Wanting a closer look at the water, and being vertically challenged, I stepped up onto the ledge which helped support the wall in front of it. Even with the extra six inches the ledge offered, Darrell was still a head taller than me. I turned to face him and he leaned closer to me, his hands gripping the rail on either side of me. Several times he turned to look at me and I could tell what he was thinking, but he didn't make a move. Finally, he spoke, his words cutting into the silence and blowing mist into the air.

"I really want to kiss you," he admitted. "But I don't want to upset you." *What unromantic idiot says something like that?* I wondered, just before I decided to show him I wanted the same thing.

Just a few days after that first kiss, I carpooled home with some other students from Ohio. We had a short break before the spring semester began. The elation of having a new boyfriend kept me positive during the six-hour drive. At home, however, my mood quickly became quite grim. Mom had told me Daddy's biopsy had not gone well. The cancer had spread to other areas of the bladder and even into the lymph nodes surrounding it. She had told me he would be having surgery to have his bladder and the lymph nodes removed the day after I returned to school. I'd chosen to push this information deep into the recesses of my brain and focus on Darrell instead. For that reason, I was completely unprepared for the depression my parents had both begun to exhibit. Daddy didn't smile, although I could tell he was putting on a brave face for my benefit. He had also begun to lose unnecessary weight. Mom looked tired and anxious.

"I have a boyfriend," I told her, once I found a quiet moment with her.

"Oh? What's he like?" Her tone remained sullen.

"He's a lot of fun. His name is Darrell. And his friends are great." Still, her facial expression was morose.

"Does he have a good relationship with God?" she asked, the expected question rolling robotically off her tongue with none of the usual teasing tone.

"Uh, yeah. He actually challenges me to pray more. We've spent a lot of time praying together and talk about God all the time. He loves music too and he's got a great voice." She had no more energy to ask questions. I escaped to my room.

The visit was over all too quickly. Daddy and Mom both dropped me off at the restaurant where the carpool was meeting to head back to school. I managed to keep my composure long enough to hug my parents goodbye. I was suddenly regretting the rushed hugs I'd offered so selfishly at the start of school. Ashamed and depressed, I curled myself into a tight ball in the back seat of a fellow student's car. There were two others riding with us and I did my very best to shrink myself into unnoticeable nothingness. As I watched Daddy and Mom fade into the distance, I could no longer stop the flood. The tears began to drip, then stream down my cheeks and I hunched in my corner of the car. Struggling to control the sobs that now soundlessly shook my body, I leaned my cheek against the window, letting the winter cold cool my hot face. All I wanted was to be alone, but for the next six hours I was to be confined to this tiny space with three too many people.

Of course it took no time at all for them to notice. My friend Roscoe was sharing the backseat with me and he was too nice not to ask. We had been high school friends and the only two from our graduating class who went to our college. We had remained friends, but rarely saw each other, so I hadn't told him what was going on. He must have been confused to see me this way. So the dreaded question was uttered.

"Abby? What's wrong?" I was no longer able to hide.

"Daddy has cancer and the stupid doctors messed up," I blurted out. Stupid did not seem a strong enough word, but I was uncomfortable swearing. I'd been taught that swearing showed a lack of creativity and a limited vocabulary, but words like "the damn doctors" felt like a more accurate reflection of my level of despair. "None of his treatments have worked because they missed an infection so he has to have surgery to remove his bladder and the lymph nodes surrounding it tomorrow." The emotions took over and I could no longer speak past the lump in my throat.

I don't remember much of the rest of the car ride. I think they prayed for me and for Daddy's surgery. I know I was angry with Roscoe for asking, but quickly forgave him when he held me close and let me use his shoulder as a headrest. It must have been pretty quiet for the rest of the time. After all, who has words in the face of such pain?

Cancer in the lymph system. Ignorant, even negligent doctors. With his medical background, Daddy must have known how grim a picture this painted for him. Yet he kept fighting. Oh the pain he must have endured! Not just physical but emotional and spiritual as well. I could no longer hide between rigorous academics and petty relationships. Cancer was too real and too evil to ignore.

Chapter 2

SCHOOL WAS THE LAST PLACE I wanted to be. But I didn't have much of an option. Darrell was glad to see me and that elevated my mood a bit. I continued to do what I needed to in order to stay busy, but I was more careful to stay in touch with my parents this time, no longer able to avoid the difficult topic of cancer. Daddy's surgery went as well as could be expected. They removed his bladder and several lymph nodes successfully. Because of the prognosis of cancer going untreated in the lymph system, they recommended that he begin chemotherapy in March. Perhaps God would still be gracious and heal him in some miraculous way. This was the hope which made it possible for me to return to my usual, bubbly, bouncy little self.

The next several months were not encouraging, however. Each chemo treatment made Daddy increasingly ill. He experienced back and abdominal pain which were severe enough to cause him to miss work. That was saying something, because I only recall Daddy having missed work once in my lifetime. With each phone call home, I became more discouraged. Yet, hope kept my faith alive—a flickering candle where there once had been a blazing torch. Darrell helped to fan the flame. We went to church and chapel together, and every Wednesday night went to a student-run praise and worship session. These treasured worship times and Darrell's unwavering, childlike faith kept me going.

One weekend in early spring, we planned to visit Darrell's parents. We were eating dinner in a campus restaurant before leaving when his mother called his cell phone. He often went out of earshot to speak to her, but this time as there was nowhere for him to find privacy, I couldn't help but overhear his end.

"Yes, Mom, my paper is done. I just need to edit it . . . I will email it to you before we leave . . . Yeah, we can look at it together tomorrow . . . Yes, I know I have a test next week. I have plenty of time to study for it . . . I've already started studying, but I have until Thursday." The conversation went on like this for several minutes, causing Darrell to become quite agitated.

"What's up?" I asked, awkwardly, when he finally hung up.

"She doesn't want us to come. She's worried I won't have time to get my work done."

"Is it me? Are they not ready to meet me?" He assured me it was just his mother being overly concerned about his academics and had nothing to do with me. He called her back after giving her a few minutes to calm down and somehow convinced her it would be ok. Before she could change her mind, we were on our way. I liked Darrell, but when he called his mom twice on the two-hour drive to his house—once to tell her we were leaving and again to tell her we had safely gotten on the turnpike—I became somewhat alarmed. This couldn't be healthy!

We arrived in his hometown in time to visit his mom's school where she was a music teacher. She seemed perfectly normal. Then he showed me his home and introduced me to his two dogs and his dad. After dinner, Darrell and I went to a movie and then took a walk at a park which Darrell frequented. It was sometime around 11:00 when we got back to his house, so I fully expected his parents to be getting ready for bed after ensuring our safe arrival home. Not only was his mom up, she was furious he hadn't called her when the movie was over to let her know where we were going and when we'd be home. If this wasn't alarming enough, she continued to berate him long into the night. I was forgotten, so I sat awkwardly on the recliner in the living room with Darrell's dog on my lap. Several times I nodded off, only to be awakened by the harsh verbal lashing of Darrell's mother.

Finally, Darrell gave in to his mother, giving up on defending himself and I was shown to my bed. The following day was just as bizarre. Darrell had to review a paper with his mom before he could do anything else. She would not let him go until it reached her level of perfection. I don't remember most of the rest of the weekend, but I was so relieved when church was over and Darrell and I went back to school.

For a few days, I avoided Darrell. He was under pressure from his mom to study for a test later in the week, so he didn't notice. Over the next couple of weeks, whenever I brought up the topic, he fluctuated between apologizing for his mother's behavior and defending it. He frequently promised it would get better, but it never did. He had to call her if he left campus and again when he got back. He had to keep her abreast of all of his academics. She scoured his syllabi, edited his papers, helped him study for tests, and shamed him if he protested. Apart from all of this, Darrell was handsome, fun, and spiritually supportive, so I put up with it, hoping it really would change.

Soon the semester ended and I was glad to be going home. I felt maybe I needed some space from Darrell to figure out the strange mother/son relationship. More than that, I was anxious to be with Mom and Daddy. The doctor had discontinued the chemotherapy, even though he had only completed three of the four prescribed sessions. It was causing such a decrease in Daddy's quality of life, they decided to take the risk that it had done the trick. In my mind, even though there wasn't anything I could actually do to help, just being home offered a sense of normalcy for all of us. I immediately went back to work at the local ice cream shop where I had spent my last couple of years of high school, taking on as many hours as they would give me.

Towards the middle of the summer, Darrell came to visit for a few days, and except for the fact that he wasn't allowed to drive and had to take the train, he was relatively free from his mother's grip. Together we went to visit my grandparents and spent the night with them. They didn't say much about him afterwards. Mom was pretty quiet about him too, except to laugh and agree with Daddy and my brother, Tim, when they said he was obnoxious.

"He doesn't ever shut up!" Daddy said, in a rare moment of criticism. Apparently Darrell had blathered on about something completely uninteresting instead of helping while Daddy was working on the pool. This had made it difficult for Daddy to concentrate on the job at hand. There wasn't much worse of a sin Darrell could have committed against him. Tim really couldn't see what I liked about him either. He thought he was lacking some intelligence, which was perhaps true. I had had a fun time with him though, and he seemed oblivious to my family's misgivings.

In any case, he returned home and I didn't see him again for the rest of the summer. I missed him and thought that was a good sign we should continue our relationship. When the fall semester began, we picked up where we had left off. I wasn't sure where things were headed with him, but I knew I needed him to keep me grounded.

LIFE WAS STATUS QUO for a couple of months. Daddy had some continuing pain, but he was able to go to work and engage in his normal activities, which was an improvement from last spring. Darrell and I were doing well as long as we steered clear of the topic of his mother. His spiritual strength was his biggest asset and it was one of the few things keeping me from bursting into a million pieces. School had become an enjoyable diversion for me. I had a lot of friends. I had asked for prayer for Daddy's healing in my small vocal ensemble, College Singers, and in Concert Choir. Students and professors alike were very supportive and I continued to clutch anxiously to the belief that Daddy would grow to be a very old man.

OCTOBER MARKED MOM'S 60th birthday, and my sisters and I decided to kidnap her and take her on a mini vacation. Without knowing why, she drove Grandma and Grandpa's minivan to Jennifer's house and then Jennifer and I drove her to Charlottesville, Virginia, where we met up with Katie. When we arrived in the late afternoon, we did some shopping and touring in the historic area of town, then took Mom out for a nice dinner before settling into our two rooms at a local bed and breakfast. Not quite ready to head to bed for the evening, we gathered in one of the bedrooms to chat for a bit. After lots of silly, girlish banter, Mom began to grow tired and looked to wrap up our conversation.

"How can we pray for each other, girls?" she asked us. Katie and Jennifer each shared a request and then it was my turn.

"Well, let's see. I need to figure out what to do about Darrell," I said, after a thoughtful moment. "His mom is very controlling and manipulative. He has to call her anytime he leaves campus and again when he comes back. He says it's because his cousin was killed in a car accident and she just has to know he's okay, but it's weird." It didn't seem like such a big deal when I said it out loud, so I kept talking in an attempt to justify my need for alarm. "He has to email her all of his syllabi and every assignment so she can check it for him and make sure he's getting all of his work done. She edits every paper. And if he ever has an argument with her, he's not allowed to go to bed until they resolve it. She uses the verse that says 'Don't let the sun go down on your anger' to justify it. Sometimes they are up arguing until 2:00 in the morning. His roommate says he can't sleep because he's always up talking to his mom—usually about homework. When he goes home, he doesn't get any sleep because his whole family is constantly fighting. But nobody ever wins except her."

I concluded my diatribe and pretended to study the antique quilt wrapped around me. I was internally cringing at the sound of my own words. Surely these were silly reasons to be considering ending a relationship. After all, I was dating Darrell, not his mother. Surrounding me were three women who had all been married for several years. Jennifer's belly was beginning to show evidence of her third child growing inside of her. Katie had two of her own. Mom had raised seven and was now helping fight a battle against cancer with her husband of thirty-five years. My misgivings about Darrell's relationship with his mother seemed infinitely trite in comparison.

I sheepishly looked up to see three sets of eyes staring widely at me in disbelief.

"She's crazy!" Jennifer was furious. Relief washed over me. Maybe it wasn't so ridiculous a thing to be cautious about.

"I know! Right?" I looked to Katie and Mom to confirm similar reactions apparent in their facial expressions.

"Abby," I could hear the finger-wagging tone in Mom's voice, "you've got to get out of this relationship. You know I struggle with anxiety too, but I try to never use control or manipulation to deal with it. This is a very dangerous behavioral pattern."

Katie quickly chimed in, "If she doesn't know how to effectively deal with anxiety and fear, she certainly hasn't taught her children to either. Even if he thinks his mom's behavior is wrong, that doesn't mean he'd be willing to stand up to her or know how to act differently himself." I knew they were right. I went to bed with a new resolve to discuss the matter with Darrell. Either he would stand up to his mother or we were through. My brain could finally rest, knowing I was at least headed in the direction of a resolution, thanks to the wisdom of my mom and sisters.

Chapter 3

I HAD A TALK WITH DARRELL, who in turn spoke with his mom. For a month or so, it seemed as though it was actually working. Darrell's mom toned it down a bit and promised to work on her anxiety issues that were at the root of the problem with their strange relationship. She didn't call as much and she allowed him to leave campus without notifying her. But as Christmastime drew closer and finals were looming, it became evident she could not keep this promise. The panicked calls started up again and the level of control was beyond what I had ever seen. How could she not see that she was setting Darrell up for major failure, if not now, perhaps in a few years when she could not control his performance in a professional environment? And didn't she realize that no woman would want to marry a man who was indefinitely chained to his mother? I was becoming more and more certain I did not want to be that woman.

Much more disturbing to me, however, were the reports of Daddy's continuing pain in his abdomen and lower back. The word remission had been uttered by the medical professionals, but we were all skeptical. Still, he was able to work and seemed better than he'd been before the surgery last winter and the chemotherapy that followed.

I was too busy studying for my own finals to have time to worry about either situation. As usual, I had procrastinated on several major projects. Many a sleepless night passed as papers and projects were completed and tests were studied for. The last week and a half of the semester were a blur, but I finished. I was satisfied with how I had performed at each task.

Before I knew it, I was back in Ohio helping Mom prepare for Christmas. My jobs always included the vacuuming throughout the house and polishing the silver, in addition to cleaning my room and bathroom, which I would need to give up for Katie and her family to use. Over the years, I had learned not to mind the chores. This year, in particular, the responsibilities offered a welcome sense of normalcy. There was an air of expectancy which overshadowed any Christmas before. The anticipation of hearing the little ones' cheerful voices and their little feet running back and forth through the house was such a happy divergence from the anxiety of the last year and a half.

All my siblings were coming, just like they always did. Dave, who was working on his M.D. at a nearby teaching hospital, didn't have far to travel and would be home each day. Tim was living at home with Daddy and Mom, and his fiancée, Leslie would be joining us for dinner on Christmas day. Andy was coming from Michigan, where he worked at a tutoring center for inner city kids. He'd be bringing his girlfriend, Mary. Jennifer and Katie would arrive with their husbands and children a day or two before Christmas. Pete and his girlfriend, Lisa would bring the total to eighteen.

Everyone arrived in turn, the large house quickly filling to overflowing. The presence of Tim's fiancée Leslie, and the baby forming in Jennifer's belly represented a healthy, growing family. We soon learned that Katie was expecting her third child as well. Had I believed in omens, I would have considered these positive ones. Daddy was walking less gingerly and there was more of the old ruddiness to his cheeks under his thick grey beard. Even Mom seemed to relax and enjoy the chaos. Seeing her that way must have done much to ease Daddy's pain.

Christmas Eve arrived and we practically had to form a motorcade to make our way to the little country church where Mom and Daddy were members and where Dave, Andy, Tim and I had spent every Sunday morning and Sunday and Wednesday evening of our adolescence. Now, with the addition of Grandma and Grandpa, we needed two pews.

"Grandma, get ready to grab a kid!" Andy joked. We all laughed at the reminder of the Christmas Eve just a few years ago when we decided to all perform a Christmas hymn together. Katie's husband Jake had been recruited to sing with us, so we had left Jennifer's husband Rodney, along with Grandma and Grandpa in charge of the two grandchildren, Ellie and Stephen. They were both about one and a half years old. Stephen was happy to sit with Grandpa, who was probably bribing him with Tic Tacs conveniently hidden in the inside pocket of his blazer for just such an occasion. But Rodney had taken the more energetic Ellie to the back of the sanctuary to keep her from disturbing the rest of the congregation. In the midst of the second or third verse of the hymn, we were interrupted by Ellie's happy voice as she ran down the center aisle towards Jennifer.

"Mommy!" she shouted, arms open wide as though they were wings. Her little legs propelled her toward the altar at an alarming speed. Jennifer, who was soloing on this verse, tried to focus on her performance. Rodney was running in a crouched position behind Ellie, trying to be as inconspicuous as possible, ready to scoop her up if only he could catch her. Suddenly our petite, fragile Grandma stepped stealthily out of the pew as Ellie toddled past, grabbed her up in an effortless motion and carried her out of the sanctuary. Those of us in the front made an attempt to continue singing, but the damage was done. One by one we fell prey to the laughter. The congregation was in stitches.

We had not attempted a group ensemble since then. Andy baited Rodney that it was because we no longer believed him capable of containing the children. Perhaps there was some truth to that, but only because of the addition of Sammy and Jenna to the youngest generation. Jen did sing a solo, uninterrupted this time, and Daddy took his normal place at the podium "waving his arms" to direct the Christmas carols. At the end of the service, the congregation encircled the perimeter of the sanctuary, lit our candles, and turned out the lights. We began to sing "Silent Night," with Daddy's voice leading the melody. His deep baritone rolled out across the sanctuary like a carpet and I was immersed in a flood of joy. There was snow on the ground outside and the wind blowing south from Lake Erie was bitterly cold. But my family was here, together, big and growing bigger.

The sound of tiny feet on the floor above woke me the next morning. Lisa and I had slept on the two couches in the basement rec room. Jennifer's family had commandeered David's room. Clearly the children had been up for some time and were hyper with the prospect of opening presents so close at hand. I fumbled my way upstairs to get my cup of coffee. The children seemed to be planning some sort of play for the grown-ups. As usual, Ellie was in charge. Stephen didn't seem to care as long as she wasn't making him do anything he didn't want. Jenna, who was three, was thrilled to be included and obeyed every word from her six-year-old cousin. Sammy, also three, who was immune to being bossed around by his big sister, and who had a habit of escaping into his own world of make believe, was a bit more difficult for her to direct.

It was entertaining to watch their preparations, paying close attention to the developmental, gender and personality differences which contributed to the chaos. Before long, however, I was asked to help with brunch. Grandma and Grandpa arrived shortly after that, just as Jake was finishing the traditional scrambled eggs with ham and gouda. Tim, Dave and Rodney helped bring in Grandma and Grandpa's abundance of gifts, nearly half of them Talbots boxes for Grandma from "Santa." After they were deposited, we all gathered around the tree to eat, open gifts, and listen as Daddy read the Christmas story from the Gospel of Luke. Everything seemed to go off without a hitch. Andy, Dave, and Tim kept us laughing, as they always did. Jake, Rodney and Daddy chimed in at times. Even Grandpa offered a joke now and then, which was always followed by a declaration of, "Oh Harold!" from Grandma.

"It's due back in two weeks!" Andy commented with every book that was opened, a throwback to the time he had wrapped up a library book and given it to Dave. Slowly the pile of gifts shrunk and the food was eaten. The children began to be concerned there were no more presents for them and my sisters had to remind them of the need to be grateful. After the last gift was opened, we all dispersed to enjoy what we'd been given until it was time for the mid-afternoon dinner. Mom and Grandma disappeared into the kitchen. Katie and Jennifer were busy opening new toys and explaining how to operate them. The men gathered around the last bits of food and chatted about their jobs.

A few hours later, as we gathered around the table, there was again that familiar feeling of joy and comfort. I found myself on Andy's left and Grandma was on his other side. It was common knowledge that Grandma ate like a bird, yet Andy was persisting in taunting her, saying she had taken way too much food. Each time he made a comment, the laughter would begin and he would use the distraction as an opportunity to snatch food off of her plate. She in turn smacked his hand away. Finally, she turned to him with a somewhat frustrated smile on her face and exclaimed, "You smart A-S-S!" She was too straight-laced to say the word, so she reverted to spelling it out. For a moment, we all glanced at one another. Had she really said that? To Andy? One by one our faces broke into smiles and the laughter rippled around the table. The dimples which appeared each time Andy smiled seemed to be a constant fixture and his thick, curly, dark brown hair seemed to bounce with joy when he laughed, which was always. Grandma guarded her dessert plate quite carefully after that. Not only was she concerned her food might disappear into Andy's bottomless stomach, but she had certainly created too much of a scene with herself as the unwitting center of attention.

Dinner ended eventually and soon after, a magical Christmas break came to a close. Everyone had to return home. I watched sadly as the kids' presents were packed away and Mom doled out leftovers according to how many were in each family. Hugs and well wishes were given and received. It would not be long before we were all together again. Tim's wedding was less than six months away, but the days we'd spent together seemed too short. Daddy's illness had taught us not to take time together for granted. Mom and I spent a few days cleaning up from the bedlam and then it was my turn to go.

Chapter 4

I NEVER LIKED ROUTINE very much. Change and adventure always invigorated me. For that very reason, January term was a welcome break from the monotony of a semester-long schedule. The class-class-lunch-class-voice lesson-class-rehearsal-dinner-practice-work-homework-bed repetitiveness was much too boring. This year I was taking a plant biology course as a general education requirement. It met every morning, so after lunch I had plenty of time to practice, do homework and hang out with friends. Darrell was too obsessed with homework and his brother's upcoming wedding to spend much time with me. I was surprised to discover that I viewed this as another welcome change.

I spent many afternoons in the fine arts building because there were people there I didn't normally see in my music classes. Most of the other music majors were also taking general education courses, and several non-music majors were involved in the annual musical production—this year they were performing *Joseph and the Amazing Technicolor Dreamcoat*. They rehearsed all day during J-term so that they could put on the show in mid-February and they took over the building.

I found myself spending a lot of time with my friend Shaun whenever the actors had a break. Right or wrong, I was flattered that he seemed more receptive to my flirtations than Darrell lately. In truth, I was shocked Shaun found me interesting at all. He was a junior and hung out with all the "cool people" in Concert Choir and College Singers. His group of friends had a reputation for enjoying occasional drinking binges. Although he wasn't the sort I was typically drawn to, he was funny, smart, and a good singer. Everyone referred to him as the honorary music major because he was in enough vocal ensembles to fulfill the academic requirements, so I'd known him since the very beginning of school.

One afternoon, Shaun and I were sitting on a bench in the atrium chatting, most likely flirtatiously. Geno, one of the other cast members, sauntered over to talk to Shaun.

"Is this your sister?" Geno asked Shaun as he slumped onto the bench next to Shaun.

"No!" we both replied, in somewhat surprised tones.

"Oh. Dating?" He must have noticed our embarrassment, because he began to mutter and stammer, "I mean, you just look good together or something." The sight of Shaun's blushing face overwhelmed me with shame. I didn't want him to get the wrong idea, even though the sight of him caused more of a flutter in my stomach than that of Darrell lately.

"I have a boyfriend," I muttered and stood to find someone else to speak with. The words were as much to remind Shaun and myself of the platonic nature of our relationship as they were for Geno's clarification. Despite this embarrassing encounter, I continued to seek Shaun's attention regularly.

NEWS FROM HOME was Daddy's pain had reached an alarming level. He was scheduled for a CT scan in February. When Mom shared this news with me, I sank in my chair feeling weary of it all. *Will this ever end? Is there really nothing I can do to make it stop,* I found myself thinking. Praying seemed less than trite at this point. *Does God really even care?*

At the same time, Darrell began accusing me that I didn't really care about him. He seemed to think I should accept his family the way it was, without expecting them to change. I was unwilling to compromise. His mother made it clear she wasn't planning to change, so I insisted that either he needed to put some healthier boundaries between the two of them, or I would need to end the relationship. He asked for time to think about it, and in the meantime, became miserable to be within ten feet of. We tried studying together and meeting for dinner in the dining hall as we normally did, but he was increasingly moody.

His birthday was in the beginning of February, right after we returned from J-term break. I spent my few short days at home pondering what gift would best brighten his mood. Knowing how much he missed his dogs while he was at school, I decided to get him a beta fish with a bowl and some decorations. When the day came, his roommate snuck me into his room to set up the fish tank as a surprise. Then, I straightened my hair the way he liked it, put on his favorite outfit and met him in the dining hall. For a poor college sophomore, I was pretty proud of what I had accomplished for him.

Expecting a brilliant grin and open arms upon seeing me, I was disappointed when he barely cracked a smile and then quickly returned to looking dejectedly at his dinner. Throughout the awkward meal, he showed no sign of appreciation. He did eventually say I looked nice at one point and he liked the fish. Even then, his expression and tone made it clear it wasn't enough. Later that night, at a study group, I asked him what I had done wrong.

"I don't know, but you need to *show* me if you really care about me." He barely looked up from his textbook as he muttered the words through his teeth.

"You know, you don't have to be so mean to me. I'm *trying* to show you, but apparently you don't appreciate it."

"You have devastated my family. I have a right to be mean to you." His expression showed how deeply he really believed these words. For a moment I pitied him, but the anger took over and I quickly gathered my things and stomped away to my room. I had to go to Climenhaga for my nightly cleaning job anyway.

My warm winter jacket did little to take away the sting of my tears or of Darrell's words as I walked the half mile on the cold, deserted sidewalks. Dim lamps cast eerie shadows across the frozen ground. Every once in awhile, a street lamp flickered menacingly as I passed under it. My mind was taking even darker paths than the concrete one I was following. *Perhaps Darrell is right and I just don't know how to show affection. Maybe I was wrong for insisting things change. Maybe I was the mean one. Maybe I'll never find anyone better than Darrell.*

As I passed the library, a car drove by; its speed indicating it was clearly being driven by a student. I was reminded of Daddy's careful driving instruction and then of his health predicament. *He's going to die. I made God angry because I flirted with Shaun while still dating Darrell. I spent most of my teenage years flirting; looking for approval from the opposite sex. God's going to make me pay for such crimes with my precious Daddy's life. But what if . . .*

Headlights were coming towards me from the bottom of the hill. Was it going fast enough? I estimated its speed to be around 25 miles per hour. That would merely land me in the hospital and my parents in a panic. The potency of the jalopy's exhaust as it whooshed past me snapped my brain into reality. What absurdity! There was a person behind that steering wheel. Jumping in front of them could harm them physically and emotionally. Killing myself would do nothing for Daddy except cause him and Mom more unnecessary pain. As for Darrell, the word Grandma had used for Andy at Christmas seemed quite appropriate in these circumstances. He was a total ass. There was no reason for anyone to be treated the way he had just spoken to me. I had enough self-respect to know I couldn't keep allowing it.

I reached the fine arts building with my mind determined. Darrell and I were done. For once I was grateful for the solitude of the empty music building. I struggled to overcome the tears which were threatening to spill over. My decision to break up with Darrell was a relief, but I would miss the fun we used to have. Recently it had been more of a roller coaster ride through Insanity Land than anything resembling fun. More than the loss of a boyfriend and good friend, however, I felt scared that my mind went so readily to suicide as a solution. Fortunately, I had realized the irrationality of my thinking before I was able to follow through.

When I returned to my room, I dialed the number to Darrell's room. He answered, sounding glum as always, and I told him we needed to talk.

"Can you meet me downstairs in the lobby so we can take a walk?" I asked.

"I think we should pray about it for a day and meet tomorrow evening," he answered, clearly uncomfortable that I currently had the upper hand. I was too tired of arguing with him to disagree.

The next day was severely cold and I was grateful for the indoor location we had chosen; an isolated lobby on the third floor of an academic building. Confrontation was my least favorite thing, yet I was oddly very calm. I had spent the day praying for the wherewithal to stand my ground. I didn't want to stoop to his level of spite, but I wanted to remain resolute. I had rehearsed over and over what I wanted to say. I needn't have prepared, however.

Darrell arrived, fifteen minutes late, as usual, and immediately began to reprimand me for causing his mom such anxiety. After several minutes of verbal abuse, he finally spoke the words I had planned to say.

"We can't be together anymore. We need to break up." He paused for a moment and I took full advantage.

"I agree. I can't be with someone who doesn't respect me." I was not about to let him control the entire conversation. "I refuse to date your mother and that's what I've been doing for a long time. As horribly as you have treated me for the last few weeks, I still care about you as a person, so I have to tell you that unless you set appropriate boundaries with your mother, you are going to be hard pressed to find a girl who will marry you. She has complete control over you. Don't you see? How can you be free to make your own decisions if your mom doesn't lighten up?" I probably overstepped my bounds, but I just had to say it. I simply couldn't control my urge to right a perceived injustice. He was not appreciative.

"Now it's none of your concern!" His voice was teetering on the verge of fury. His jaw tensed and his shoulders squared. His fists clenched and unclenched several times. For a moment I was frightened he might hurt me, but I reminded myself that he was too submissive. His rant went on for several minutes. I was beginning to feel trapped. In his family, it was customary to argue until a resolution could be agreed upon—or someone just gave up—but we were never going to agree.

"Darrell, let's just stop now. We aren't going to get anywhere by arguing. Let's just agree to disagree and be done with it. It doesn't matter anymore anyway. Our relationship is over. Just forget it." This brought on several more minutes of admonishing. He insisted that I needed to walk in his shoes and that I was being utterly selfish. I tuned him out pretty effectively, knowing he would be satisfied with nothing less than me apologizing and confessing I had been wrong to speak ill of his mother. I was too proud of my wisdom so I just stood there and cried.

Somehow I managed to escape his tirades in less than an hour, using the excuse that I was late for a Singers' rehearsal, the small vocal ensemble that was perhaps my favorite activity. I had not put any stock in Darrell's angry words, but they still lingered. My face was tear-stained and puffy as I tucked my head against the cold wind. Fortunately, this group of singers was not like the group of random students on the car ride home a year ago. These fifteen other musicians were some of my closest friends, and Shaun was among them. We traveled together and shared fond memories of making music together. So after stopping in the bathroom to splash cold water on my face, I took my seat next to Shaun. When he asked if I was okay, I told him Darrell and I had just broken up. He was genuinely sympathetic, but I thought I detected a slight smile at this news.

A few hours later, back in my dorm room, the voicemail light lit up, though no call had come in. The college had somehow wired the phone network so that you could send someone a message without having to risk them answering their phone. I'm sure these "silent messages" were misused, but in this case, it was a perfect way of conveying what Shaun was too shy to say over the phone, let alone in person.

"Hi Abby. It's Shaun. I just wanted to say I'm sorry about your breakup with Darrell. Let me know if you ever need to talk. I'll be here." Oddly, his voice sounded sincere, although I knew he was not really sorry about our breakup. He did seem to be sorry I was hurting, which was sweet. But it was too soon and I wasn't sure what I thought about him. Yes, he was funny, smart, and popular among our mutual musician friends. I had witnessed his sensitive side, too. Once at Concert Choir, which was a much larger group than Singers, he had shed tears when he asked for prayer for the family of his best friend from high school who had been tragically killed in a car accident. Then on September 11, 2001, I had been sitting near him at a chapel service to pray for the victims of the attacks and their families. He was from Long Island, New York, and he was unable to get ahold of his family. I learned then that one of his father's best friends was a New York firefighter. Again, the tears had stung his eyes and spilled over onto his cheeks, despite his obvious efforts to keep them at bay.

A week passed and I ignored Shaun's message. He didn't follow up. When I saw him at Concert Choir or Singers, we flirted as we always had, but neither of us mentioned his invitation to enter into a deeper relationship. It may have been awkward for him, but I had no problem with this arrangement. Besides, it turned out I was not as free from Darrell as I had initially thought.

Returning to my room one evening, a few days after our breakup, weary from classes and rehearsals, I was surprised to find a scathing voicemail from him.

"You have destroyed my family. We are all hurt and my mother is depressed. And all while we're trying to get ready for my brother's wedding! How could you be so insensitive? God is going to punish you for the way you've treated us!" A crash followed by a dial tone indicated he'd slammed the receiver down.

In a tearful panic, I called my parents, hoping that despite it being past 9:00 in the evening, they would still be awake and willing to answer the phone. Daddy answered and the words tumbled awkwardly out of my mouth.

"Darrell left me a really nasty message. He says God is going to punish me for hurting his family. What did I do wrong, Daddy? Why can't he just leave me alone!" When my voice trailed off into sobbing, he cleared his throat and soothed me as only he knew how.

"Sweetheart, you did nothing wrong. You are not a bad person. You made the right decision. Would you really want to still be in a relationship with someone who is capable of treating people this way? Besides, his theology is messed up. God doesn't punish people like that. You know that, right?" Sensing I was calming down, he started to develop a plan of action.

"You need to send him an email. Don't call because he will try to trap you into an argument. Send him an email telling him not to contact you again. Tell him if he does, he can expect a call from me. If he sends you any emails, don't read them, just send them to me. If he calls you, hang up and call me. You need to give me his number." I did as he asked and hung up the phone. Calm and confident, I composed a short email which I sent to Darrell and blind copied my father. Then, with Daddy's reassurances still anchoring me, I began to work on some homework. Finishing an assignment, I went to my computer only to discover a reply from Darrell. The message appeared to be an equally accusatory diatribe of immense length. I read only the first sentence before responding that I would not be reading or listening to any further communication from him. It took no time for him to shoot a response back, just as nasty as the first message.

Now I was enraged. *How arrogant of him to think he can belittle me like this!* But I was also afraid he would never stop. Part of me even considered that he could be right about me. I called my dad again. This time it was well past 10:00 and the phone woke him. The update made him even angrier than I was.

"Forward the emails to me and then change your email address immediately. I am going to call him and I don't want him to be able to get through to you anymore." I didn't hear anything else from Darrell that evening. Much later, Daddy called to let me know the situation was taken care of and I assured him I had changed my email address. Then I fell into a restless sleep plagued by dreams that I had murdered Darrell's family and all my family and friends had disowned me for my heinous crimes.

I found out the next day that Darrell had tried to argue with Daddy, forgetting, or oblivious to the fact that Daddy was his intellectual superior by a very wide margin. Daddy had told him he would call campus security and the local police if he did not leave me alone. Eventually he had been forced to hang up on Darrell because he just wouldn't stop arguing. Only moments later, Darrell's father called Daddy and told him to stop harassing his son. But Daddy always had the upper hand because his voice imparted his large stature, even over the phone, and because there were few people who could outsmart him. Despite weightless arguments, Daddy won out by saying he would leave Darrell alone when Darrell left me alone and he was being beyond rude to be interrupting the precious sleep of a very sick man. I never heard from Darrell again.

Chapter 5

ON FRIDAY EVENING of that same week, I was in my room alone when my phone rang. It was Mom, reporting the results of Daddy's CT scan.

"He's pretty sick, Honey. The doctor said there are several lymph nodes which have increased in size and there is hydronephrosis in the kidneys. His creatinine levels are a little higher than they like to see as well." I had become pretty familiar with medical talk. Enlarged lymph nodes could indicate more cancer, but the rest of this was no more than jargon to me.

"What are hydronephrosis and creatinine?" I asked her.

"Hydronephrosis means there is scarring on the kidneys and ureters. Creatinine is a chemical naturally produced in the body, but too much of it is toxic and can indicate kidney failure."

"So they think the cancer has metastasized to more of the lymph nodes? And the scarring is possibly causing his kidneys to shut down?" Mom confirmed this was their theory. "Ok, so what are they going to do?" I was feeling overwhelmed with the gravity of this news but certain there was always a medical solution. For Mom's sake I attempted to hold it together.

"He's scheduled for surgery on March 14. They will try to remove the scar tissue and any cancerous nodes." It was still February. March 14 seemed like a long way off to me, but I didn't want to discourage Mom, so I kept that thought to myself. We chatted for a few minutes and when she hung up, I immediately called my best friend, Melody.

"I need you. This week has been awful," I told her. Within a few minutes, Melody, her boyfriend Ryan and our friend Seth were in my room. Soon the smell of popcorn and the sound of laughter filled the room as we put some ridiculous romantic comedy into my tiny TV/VCR combo. Melody and Ryan were certainly cozy all cuddled up on my floor. It made me lonely to be the odd one out. I tried to flirt with Seth, but he wasn't biting. I was relieved when visiting hours were over and the boys had to leave.

My roommate was MIA so Melody stayed to help cheer me up. Before long we were laughing about how silly boys were and Melody was plotting a way to get Seth interested in me. By the time Melody left around 2:00 a.m., I was feeling much better. I climbed into bed, too exhausted to think about anything serious—like cancer.

BRRRRRRING! The phone woke me with a start early the next morning. I leaped out of bed, thinking the worst. It wasn't Mom, though. It was Ted, a member of Concert Choir's leadership who sounded quite irritated with me. We had a concert that morning and I had missed the bus. He arranged to pick me up in twenty minutes outside another choir member's apartment who had also slept in. I hung up the phone and quickly grabbed my dress, shoes and panty hose. I also grabbed my straightening iron as I rushed to the bathroom. I wouldn't have time to take a shower and my curly hair was unforgiving without the reset button of a good wash. I got myself ready as quickly as possible, deposited my things in a heap in front of my dresser, grabbed my coat and ran down three flights of stairs and across the street where Ted's car sat waiting. The other choir member, Tracy, rushed out shortly after me and sat in the front passenger seat, but we didn't pull out. When I asked, it was explained that Melody had also slept in and we were waiting for her. Within a minute or two she was in the back seat next to me and we were on our way.

Exhausted, Melody and I leaned on each other and started to nod off to sleep. Before I lost consciousness, however, I heard a question from the front seat which piqued my interest immediately.

"Can you believe Shaun and Wendy last night?" Tracy asked Ted. Both were among Shaun's closer circle of friends. I remained as still as possible, hoping they would think I was asleep. *What happened? More intriguingly, why am I so concerned about it?*

"Yeah, what a night for them," Ted exclaimed. Inexplicably, I felt my heart sink.

"Do you think anything else happened?" Tracy wondered.

"No, they both passed out pretty quickly. But they were definitely making out for a while."

"Do you think they'll get together? They don't seem right for each other somehow."

"Yeah, I don't think they really like each other, they just had too much to drink," Ted agreed. "How long has Shaun had a thing for Emily?"

"Oh, he knows nothing will ever happen with her." Tracy's voice became a whisper, but I could still hear her easily. "Besides, I'm pretty sure he likes Abby. Have you seen him when she's around? He's a mess!"

The topic of their conversation changed but my brain refused to move on. Tracy's suspicions gave me butterflies, but at the same time I hated that Shaun had made out with someone else. I found it even more frustrating to have additional evidence of his drinking habits. Perhaps I thought him to be more mature or more intelligent than that. Somehow I felt personally insulted, even though I had no claim over him. I wasn't even supposed to like him.

My mind whirled for another half hour before we reached our destination. We arrived just before our director began warm ups. I scanned the sanctuary of the unfamiliar church and was relieved to find that Shaun and Wendy were nowhere near one another. As we climbed onto the small platform, there was a need to adjust our usual arrangement. By some coincidence or divine intervention, Shaun ended up right behind me. I turned halfway backwards to glance at him.

"Good morning Shaun. Like my hair?" As I turned back around, I flipped my hair just a bit to emphasize the fact that it was not in its usual curly state. I felt him reach forward to gently touch it, a bit timidly.

"It's really soft like this. It looks so much longer." Did I sense a bit of awe in his voice? Since I didn't pull away, he continued to play with my hair until the director was satisfied with our arrangement and began warming up our voices. I was fully awake now, relieved that Shaun's interests were clearly still aimed in my direction. With a slight twinge of guilt at my own duplicity, I looked for Seth. He did not give me the satisfaction of a glance in my direction.

For the next two weeks, I felt tortured. I really liked Seth but he clearly saw me as no more than his classmate and friend. Any attempt at flirtation on my part was met with confusion or awkward silence from him. Shaun, on the other hand was gaining confidence. He no longer waited for me to speak to him but started conversations. He seemed more comfortable being near me, but still blushed and beamed when we interacted. I thrived on the attention. I vacillated between wanting to know him better and not wanting to give him the impression I liked him. Yet something I could not identify kept me intrigued in him. I could not help myself.

All the while, I knew my precious Daddy was in pain and anxiously awaiting his surgery. Guilt at being preoccupied with boys, especially so soon after the fiasco with Darrell overwhelmed me. But Daddy was so far away, and there was nothing I could do. Shaun and Seth were very real and very present.

Singers was scheduled to leave for a bus tour of Florida just days before Daddy's operation. We would be giving concerts at churches all around the Gulf Coast as well as visiting beaches and shopping venues. It was difficult to justify having so much fun with such good friends while Mom and Daddy were experiencing their own sort of hell more than a thousand miles away. Of course they encouraged me to enjoy myself, but their words seemed like mere platitudes. One consolation was that Grandma and Grandpa would be in Florida and would be able to attend one of our concerts.

"Did you hear that Seth isn't going to Florida with us?" Melody asked me, a few days before we were scheduled to leave. "He has a *previous engagement.*" She emphasized the last two words as though she didn't really believe them. *Well that stinks,* I thought. *But I'd probably spend the entire time being disappointed that he has absolutely no interest in me anyway. Melody will be there, as well as everyone else. And Shaun, my own personal dilemma.* My heart skipped a beat at the thought, and I resented it. *Ug! I can't do a relationship again right now. I don't think I can handle any more drama, much less a break-up. And what if he's secretly crazy too? But he would do just about anything to go on a date with me. And it seems like he's not just in it for a pretty face. Maybe I should focus on someone who seems to genuinely and deeply care about me.*

When it was time to leave, I walked with Melody to where the bus was waiting and climbed in. I managed to pull off my usual cheerful demeanor, but I felt insecure. Melody was even more outgoing than I, and she quickly set to work making better friends with some of the lower classmen towards the front of the bus. Shaun was near the back playing a card game with the upperclassmen. I wasn't familiar with the game, so I sat in the seat in front of him and faced backwards on the pretense of learning the game.

It takes a long time to drive a charter bus from Pennsylvania to Florida. Melody was having fun improving friendships so I spent the day with Shaun. She wasn't being insensitive, that was just her personality. She was fun-loving and unencumbered by the expectations of others. Shaun didn't seem to mind that I defaulted to being near him. After the card game, he moved into the seat next to me. We laughed so comfortably together, it was as though we'd been the best of friends for quite some time. As it grew dark, our director put a movie on. Shaun pulled a blanket out from under his seat and spread it over both of our laps. As we both tugged the blanket straight, our hands brushed one another and before I knew what was happening, he had intertwined his fingers with mine.

What's going on, I wondered, partially thrilled at the closeness, and partially terrified. *Is he going to ask me out? What should I say? I should be terrified, but this seems completely natural.* There was not even one more thought about Seth after that.

We arrived at our destination in Florida just as the movie ended. Reluctantly, Shaun and I unlaced our fingers. The church where we'd be singing in the morning had asked for volunteers to house us for the evening. Melody and I reunited to spend the night in a stranger's home. I couldn't wait to tell her about my day, but didn't want to discuss it in the back seat of our host's car. Waiting until we were safely in a private bedroom was practically painful.

"Shaun and I were holding hands during the movie," I confessed, feeling self-conscious and immature.

"You and Shaun? Really?" Her eyes twinkled in amusement, despite her obvious confusion. I hadn't mentioned my feelings for him to Melody or to anyone else. She was oblivious to our flirtations, thinking we were just good friends.

"I thought you liked Seth," she prodded.

"Yeah, I thought so, too. But he doesn't like me and I guess I've liked Shaun for a long time. Even when I was still with Darrell, I think." Assured that I really did like him, she began to ask for details and giggle with me over the whole thing. This was my favorite thing about Melody. She never judged and she thrived on the silly details of life.

The next morning, I woke up with serious butterflies. Our hosts graciously offered us a breakfast banquet, but my stomach hurt too badly to eat much. My assigned place in Singers was next to Shaun. I was anxious at the thought of it, especially since we were supposed to hold hands with the people on either side of us during our benediction. *This could be a really awkward day. A really awkward week, really. What if he was just flirting and none of it meant anything to him? Holding his hand during the last song is going to be so weird!*

I needn't have been so worried. Shaun had arrived at the church first and a smile lit his entire face as soon as he saw me. I felt my heart pounding against my chest as I took my spot next to him. When it came time for the benediction, I timidly slid my fingers into Shaun's palm. But rather than the closed-finger hand hold of friends, he laced his fingers through mine without hesitation. It was still surprising to me that this caused my heart to flutter.

When the song was over, I was greeted by two familiar faces from the audience—Grandma and Grandpa. I had been too engrossed in my thoughts about Shaun to remember! Immediately after hugging me, Grandma embraced Shaun in a bear hug, winking at me as she disappeared into his arms. She was clearly onto us. *How did she know?* I could not avoid the topic when they took me out for lunch afterwards.

"Who was that boy next to you, Abby?" she asked with quite the mischievous sparkle in her eye.

"That's Shaun. He's a good friend." I tried to use my poker face, but I could feel the hot blushing of my cheeks and my facial muscles pulling involuntarily into a smile.

"He seems like such a nice boy."

"I think he wants to be more than friends," Grandpa chimed in. I could see Grandma's eyes twinkling, planning. But I got off easy and didn't hear anymore about it.

For the rest of the week, Shaun and I continued to stay close to each other on the bus. Our fingers got quite accustomed to being intertwined. Eventually, I was no longer surprised that the sight of him made me giddy. I had fallen for him, but it unnerved me that he didn't mention anything about dating. *Is he waiting for me to ask him?* I'd been taught to leave that role to the man in the relationship. But I was confused by it all. Our mutual friend and fellow Singer, Liz, was getting worried Shaun would soon miss his opportunity.

One night, late into the trip, I was hanging out with a few of the other girls in Liz's hotel room.

"Did you have the DTR yet?" she asked me. The question caught me totally off guard, besides which, I had no idea what she was talking about.

"The DTR?"

"Define The Relationship. You know, 'the talk.'" *Is she suggesting I should broach the topic of dating? Can I do that? What would my mother say?* It was clear Shaun and I needed to talk about what was going on between us, but was that my responsibility?

"Well, no. I mean, I don't know if he's really serious. I think he just kind of likes flirting with me." I was so confused. I was used to guys making it perfectly clear whether they were interested or not. But Liz knew him better. Maybe she could offer some insight into the situation.

"Oh trust me, he's interested. He's just worried you're on the rebound. Everyone knows Darrell really screwed you up. So do you really like Shaun? Because I don't want to help you if you're just going to hurt him." She certainly didn't sugarcoat things very much.

"Yes, I do really like him. Darrell was crazy. It didn't take much to get over him." Even as I said the words, I wondered if they were totally true. I was over Darrell, sure, but was I over his craziness enough to get involved in a new relationship?

"Well, Shaun needs to know that. He's not going to risk getting hurt until he's sure."

My mind was reeling when I went to bed that night. Did Shaun's misgivings qualify as an exception to the rule of letting the man lead? It didn't seem like Shaun was going to ever ask me out if I didn't make him certain I was going to say yes. Did I like him enough to risk it? Or was the real risk missing out on this opportunity? It occurred to me to pray about it, but I wasn't sure God cared about my dating life. I thought it might be presumptuous to ask for help on this topic when I'd already spent a year and a half asking for healing for my daddy. That was much more difficult a task than securing a date.

The next day, we started our journey back to Pennsylvania. At lunchtime we stopped at a Cracker Barrel and, while we waited for a table large enough to accommodate our party, we browsed the gift store. After a few minutes, Liz pulled me aside.

"I know what you need to do." She led me to a card she'd found with a cute picture and a message indicating that I wanted to discuss our relationship. "Write a personal note in it and give it to Shaun. Make it clear you're not just rebounding and he'll ask you out."

I purchased the card before I could change my mind, hiding it from Shaun as best I could. After ordering my food, I snuck it into the bathroom, wrote a few words on the inside, and gave it to him when we got back on the bus. I was horrified when, rather than opening it, he put it in the pocket of the seat in front of us and didn't touch it until we got off the bus. I tried to pretend I wasn't nervous, but the butterflies were overwhelming and I felt squirmy. My own handwriting on the white envelope mocked me from the mesh pocket.

That night, we stayed at a hotel somewhere halfway between Florida and Pennsylvania. I don't really remember anything about it because I spent the evening obsessing over the card. *Why did I put myself out there like that?* Clearly I had imagined he was giving me signals that he wanted to be in a relationship. He was just taking advantage of the trip and would forget all about me the moment we stepped back on Pennsylvania soil. I attempted to make the most of it, telling myself it had been a fun learning experience and I had gotten to know him better, but I was simply too embarrassed to believe these words.

I climbed onto the tour bus the next morning, resolved to sitting in a seat near Melody in order to avoid Shaun. Her legs had gotten so badly sunburned she needed to stretch out across an entire seat, so I sat down in front of her. I was shocked when Shaun scooted in next to me. One look at his face and I knew he'd read it. And he'd liked it.

"I talked to Liz last night," he began without wasting a moment. I was so relieved that he wasn't going to prolong this ridiculous process any longer. Yesterday had been horrid enough.

"And did you read your card?" I asked with renewed confidence.

"Of course I did," he smiled, softly. He looked handsome when he smiled like that, I noticed. "It was the first thing I did when we got to the hotel last night. So we need to talk, huh? How about tomorrow for lunch?" I'm sure I blushed a thousand shades of red. I was usually more composed than this. Why did he have such a hold on me?

"Are you asking me on a date?"

"Yes, I am," he replied, more confidently than he probably felt.

"Where are we going?"

"I hear Isaac's is a good first date location. I'll pick you up at noon."

Chapter 6

IN THE MIDST of all the goings on with Shaun, I had not forgotten about Daddy's surgery. I had no cell phone, so as soon as we returned to campus, I went straight to my room and called home. Mom must have been waiting for me to call because she answered on the first ring.

"The doctor didn't find anything!" She sounded so relieved to be able to deliver good news. "Everything looked normal." I was a bit reluctant to get my hopes up.

"How is he feeling?" I asked.

"Well, he's still in pain. The doctor could find no explanation, though. He thinks he will be fine." An almost imperceptible crack in Mom's voice led me to believe that she and Daddy disagreed with the doctor. I didn't dare ask, however. I didn't want to solidify any fears, real or imagined, so I accepted the doctor's words as fact. A shred of trust in God's ability to heal him remained and I grabbed ahold of it as tightly as I could, praying Daddy's pain would dissipate over time as his body healed from its various invasions.

The next day, after returning from church with Melody, I met Shaun outside of his apartment building. He walked around and opened the passenger door of his car for me and we headed off to get some lunch together. First dates always seemed awkward to me, but we simply laughed about the oddity of such social norms. We had been good friends for so long that I was perfectly comfortable being alone with him.

Once we'd ordered our food, Shaun dove into the topic we'd come to discuss.

"I really liked the card you gave me. I really like you too. I actually have for a long time." He was perfectly composed.

"I know," I grinned at him.

"How did you know?"

"The silent message kind of gave it away." I knew it by heart and quoted it to him, "'Hi Abby. It's Shaun. I just wanted to say I'm sorry about your breakup with Darrell. Let me know if you ever need to talk. I'll be here.' It wasn't very subtle!" Shaun chuckled.

"Yeah, I guess that gave it away, huh?"

"I knew before that though. I've known for awhile."

"Well, I like you and you said you like me." He paused, waiting for my confirming nod, then continued in a somewhat professional manner, "So would you like to start dating? I don't want to pressure you into a relationship if you're not ready."

"I would love to date you," I replied, exuding more confidence than I felt.

"Then I think we should take it slowly and just build on our friendship and see where it goes. Maybe we don't even tell people except our closest friends for a little while. That way, if it doesn't work out it's not a huge public affair."

This plan sparked a sense of adventure and mystery which I adored. I didn't mind Shaun's businessman-like demeanor. It actually reminded me of how Daddy might have handled the situation.

As excited as I was about this new relationship, I was still wavering. Shaun was different than any guy I had ever dated. Most had been guys whose opinions of themselves were much larger than necessary. They were all tall and strikingly handsome. Shaun had strong opinions, but not of himself. He was very smart, but humble and even a bit reserved about his intellectual abilities. He was tall, and although I was becoming more physically attracted to him, his features didn't initially strike me as particularly handsome. His most endearing attribute was that he cared more about me than about himself. He always considered my needs and desires first. I got the feeling he would have done almost anything if he thought it would be in my best interests.

One night in early spring, we were walking about campus, casually talking and holding hands as we went. The spring air was warm and fresh with the scent of grass and blooming bulbs. The sun was beginning to set and the light around us was just starting to fade into a purple glow. As we walked along the side of the road which ran in front of the main administrative building, a small car packed with six or eight students squealed around a corner towards us. There were several people leaning out of windows and the sun roof, presumably because there was not enough room for them inside the tiny vehicle. As the car zoomed past, they began to yell something at us. I could not make out what it was, but Shaun began to chase the car, one fist in the air. They were moving much too fast for him to follow for long and after hollering something back at them, again imperceptible to my ears, he slowed to a walk again. When I caught up to him, he was shaking with rage, his jaw was set and his fists were clenched at his sides. Images of Darrell lecturing me flashed into my consciousness. What had just happened? It had only been a few brief moments, but the intense emotions of it all made my brain fuzzy.

"Calm down, Shaun. They're just a bunch of drunk idiots," I tried to soothe him.

"You didn't hear what they said, did you?" He turned to look in my eyes, searching for any sign of comprehension. His intensity scared me.

"No. But it couldn't be worth getting so angry. It's fine." He breathed a sigh of relief at my ignorance and naivety.

"It's not fine. If they come back I'll . . ." he trailed off, suddenly realizing the effect he was having on me. He softened his voice, "You're safe with me." He put his arm protectively around my waist and pulled me closer to his side. I pulled back a bit to look in his face as we kept walking. I still wasn't sure why he was so angry.

"What *did* they say?" I asked. Disgust furrowed his eyebrows and turned his upper lip.

"Nevermind. I can't repeat it to you." He shook his head in disbelief. I relaxed into his protective arm. At least his anger was not aimed at me but at those who wanted to harm me. That was not like Darrell at all. In fact, once again, Shaun reminded me of Daddy, who always responded in protective anger to any threat that came my way. In that moment, I decided to trust that Shaun's anger had been justified. It was clear he was not going to mar my innocence by reiterating their cat calls to me. At this realization, my emotions for him matured from fascinated infatuation to cautious respect.

After this glimpse into Shaun's character, I was confident things were on an uphill swing for me. The last two years of anxiety and hardship were over and I could begin to live a more relaxed life. I was learning that Shaun was well respected by teachers and students alike. I mentioned to my voice teacher that we were dating and she practically beamed as she pictured the match.

"Shaun's such a good guy," she exclaimed. These were the words I heard over and over again. And Shaun continued to prove them to be true.

JUST TWO AND A HALF WEEKS after our first date, my sister Jennifer's baby made his appearance into the world. Mom, Daddy, and my brother

Dave traveled from Ohio to Maryland to meet him and help Jennifer as she recovered from her third cesarean section. Shaun agreed to drive me to their house one Saturday, a couple of weeks after Jack's arrival. It would be Shaun's first introduction to my family. I was relieved that, after spending a few days there, Daddy had gone back to Ohio for a doctor's appointment before driving to Michigan. I was vaguely aware that my brother Andy would be attending some of his own doctor's appointments and it didn't strike me as curious or ominous that Daddy wanted to go with him.

My mind was, perhaps selfishly, focused on Mom, Dave, and Jennifer meeting Shaun. After Daddy's disappointment in Darrell, I feared he would dismiss Shaun without giving him much of a chance and I already felt too invested in him to navigate such a huge obstacle. Dave would probably take a protective big brother stance, but he did not have as much say in my dating relationships as Daddy and Mom.

I gingerly broached the topic with Shaun on the hour-long drive to Maryland.

"So, I haven't told Mom that I'm dating anyone yet. She has said more than once that I shouldn't enter too quickly into another relationship after Darrell. I'm just not sure she's ready to see me with someone yet."

"That's okay," he answered, flashing an understanding smile in my direction, while keeping his eyes on the road. "We said we weren't really telling anyone yet anyway."

"Okay. I just wanted to make sure we were on the same page. Didn't want you to be hurt when I introduced you as my friend."

What I didn't realize was Grandma had already filled Mom in on her encounter with Shaun in Florida. Calling Shaun my friend wasn't going to fool her. As the day progressed, I was surprised to see Shaun had no problem engaging my introverted and highly intellectual brother. It actually seemed like they might be enjoying one another. This was a side of Shaun which hadn't yet been revealed to me. Dave was possibly superior to Daddy in his intellectual abilities, yet Shaun was having no problem contributing to a conversation I couldn't follow.

Later that afternoon, Mom asked me to help her clean the kids' bathroom upstairs. She didn't waste much time getting straight to the topic she wanted to discuss.

"Shaun's a really nice guy, Abby. He reminds me of my cousin Gary." This was fabulous! Mom was very close to her cousin Gary. "It seems like he really cares about you. That is what your dad and I have always prayed for you. But, do you think it's too soon after Darrell?"

"Mom, we're just taking it slow and seeing what happens. It's nothing serious right now." I had given up trying to convince her we were just friends, but even these words seemed like lies. Intellectually, I had convinced myself this was true, but my heart was pointing an accusatory finger right back in my direction. I was already falling hard for Shaun and these positive interactions with my family were not helping me hold back my overwhelming emotions.

LATER THAT WEEK, just as I was beginning to feel secure in the goodness of life again, I got an unexpected call from Daddy. He was still with Andy in Michigan. I hadn't expected to hear from him until he was back in Ohio. The voice that usually had the ability to calm me when none other could, instead caused me to fall apart.

"Abby, I have to tell you some bad news. They found two tumors on Andy's liver. A biopsy shows they are cancer." He delivered the news as though he were talking about a patient completely unrelated to himself. I must have responded strongly, because I could hear Daddy take a composing breath.

"He's not dead yet, Abby. Let's not assume that this is going to kill him." Daddy was trying hard to sound strong, but his voice was shaking. Somehow we concluded the conversation and hung up the phone. I must have been in shock because I don't remember anything except sitting in front of the closed door of my dorm room sobbing for what seemed like hours. I don't remember my roommate coming back. I don't remember calling Shaun. I just remember the feeling of helplessness, of hopelessness, of terror. I remember curling fetus-like on the floor blocking the door. Perhaps if I kept the world from knowing my pain, it would turn out to be only a nightmare.

Andy too? Why God? Poor Daddy, having to call everyone with this news. My heart ached for him, for Andy, for Mom. *How could You do this to us God? Our family has served You faithfully over the years. Andy's worked so hard to help poor city kids in Grand Rapids go to college and better their lives. He doesn't deserve this. He has so much more to give You!*

Somehow I mustered the emotional and mental strength to wash my face and walk across campus to meet Shaun at our bench by the covered bridge. I don't remember what he said to comfort me. He was missing his favorite class to be with me when I needed him most. He didn't have words and he said as much. But it didn't matter. He held me and let me cry and that was enough. I just wanted to go home and take care of my brother and my father. But it would be a month before classes were done and then I was going on a ten-day trip to Ireland with Concert Choir. *Can I fake my way through for that long?* With Shaun by my side, I felt like I could do anything. It was Shaun's dedication to me which gave me the determination to gather my mental faculties and press on. Robot-like I went to classes, rehearsals, practice sessions, voice and piano lessons, work, church. None of these things mattered or made sense anymore, but I knew I had to do them.

I felt too numb to fully process an email which Andy sent to hundreds of people only days after his diagnosis.

> Dear Friends,
>
> I woke up at 3am a few nights ago and looked out my window. Shrouded by trees and mist, I saw a lamppost, burning brightly through the night air. It so struck me that I stared at it for a few moments.
>
> It reminded me of C.S. Lewis' "The Lion, the Witch, and the Wardrobe," where the kids enter the hidden world Narnia through a wardrobe. After entering, the hanging fur coats in the wardrobe turn to fir trees, and eventually they see a lamppost ahead. The lamppost becomes the symbol of their entrance into the new world, and the wardrobe the symbol for the old. Well, I feel kind of like Lucy entering the wardrobe and an unknown world for the very first time. Only I didn't want or ask to go in; I was sort of hurled in and the door locked behind me. What is in this world? I don't know; it's all foreign to me. And somehow, I have to find another way out. But as I walk on, I see the lamppost ahead, burning brightly. I have a feeling the lamp will be walking ahead of me for some time now, until I get out of this dark forest, maybe even longer. If I turn to the side or the back, I stare at the trees and the darkness and I grow scared: these trees are so big, and what could be behind them?! Why am I here?
>
> But if I turn again to the light, I see the lamppost out in front again, almost waiting for me; if I look closely, the lamppost is shedding tears for me, relieved that I have turned back. Whatever questions I had that were so pressing only seconds ago are gone with the mist, and my hope is restored again, for this, indeed, is God in front of me.

And, I do feel a thousand voices cheering me on and lifting me up in prayer.

My family and my girlfriend, Mary, are right there, holding my hand. I cannot thank you all enough. Thank you to everyone who has expressed their love through mail, email, and phone messages. I cannot tell you how much each heartfelt word does for my spirits and for those around me.

Yeah, I thought cynically, *prayers and heartfelt words are gonna do a whole hell of a lot! I just want to get out of this world. The old world was perfectly fine in my book!* Angrily, I read the rest of his email.

To those struggling with Why:

I know a lot of folks are struggling with the Why, God? question in all of this. Is it God's will?

Well, I'm not a seminarian or a pastor, but I've had to work out my thoughts on this in a hurry. One of my good friends gave me the image that God is crying and pounding his fist on the table because of this cancer. I love that image, and I think it is right. Somehow, to me, that image seems inconsistent with it being God's will, or at least that he wanted it to happen this way. I may be toying with semantics, but that's how I feel. God did not want this anymore than he wanted Satan to inflict Job. However, God did ALLOW my cancer to happen. I also believe firmly that he will, as Romans 8:28 proclaims, use it for good. Though he may be crying at our pain, he may also be joyfully crying in anticipation of how this may affect his kingdom. I think my little brother Tim stated it best, "I consider it an honor that our family can suffer for God," first in my father's cancer a year ago, and now in this time.

Finally, I don't feel like asking why of God will get us anywhere, for two main reasons. First, for me task the question, "God, why me?" is basically to ask the question, "God, why not someone else?" With God as the only judge of human value, how could I ever dare to assert that my life is of more earthly value than anyone else;s? Secondly, I look at Job who kind of asked God why in the last several chapters of the book. Did he get anywhere? No. Except maybe smarter because he got a lecture from God on who was in charge.

There may be moments where I break down and start to ask God why, but where will it get me? Nowhere but back to leaning on God. For my family, Mary and I, that is our challenge: that through this suffering, we will be able to stand up and say that God is still in charge. I know there will be moments where we will be tested, but, as one of my high school friends pointed out to me this week, there will never be more temptations than we can bear (I Corinthians 10:13)

God bless you all.

Love,
Andy Schrier

If I was honest with myself, I hadn't even thought of why. I hadn't thought of much of anything. I was just numb; trying to pretend Andy's cancer wasn't real. But his email was difficult to ignore. The thought of God allowing Andy's cancer made me angry, and that scared me. I was supposed to have unshakable faith and suddenly I felt duplicitous. Not knowing how to process these feelings, I tried to focus on just putting one foot in front of the other, every moment of every day.

My robotic state did not go unnoticed. One day, I pulled a note with unfamiliar handwriting from my mailbox. Assuming it was innocuous, I tucked it into my backpack with its companions and didn't consider it again until I returned to my dorm room later. Rather than the innocence I expected, the note required me to make another emergency meeting with Shaun.

When I met him at the benches by the stream, I handed him the offensive piece of paper. He read it out loud.

> Dear Abby,
> You don't know me, but I've been watching you and you are a hypocrite. You say that you are a Christian, but you are just putting on a show. You just want to look good for anyone who might be watching. Well, I see you and I'm not fooled. You're nothing more than an empty, miserable person.

There was no salutation or signature.

"Do you think it's true?" I asked, when he had finished reading. He was scowling.

"I think you should tear it up and throw it away." This was not what I had expected him to suggest. "Abby, no one with pure motives writes a note to tell you how terrible of a Christian you are without identifying themselves. She even admits she doesn't actually know you. How can she judge you without knowing you or anything about what you're going through?"

He was right, of course. Whoever had written the note could have no idea my dad had cancer and my brother had just been diagnosed with it as well. Still, I had to wonder if she might be right that my particular form of Christianity was rather superficial. In truth, I felt as though I was blindly clinging to words I'd been taught all my life but was increasingly unsure of their validity. It was an extremely uncomfortable process, not unlike treading water with no hint of land in sight and a half rotted piece of driftwood as the only available floatation device. Shaun wouldn't allow me to belittle my faith so quickly, however, when I voiced my thoughts to him.

"Sweetheart," he soothed, patiently wrapping an arm around my slumping shoulders, "if your faith wasn't very important to you, it wouldn't bother you so much when it's called into question. You have no idea how much your faith has made mine stronger. Please let me rip this up and throw it away for you. It just isn't true or fair."

"Okay," I finally consented. *How does he always seem to know exactly what to say?* I watched him calmly tear the note into small pieces and drop it in a nearby trash can. Then he gently took my hand and led me back to my dorm.

Ripping up the note had only slightly diminished the effect of its words on my mind. On one hand, I was confused about my own faith. Shaun's words were comforting and helpful, but I had never been challenged in my beliefs as I was right now. He also wasn't exactly on the best terms with God right now since his friend's death and 9-11. But somehow, my wrestling match with God's role in suffering was impacting his struggle in a positive way. Sure, I had made it clear that dating me meant going to church with me. He had not fought me on this and actually seemed to be more invested than I had expected. In fact, after one of our required chapel services on campus, he had asked if we could not hold hands because it was too much of a distraction to him. Yet, I was unsatisfied with his progress in making lifestyle changes. He still liked to drink when he spent time with his other friends. I had broken up with guys for less. Unable to mentally resolve this issue, I turned my attention to a second email from Andy.

May 10, 2002
Dear Friends,
    David Wilcox, a songwriter, performs a song called "Farthest Shore." In it, he writes these words:

Let me dive into the water,
Leave behind all that I've worked for
Except what I remember and believe
And when I stand on the farthest shore
I will have all I need. (Wilcox)

I've tried to live the last few years of my life by a Christian creed of that nature. i've always known that you can't take it with you when you go. But I always thought this meant material possessions. Especially in the last two years of my life, I've tried to not worry at all about material possessions and throw my all into the Hatty Beverly Center, that tutoring program in Grand Rapids that I worked so hard for. I've tried to invest my very fibers in something worthwhile, not seeking to get anything back. In doing so, to use a cliché, I've found myself.

I'm not trying to boast but to be real. But even this, this thing that i've labored long over, the young people and tutors I love so much, the countless hours, the success, the pride-I can't take any of that with me either. It all has to stay behind-even what I've worked for in this life.

Now I stand on the farthest shore, and I truly have all that I need. I dove into the water and left behind so much and so many that I love. I can still see all of it on the other shore. But now that I've left everything, I stand here alone, naked, not ashamed, yet vulnerable. I truly have nothing that I came here with. I turn my back on the other shore, wide-eyed into the wilderness, ready to face . . . well, I don't know what.

But I do have something: what I remember and believe, what I've learned in my life's journey so far.

It's funny how God uses places to teach you things. For example, he has always let me struggle here in Ohio. I've fought several battles here. When I first moved here, I struggled with shyness, popularity, not being good at sports, fitting in, and owning a faith that was really my parents' and not mine. Then, during college, I came back here for the summers. One summer, I wrestled my toughest battle ever against depression and anxiety brought on by my RA year at college and a breakup. And now, I'm here again to fight this battle.

And through it all, God used Grand Rapids to teach me the stuffing in the middle of the oreo, what I needed to know in between. In Grand Rapids, I learned the life lessons I needed to know to not care about popularity, to take ownership of MY faith, to conquer anxiety and depression, and to find the passions in life that make me tick.

It's a tale of two cities, if you will, the best of times and the worst of times. But I will always have those experiences as I go through this.

Finally, I realize that I have my family and friends. I'm not sure how the analogy fits, but this great cloud of witnesses is cheering me on, praying for me, encouraging me, crying for me, telling me wonderful things about myself, showering me with gifts and mail, and above all, time. If I ever struggled with popularity in my life, my diagnosis with cancer sure has cleared that right up. And I'm not really sure why. I don't feel like I deserve all this attention. I'm really just a messed up sinner like everyone else.

Someone told me that I don't deserve to go through this. I agree. No one does. We all deserve a lot worse. Only because of what Jesus did on the cross are we able to even limp through one day of life on this earth. He's given me 25 beautiful years, and often, in the words of another favorite artist, "this blessedness of life sometimes brings me to my knees."

Because of this, if I have to leave everything on that shore and say goodbye forever, I'm okay with that. Yeah, I've got dreams that I haven't realized, but that will probably be true even when I'm 80. If it comes down to that, I hope to see you all in heaven. (By the way, this is not a stance that I developed in the last few weeks in reaction to my situation. It is, however, a stance that I have kept strongly since the developments in the last few weeks. Maybe that matters to someone.)

As I see it, this is not a time for weak-kneed or pew-padded Christianity. Not that there is really any time or tolerance on God's part for such things, but for me, this is more urgent of a time for sincere belief than ever. You see, I'm about to look death in the face and say, "Do what YOU will, but unless GOD will, YOU will NOT." I can't say that with a shaky voice or with any wavering in my belief. I truly pray and believe that if we, as a prayer army, can challenge ourselves to be true Jesus followers, the we will be more than conquerors through Jesus Christ, in any trial, not just this one.

Thank you all for everything! As always, we feel surrounded and uplifted by your prayers and support.

Love,
Andy Schrier

I couldn't process this email. I read the words, but I couldn't expend the emotional energy required to tackle their meaning. I had looked to the theological concepts I was sure to find in Andy's email as a distraction. Instead, I found another dilemma I could not bear to face —Andy's illness and possible demise.

For a couple of days, I ignored both issues until circumstances forced me to turn my attention back to my romantic relationship. Shaun was planning to go to a family wedding in Minnesota. I hadn't yet met any of his family, but he'd told me enough about them that I was sure there would be an open bar at the reception. As I hugged and kissed him goodbye, I nearly begged him. "Be good? Please? For me?" His response was mischievous and noncommittal.

"Depends on what being good means." There was a twinkle in his eye, but his meaning was clear. He was planning to fully enjoy himself. Hiding my emotions was not a skill I'd ever acquired, so I was certain he saw my disappointed expression as he hopped into his car. That night, I lay in my bed, silently arguing with God.

I need to break up with him, God. The tears were already flowing freely. *I think I'm falling in love with him, but I don't want to end up marrying someone who could become an alcoholic. Everyone says he's a great guy, and he really is. Everyone says we're a great couple, but I just don't like the drinking.* I spent several minutes monologuing about my dilemma until the memory of the anonymous note interrupted my thoughts. So much of it was true—I did doubt God.

"Who are you to judge him?" God seemed to say in silence, as my mind quieted enough to listen. "You doubt my goodness and my love for you, but I have put Shaun in your life at this particular time for a reason; because I love you. I am capable of overcoming your doubt. Let me take care of Shaun, too." These words were not spoken audibly but overcame me like a flood. They were a soft, gentle hug filling me up from the inside. I could not argue, so I closed my eyes and let sleep come.

When Shaun returned, I did not ask if he had drunk or how much. I already knew the answer and I knew he didn't need a guilt trip from me. I clung to the promise God had given me.

Chapter 7

BY MID-MAY, most of the students had gone home for the summer. Those of us in Concert Choir, however, were excitedly preparing to travel to Ireland for a ten-day tour of Dublin and Galway, giving concerts at churches along the way. We had an extra day to kill before our departure. That night I received Andy's third mass email.

> May 16, 2002
> Dear Friends,
>   Before Daniel went into the Lions' den, he must have been a wreck. Oh, I'm sure he prayed like crazy beforehand, trusting that the Lord would protect him. But I don't think there is a human alive who could have enough faith in God to walk into that den without a serious degree of fear and trembling.
>   I guarantee you that Daniel had nervous diarrhea that day. Of course, he trusted that God would save him, but look at those fangs, those teeth, those huge, majestic, and hungry beasts. Look at the piles of bones strewn around the den. Everyone in the kingdom probably knew criminals that had been ripped apart by those animals.
>   After a while, when I imagine that those things started purring like kitties, Daniel probably relaxed and became amazed at something that he had known all along: that God would take care of him. In my imagination, there are countless people of faith who, though they believed in God's provision to the best of their human faculties, probably trembled with anxiety and questions at the moment of truth. Well this is my moment of truth, and I'm scared. I have faith, but I also have fear and trembling.
>   We were planning to start chemotherapy on Monday, May 20, but a phone call from my oncologist changed that just a few

hours ago. The tumors appear to be growing fast and she wants to start tomorrow. Friday, May 17th, a month and a day after I was originally diagnosed in Grand Rapids, will be the first day of chemotherapy. I will be in the hospital for five days, receiving the first drug in doses as much as my system can handle.

I will be miserable at times, nauseated, puking, and without energy. Eventually I will lose my hair, and my 150 pound frame will probably do some shrinking.

I'm scared. It is indeed a terrible thing not to be able to have control of one's body. If you think about it, which I have, cancer and chemotherapy are really very interesting, and perhaps ironic enigmas. Germ cell cancer is really my own cells, from my own body, growing without supervision and organization in a way that threatens to take over the very mass that allowed their existence. They're like the prodigal son in a way.

Chemotherapy, on the other, hand, is a technology that God has revealed to man about how to combat this phenomenon of cancer. It is a series of chemical treatments that poison the cancer. But the chemicals are so strong, and often poisonous to certain parts of the human body, that they must be delivered with caution, anti-nausea drugs, and a lot of fluids to flush them out of certain organs. Some folks, after enduring chemotherapy for so long, prefer to die of cancer before the drugs kill them. While a miracle, and often successful, chemotherapy often weakens the spirits of those who receive it, sometimes more than they reduce the cancer.

My chemotherapy is not one of the worst, nor one of the easiest. At times it will be very miserable and difficult. I will be on four three-week cycles that last from now until the beginning of August. This process, standard for germ cell cancers of my sort, is 48% successful in blasting the cancer into remission, which is a far cry from liver and pancreatic cancers that are virtually incurable.

So, while I am scared, I also still have my faith, and I hope and pray that I will never seriously question it as I go through this process. So please forgive me if this email is a little longer than the last. Tis is the last day of my normal life that I will have for a while. In the meantime, i don't know if I will feel well enough to continue my lengthy updates; they may have to become shorter for a while. i'm just not sure. When I come out of this in August, I will be done. I will have turned 25 during the process. As I said at Madison Square Church the day I left Grand Rapids, there aren't many 25-year old cancer survivors walking around, but I intend to be one.

Prayer List
1) Please pray for my strength and my faith.
2) Pray for my thought life to stay positive and joyful.
3) Pray for Mary and my family, as well as any friends who may see me; it may be more difficult to watch someone go through this than to actually be the person who goes through it.
4) Pray for my relationships with Doctors, nurses, and other patients; I want to have a good attitude and represent Christ in this process.
5) Pray for the medical community at the hospital to have keen attention to detail and wisdom to see things that they need to.

Finally, I am by no means the greatest poet on earth. But my poetry means a lot to how I express myself. I would like to share this poem with everyone, and it follows after my postscript. To me, it captures my struggle, my relationship to God (Daddy), and the standards I'm setting for my own outlook on this whole ordeal. If it makes sense to you: great. If not: sorry.
Thank you for everything.

Love,
Andy Schrier

P.S.: I will have constant email access while in the hospital, with my laptop by my side, so please continue writing. I will respond to as many as possible.

TO DADDY

Daddy, daddy,
This I pray,
Which mountain shall we
Climb today?

My burden's heavy
And my faith -so small -
Next to those mountains
That you built so tall.

Daddy, daddy,
This I cry:
How could you lead me,
So young, to die?

I've followed you as close
As anyone, I guess;
So how could my journey
Be so much less?

Daddy, daddy,
This I know,
I've got more questions
When I'm feeling low.

Now Daddy listen here:
It's hard for me to be brave,
On my knees in a hole
That may soon be my grave.

Daddy, daddy,
A joyful life I've known;
Did I use up my quota of joy
With fifty years to go?

Just give me another fifty
And I'll spread your joy like seeds,
It'll grow faster than cancer,
with deeper roots than weeds.

Daddy, daddy,
One more thing to say:
Don't leave me all alone
And then go on your way.

This pain is a burden
And my fear is at its height
I can only bear it daddy,
If you stay tonight.

Daddy, daddy,
This I pray,
Which mountain shall we
Move today?

A mustard seed,
Is that faith enough?
You rewrote the book
On how men are to be "tough."

Daddy, daddy,
I ask you one more thing:
You healed so many people,
You stole from death its sting.

I know you can heal me
And how will you choose?
My feet are way too small
To wear any of your shoes.

Daddy, daddy,
This I choose:
Enough of my silly questions-
We don't have time to lose.

As long as I live this moment-
Perhaps more down the way-
I'm gonna live each minute
With such joy to burst a day.

But Daddy, daddy,
May your will be done.
I'm happy to walk with you,
Until another day is done.

And knowing that you treasure
Each minute you walk with me
Is enough to boggle my mind;
I have to believe it before I see.

Andy's words were jarring. I felt as though I was in a fog, driving towards a distant light which threatened to reveal the dangers all around me. I had a choice—drive toward the light into the danger I knew lay ahead, or veer off into the dark, risking the unknown.

Feeling utterly confounded, I turned off my computer and joined Shaun in one of the many student lounges. It was eerily empty, now that all of the students had gone home for the summer. As I sat down next to him, he looked at me awkwardly for a moment, then began to stutter over his thoughts.

"I . . . I . . . um . . ." he started. Stuttering was very uncharacteristic of him and it made me squirm inwardly, if not outwardly. I hoped he wasn't going to say "I love you." In fact, I was surprised to find that I was dreading hearing such a declaration. How could I respond? I was pretty sure we were quickly headed toward falling in love, but I wasn't positive that was the best direction, considering my misgivings about him. All of these thoughts went through my mind in a mere moment as I observed Shaun's uncharacteristic discomfort. He stammered on, oblivious to my concerns.

"How should I say this? Um . . . well, I'm sorry if I haven't said something and you are expecting me to say it." The words tumbled out as though escaping from a long captivity. He paused to glance cautiously at me and relaxed when he recognized a look of relieved amusement on my face. Then he continued.

"I'm just not sure. I mean, I think I do . . . you know, but people say when you do, you just know and I don't think I've felt that yet."

I responded quickly to ease his mind, "I agree. I'm not ready yet either and I don't want us to ruin it if and when the time is right." The mental capacity to formulate thoughts around this conversation eluded me. Yet, somehow, in avoiding pressuring me into a deeper commitment than I was ready to enter, while at the same time being considerate of my emotions, Shaun solidified a greater respect for his character in my mind.

THE NEXT DAY, all the members of Concert Choir gathered outside of the music building to receive our final instructions and load our things onto the bus. Our director and three chaperones were as jittery as we were. As the bus rolled out, and each of the chaperones gave their instructional speeches, the excitement level began to climb, along with the noise. I held back somewhat from the hubbub, feeling as though I was betraying my family, or at least ignoring their needs. Andy was home with Mom and Daddy in Ohio for the summer. His girlfriend, Mary, was there too and would share my bedroom with me when I returned. While I was gone, he would start his chemotherapy. At least I knew he was well cared for until I got home. *Thank you, God,* I uttered under my breath.

All at once, I remembered Tim's wedding which would be taking place shortly after I got home as well. I had only met Leslie a couple of times and she was fairly quiet, but Tim was crazy about her. A wedding would be a very welcome distraction from the illness which plagued my family. *Thank you, God,* I repeated. It was all I could manage.

The hustle of the John F. Kennedy Airport helped to take my mind farther from the internal struggle. But as the plane began to ascend into the sky, and the ocean stretched out across the horizon, in front and behind, my heart began to race.

"Are you okay, Abby?" Shaun looked at me with concern.

"My ears are just hurting from the pressure." It was true, but more immediately, I was panicking. My chest felt tight and my palms were sweaty. Short, shallow breaths felt like stretching a rubber band just shy of its breaking point. I squeezed my eyes closed as hard as I could.

"He's not dead yet. Not dead yet. Not dead YET." Daddy's words began to pound in my head. I couldn't hear what was going on around me, only Daddy's voice, dripping with fear. I gripped both arms of my seat and took several deep breaths, willing myself to think positively. *He is okay for now. There's nothing I can do from here. I'll have plenty of time to care for him in a few days. He'll still need me when I get home.*

By the time the airplane had reached its intended altitude and the seatbelt light flickered off, I was able to gain control over the fear in my mind. At the moment, my friends were having too much fun to not join them. I forced myself to enter into a card game and the interaction quickly helped me recover from the panic attack. Seeing that I was okay, Shaun traded seats with Melody so she could join our game and he could spend some time with some of his friends.

I'm sure the other passengers on the airplane were more than a little irritated by our antics, which lasted well into the night. Eventually, Mrs. Tedford instructed us to get some sleep before our flight landed at 6:00 a.m., London Time. Then we would only have a couple of hours to settle into our hotel before our tour would start. Completely exhausted, I curled up in my seat and slept on Melody's shoulder until landing.

Shortly after arriving in Dublin, I stopped at a phone booth in an attempt to call my family. I had a calling card which was supposed to have worked internationally, but it was giving me a good bit of trouble. Being totally unfamiliar with international travel, I decided to call collect instead. After going through the procedure, I heard my mother's voice accepting the charges. I quickly spoke to her, then Daddy and Andy. I even spoke to Mary for a moment, who thanked me for sharing my bedroom with her for the summer. As usual, Andy's arrival at home seemed to have cheered everyone dramatically, despite the reason for his being there. The few short minutes on the phone with them was enough to reassure me that they were okay for the moment. I learned later that the last call cost my parents $50. We all laughed about it, agreeing that it was a small price to pay for mutual peace of mind.

The days in Ireland were filled with sightseeing and concerts. It was not difficult to put the worries of home behind me. The first few days we spent in and around Dublin, visiting the landmarks and singing in local churches. One evening, we had some free time and Shaun took me out for a posh dinner. We sat at a candle-lit table by a window overlooking the famous St. Stephen's Green, an expansive park which we'd explored earlier that day. As we sat talking and enjoying the delectable meal, he reached across the table and took my hand. I looked up into his eyes and an unknown warmth spread through me. Was it merely the flame of the candle reflecting in his eyes, or was there a glow there I hadn't seen before? We smiled at one another at the same moment. The warmth deepened, causing my fingers and toes to tingle, and settled in my chest, where it felt as though it might overflow. Suddenly, I realized we were both grinning. Tears came from nowhere and threatened to spill over. The words Shaun had said a few days ago popped into my head.

"People say when you are . . . you just know." It was easy to see that at the moment Shaun had reached for my hand, we both knew. There was no going back. *I'm in love with him,* I thought. *This is the man I want to spend the rest of my life with.* We didn't speak for the rest of the meal, for fear of interfering with the magic. When dinner was over and the last crumbs of a shared dessert had been licked off of our forks, we agreed to head back to the hotel. It was just a short walk and the boisterous sounds of the first-floor pub broke our awed silence. Not wanting to miss a moment of the supernatural experience, we headed to a couch in a quiet corner of the hotel to be alone for a few more minutes. For a time we simply looked into each other's eyes. There was no need for words. It was clear we both were thinking the same thing. Slowly, Shaun leaned forward and kissed me. We had kissed before, and many past boyfriends had also kissed me. But no kiss had ever given me goose bumps over my entire body as this one did. I rested my head on his chest, content to just be with him. His arms held me close; I could imagine no better place. Finally, he pulled me up so he could look into my eyes again. His eyes were wet with emotion; a rare thing for him.

"I still want to wait. I want us to be completely sure." I was briefly disappointed, but I didn't need him to say the words. I knew his hesitancy was an attempt to preserve our integrity, just in case it didn't work out. I was too happy to be annoyed and rather respected his restraint. Besides, what if this glorious feeling faded once we were apart for the summer? I smiled back at him and nodded my consent.

Glad he hadn't upset me, he continued, "When we get back to the States, you have to go to Ohio and I have to go to New York. It will be hard, but I think we should wait until the end of the summer when we see each other again." I loved challenges and I felt certain nothing could come between us, so I agreed.

Chapter 8

ALL TOO SOON, I was back in the U.S., driving my Oldsmobile in the direction of Ohio. Saying goodbye to Shaun had been one of the hardest things I'd ever done. We couldn't say what we so desperately wanted to. So, instead, he took a picture of me by my car to keep as a souvenir, kissed me and whispered in my ear, "Those three little words are all I want to say to you right now." How could a girl drive three hundred miles in the opposite direction after that?

And then there was the looming reality of what I was driving home to. My job was going to be to take care of the cooking, cleaning, laundry and gardening while Daddy continued to recover and while Andy was getting treatments. Mom and Mary would take care of the men. It was helpful to have a plan in mind, but it seemed like a lot. I had done each of those things, but had never been fully responsible for all of them. And what about Mary? What would she be like? What if I didn't like her? What if she didn't like me? What if she wasn't good enough for Andy?

I tried to put the more obvious concerns out of my mind. I didn't allow my mind to linger on the possibility that both of these two men would be drastically different than I remembered them. I preferred to imagine the best and face the reality when it slapped me in the face. Besides, how could I prepare for the unknown?

There was a small greeting party awaiting me when I arrived home. Daddy and Mom were the first to hug me and Andy was close behind. Daddy's hugs always enveloped me totally, making me feel as though he would never allow anything to harm me. But today I was shocked to find that his hug seemed weary and frail. It was I who attempted to impart some extra strength into those brief seconds. Mom's hug was anxious. Recently it seemed this was her default setting. Andy's hug, however, was as robust as ever. His curls covered his head as always, and though he was not much bigger than me, his athletic frame easily lifted me off the ground and swung me around. At times, this exuberant brother of mine had been the best friend I had. I could not comprehend that he had just endured six days of chemotherapy. Clearly he had recovered well. I didn't ask him how he was faring so well in the face of such adversity because Mary was waiting shyly beside him.

The next few days were telling. Mary and I clicked and I found myself opening up to her about Shaun more than I had anticipated. I needed someone who would share my joy and Daddy was certainly not joyful about me being in love. Mom just didn't have the emotional capacity to listen to all the details of my romance. But Mary seemed to need the distraction as much as I did and she, in turn, told me bits of her relationship with Andy. It became quite clear that this shy, detail-oriented girl perfectly complimented Andy.

ONE MORNING, a few days after I arrived home, I noticed Andy had chunks of hair starting to fall out of his head. I didn't know what to say about it and it seemed no one else did either. We all remained silent, but I think we were all relieved when he began to joke about it, shaved his head and gave the owner of a local hat shop a modest amount of business, buying various headgear for various occasions. He bought a particularly dapper top hat for Tim's wedding in just a few days. I inwardly marveled at his steadfastness but didn't dare comment about it for fear it would shatter under the pressure—or I would.

A few days later, I received another group email from Andy. The contents helped to explain Andy's state of mind. It read:

6-6-02
Dear Friends,
    The name Israel means to strive or struggle with God. Jacob, a patriarch of the nation of Israel, won the name after wrestling all night with a man that turned out to be either God or an angel. The story seems oddly placed in Genesis 32: one moment Jacob is very concerned with avoiding Esau's wrath and getting his family home and across a river quickly, the next moment he is wrestling with some random guy in the desert. Now I'm a wrestler, but I prefer not to stay up all night fighting folks that I just happen to meet in the desert at midnight.
    Whatever details are clouded here, it is clear that this man was not able to defeat Jacob, so he touched his hip and dislo-

cated it, and gave him the name Israel. In fact, Jacob would not let the mysterious stranger go until he had blessed him. So the man blessed Jacob; after the man left, Jacob realized that he had wrestled with God himself. Jacob, however, walked away with a limp.

Honestly, this story shocks me sometimes: how is it that God can get away with blatant physical damage of one of his children? Doesn't this pose a serious problem to those of us who believe in God as a compassionate and benevolent lover of his people? How can I trust a God who blesses and physically harms within the same breath of his almighty power?

I think I understand this passage a lot better after this week. If I can make an analogy that a hip is something we stand or rely on for emotional stability, then God has dislocated one of my hips this week.

In his own unique way, God made me aware that in the last week I have placed too much hope and trust for my healing in the medical process. After all, my prognosis is favorable compared to most other cancers. Also, my chemotherapy isn't one of the toughest treatments being used. From a medical perspective, this is a favorable cancer to have.

And, in God's equally unique way, he has dislocated my hip; he has violently severed me from the hope that medicine will cure this cancer. Why? So that I can be totally reliant on Him for the cure.

Now some may say that I shouldn't even proceed with chemotherapy in that case. However, there is an important distinction to make between such stance and one that places all hope in God for healing, acknowledging that God can use chemotherapy and medicine as weapons in his vast arsenal. Indeed, he allowed "science" to "discover" this knowledge in the first place, in order that his people be less afflicted.

To some, this may seem like a total contradiction, or a paradox. "What is the difference," you might ask, "you're still receiving chemotherapy?"

The difference is in my attitude and my allegiance. God has made it mentally impossible for me to continue trusting in anyone or anything but Him for healing. As far as I'm concerned, I have cancer in my body that will kill me unless God intervenes on my behalf.

Back to Jacob, I believe that something similar happened to him. Perhaps God desired Jacob's trust. So, at a moment when Jacob needed speed and physical ability most for survival, God interrupted his hope, blessed him, and made it impossible for Jacob to trust in his own physical ability. Why? So that Jacob would be totally dependent on God for survival in a tough situation. Instead of running, Jacob had to trust that God would protect him and fight for him.

We serve a jealous God who deserves and desires our affection, trust, and total reliance. As one of my pastors remarked in a sermon a few weeks ago, those of us in middle and upper class America live in the wealthiest, most plentiful society ever. It is extremely difficult to rely on God when we live in green pastures as we rely on God when we journey through the deserts of life. We place a lot of trust, hope and faith in our own abilities, diligence and finances, rather than in God who allowed us to acquire them.

I would like to challenge that maybe we need to boldly pray for God to dislocate our "hips," or the things that we stand on aside from God. I will warn you, weak-kneed or pew-padded Christians should not pray this prayer, because it will mean a total paradigm shift in your hopes and trusts. For those who are bold enough, I think we will change radically from a pat-myself-on-the-back, sometimes self-worshipping brand of Christianity to one where we are totally dependent on God for survival, and totally in awe of the fact that he provides for our needs.

And isn't that exactly where we ought to be?

Mary has moved in safely. She is getting along well with her roommate, my sister Abby, who is also home from college from the summer. Mary's addition to the family during this time is priceless. God has blessed our relationship, along with her relationship with the rest of the family. It is also extremely good to have Abby back.

My hair started to fall out on Monday morning, so I shaved it off along with the facial hair. Being bald is both an adjustment, as well as a poignant physical reminder of the battle itself. It was a difficult wake-up call at first, but we are able to laugh about it now. I wear a lot of different hats (when you usually hear people say that it means something else!).

Finally, on Sunday June 9th I begin the second cycle of chemo. I will write again as soon as I get home from the hospital. Thank you for all your prayers and support.

Love,
Andy Schrier

There in those words lay the key to getting through the trials of Daddy's and Andy's sicknesses. Andy had grasped more from that bizarre Bible story than I could have imagined possible. I felt just like Jacob, wrestling with God when I was in such desperate need of His help. Could Andy be right that the God of the universe, who knew my every thought before I was even born, intended this hardship to strengthen me? I felt so torn down, not strengthened. But I was not even the one who was sick. If Andy could muster so much faith, couldn't I? Somehow I found myself taking emotional and spiritual support from the very one whose suffering was causing me to stumble in the first place.

Chapter 9

HUMMING COULD BE HEARD from many corners of the Schrier house. The rooms began to fill with my siblings and their families. Laughter was everywhere—real laughter, not awkward, forced, half-hearted laughter (although there was still some of that too). It was the day before Tim and Leslie's wedding. Tonight we would all gather for the rehearsal dinner. Tomorrow there would be dancing, singing, and celebrating. My only reservation was Shaun was not with me. How appropriate it would have been for him to be included in the festivities. One day he would be a part of this family, after all. I was sure they would all like him very much. Mom gave me a hesitant smile when I shared this with her. Daddy scowled and I could see in his brooding green eyes that he still pictured me as the pigtailed little girl who climbed through the hay stacks in the barn at Laughter Farm in search of new kittens.

Despite Daddy's misgivings, the rehearsal dinner for Tim's big day served only to solidify my plans with Shaun. I could not keep my mind off of what I would want for my own wedding, which seemed impossibly far away. I knew I would not be given my parents' blessing to get married before I graduated. I daydreamed about Daddy walking me down the aisle between rows of folding chairs on the lawn of our treasured farmhouse in Maryland, healthy and robust. I envisioned Shaun waiting for me on the front porch and saw Daddy happily placing my hand in Shaun's before the two of us climbed the porch steps together. The image brought stinging tears of joy to my eyes. A sudden sense of impatience came over me and I desperately wanted a remote which possessed the ability to fast forward time.

No, no! I mentally regrouped. *This is Tim's day. One day it will be our turn, but I still have two years of college to finish. And Daddy needs time to warm up to Shaun and get used to the idea that I'm not a child anymore. I'll always be his little girl, but I'm not a child.*

My mind vacillated between planning my wedding to Shaun and forcing myself to be mentally present for Tim. The rehearsal dinner was held at a beautiful outdoor setting with delectable food and even better company. Tim and Leslie seemed to float on air in their anticipation of the next day's festivities. Our larger, louder family dominated the evening. Leslie's family was significantly smaller in number and the majority of them seemed to be fairly reserved, like Leslie. Andy was, as usual, the hub around which the excitement of the evening centered. His top hat poetically shielded our minds from the evidence of his disease. His usual boisterousness and magnetism caused everyone to forget their concern about him and Daddy. I admired this about him. He always had the ability to cheer everyone in a room, no matter the circumstances.

The next morning, I pampered myself, straightening my hair the way Daddy liked, and getting dolled up for the wedding. As I prepared, I warmed up my voice for the duet I would be singing with Daddy during the ceremony. Andy, Dave, and Pete were putting the final touches on a song they had written for the reception. Andy, challenged with the task of making an audience laugh, was even more chipper than he'd been the evening before. Daddy and Jen, who would also be singing in the ceremony, were also warming up.

Daddy emerged handsomely suited from his room. His tall frame seemed to be moving more gingerly today than I had noticed before. He looked pale and seemed much older than his sixty-three years. Everyone in the living room gasped when Mom stepped out of her bedroom, strikingly adorned in the gold lace gown she and I had found together. She was a humble woman, not one who was prone to vanity, but she was beautiful and could easily pull off such elegant attire when the occasion called for it.

"Mom! You look amazing!" I declared. Daddy was beaming at her. For a moment, she smiled cautiously at the praise. Then, looking at Daddy, her worry lines reappeared. His admiring smile didn't hide his pain. She knew him too well, and so did I. In that moment, I wanted desperately to snap my fingers and take all the cancer away—from him and from Andy. No more cancer, no more worry. But I was helpless.

The rest of the family seemed to notice the interaction between Mom and Daddy, too, and everyone awkwardly returned to what they had previously been doing. We all distracted ourselves with the preparations until it was time to pile into cars and head to the church. But there was no more humming, and no more laughter. No one spoke of what had happened; the joy of the day was now muddled as though someone had smeared a muddy brown hue over a vibrantly painted, flowery landscape.

The ceremony went smoothly and a fine outdoor reception followed. Andy's song procured many laughs. Everyone outside of our family danced and carried on as though nothing was amiss. Perhaps I had merely been blind to it before, but Daddy was clearly not in remission. His every move was tempered with the severity of his pain. Last night's wedding day-dreaming seemed selfish and trite. Daddy was my number one man right now and I felt an urgency to appreciate the time I had with him.

"Can I have this dance?" Daddy held his hand out to me. *I might not have another chance. This dance is a gift, just to be close to him.*

I don't remember the song. I think it was an old jazz standard. I just remember snuggling comfortably into his chest. My five-foot three-inch frame barely brought me to his shoulders. He placed his chin gently on the top of my head, making me feel safely tucked into him. In that moment, I rejoiced that there was no reason to scramble to repair our relationship as so many people did when a loved one was in their last days. We had always been close. I was blessed. But how could I be without him? How would Mom survive? How would our family hold together?

The song ended and I handed him over to Mom, who had been watching us with a sad sort of smile. Shorter than me by an inch or two, Mom had to stand barefoot on top of Daddy's feet to reach him. As I watched them sway together as if they were one body, I marveled at their deep love for one another. Their thirty-some years of marriage had wizened and seasoned them. I lost myself in admiring the beauty of their relationship. *They are not star-crossed lovers anymore, although sometimes I do see glimpses of that—like when Daddy first saw Mom in her dress today. More often, they just seem to admire and respect each other so deeply. They work so well as a team, because they know each other's strengths and weaknesses. God, help me learn from their example.* I marveled at the analogy hidden within this dance. They moved together in the give and take of life, just as they were doing now on the dance floor.

Before long, someone noticed that Tim and Leslie had mysteriously and conveniently disappeared. Reluctantly, I returned home with my family. The end of the wedding meant the entrance back into reality. Time seemed to have frozen when I was in Daddy's arms, but now it continued its relentless march forward.

Chapter 10

A LAZY WEEK WENT BY with no spectacular events. Daddy and Andy were both exhausted after the wedding and had to rest for a few days. With the wedding in the past, we began to develop a routine. Mom led Mary and me in a daily Bible study on the book of Ruth. We cared for the men, did chores around the house, swam in the pool, cooked meals, and generally stayed busy. Mary and I were developing a unique friendship, and I was seeing Mom in a new light. While I'd always been close to Daddy, Mom and I had been too similar in personality to be terribly close before now. My preteen years had been particularly tumultuous. But now, we had a common cause. A very special bond was developing between us as a result.

We adopted Psalm 91 as our theme chapter in the Bible. It had become a special comfort to Mom and she shared it with Mary and me. Its rhythmic verses stoked the fire of our hope. God would rescue our beloved men from their diseases. Whenever we felt particularly challenged, Mom would read it out loud to us.

> Whoever dwells in the shelter of the Most High will rest in the shadow of the Almighty.
> I will say of the Lord, "He is my refuge and my fortress, my God, in whom I trust."
> Surely he will save you from the fowler's snare and from the deadly pestilence.
> He will cover you with his feathers, and under his wings you will find refuge;
> his faithfulness will be your shield and rampart.
> You will not fear the terror of night, nor the arrow that flies by day,
> nor the pestilence that stalks in the darkness, nor the plague that destroys at midday.

> A thousand may fall at your side, ten thousand at your right hand,
> but it will not come near you.
> You will only observe with your eyes and see the punishment of
> the wicked.
> If you say, "The Lord is my refuge," and you make the Most High
> your dwelling,
> no harm will overtake you, no disaster will come near your tent.
> For he will command his angels concerning you to guard you in
> all your ways;
> they will lift you up in their hands, so that you will not strike your
> foot against a stone.
> You will tread on the lion and the cobra, you will trample the great
> lion and the serpent.
> "Because he loves me," says the Lord, "I will rescue him;
> I will protect him, for he acknowledges my name.
> He will call on me, and I will answer him; I will be with him in
> trouble,
> I will deliver him and honor him.
> With long life I will satisfy him and show him my salvation. (NIV)

We began to claim these words, confident they applied to Daddy and Andy. They were both men who loved God, who acknowledged Him and called on Him. Certainly the Lord would rescue them in their trouble and satisfy them with long life.

Mid-June meant it was time for Andy's next chemo treatment. Our seemingly lazy home became frenzied with activity. I helped pack lunches and assured Mom I would be ok with the house, garden and dog. Still, she fussed over having everything just so and being sure I knew all I needed to know. She was only going to be gone for the day. I was neither incompetent nor inexperienced, but I let her fuss anyway. This unusual nervous energy from her was a distraction from her reason for leaving.

"Daddy will be home from work around 6:30, and there is chicken for you to make for dinner. I'll try to be home around then, too, but the traffic is horrible because of the construction. Oh, I forgot to water the plants." She bustled towards the back door, but I stopped her with a gentle hand on her arm.

"It's okay, Mom. I'll water them. You don't want Andy to be late." She turned around to walk out to the garage in agreement, but threw out one last instruction, "Be sure to do it right away before it gets too hot."

"I will, Mom. It will be fine." She seemed to be satisfied and left with

Andy and Mary in Andy's little tan Toyota Corolla. Mom would return that evening, but Andy and Mary would stay at the hospital for the full five days of the treatment. It would be a long week for them and the anxiety showed on Mary's face. But not Andy's; he was a rock. His faith seemed to never waver, nor did his sense of humor. I was jealous of these attributes, but no matter how hard I tried, I could not make them true of myself. My emotions seemed to shift with every crashing wave.

Finding myself alone in that big house brought on deep loneliness. Being alone was one of my least favorite things. As I filled Mom's repurposed milk jugs with water for the plants, I pondered what I would do to make the time go more quickly until I had to fix dinner. I could walk Zaccheus, our giant white dog, go rollerblading in the driveway, work on my tan, and I could always check my email. I would probably have something new from Shaun. At that realization, I decided to head to the computer as soon as all the plants were watered.

Even though it was completely expected, my heart skipped a beat to see the waiting message from Shaun. Just as I did each day, I treasured every word. Poor Shaun had developed mono and was suffering from fatigue and high fevers. But he was resting up so he could drive from New York to Ohio for a visit in a month and a half. It had become our habit to end our emails by saying "those three little words," since we had agreed not to actually say them until we saw each other again. In the past, the new relationship jitters went away after a few days for me, but this time they just seemed to get worse with the passing of time. I had actually lost some weight without even trying just because my stomach was in such a nervous state that my appetite had waned significantly. I didn't mind being a little thinner, but wished I didn't feel queasy every time I thought of him—which was nearly all the time.

After sending a get well response, being sure to use our special salutation, I practically bounced through the rest of the day. He was coming! When Daddy came home from work, I had dinner ready, but I don't remember what else I did that day. I was too excited to think about anything but my love. *He's coming! I'll have to ask Mom and Daddy, of course. Well, I'll ask Mom. She'll convince Daddy. I should get Shaun something, or do something special for him. But what would he even like? I could get him a book. He's always reading, always learning. But that's too boring. I think I need to make him something. Something that will really show him I love him.* I spent the day doing who knows what while I pondered this conundrum. After dinner, I brought my large stack of pictures from Ireland to the table, hoping something in them would spark my creative juices. *It would be fun to make some kind of collage with all of the best pictures. But how can I choose between so many? I'll make him a scrapbook!*

Scrapbooking was a fad in the crafting world at the time. I'd tried my hand at it, but didn't love it. I found my attention span lacking. But for Shaun, I felt I could do just about anything if it would bring a smile to his face. Over the next few days, I visited some local craft and art stores to gather supplies and began organizing all of my photos. I spent all of my spare time carefully constructing each page as a visual souvenir of each memory from our trip. I used the internet to find out how to say "I love you" in Irish Gaelic and practiced writing it in calligraphy. I planned to use it as a heading for the very last page of the scrapbook.

In the meantime, Mary and Andy returned home. Andy was not too worn down from his chemo treatment and remained hopeful that it was eliminating the cancer cells. He had a CT scan on Friday and then an appointment on Monday with his oncologist to review its findings. Daddy was still in tremendous pain in his lower back and kidney area, but he had an appointment with Dr. F. scheduled for next Thursday to determine the cause and try to fix it. The atmosphere in the house was one of cautious optimism. In just a few short days we hoped to have two very positive reports.

With that hope in mind, I allowed myself to get lost in perfecting every little detail of this special project for Shaun. Joy awaited me each time I sat down to work on what would normally seem like a very tedious task. As I worked, I contemplated Andy's latest email.

6-20-02
Dear Friends,

Mary and I have a favorite spot here in Ohio. We call it the town's best kept secret. It is a huge reserve of flowers and trees, elegantly landscaped by a local division of Ohio State University. While azaleas were in bloom, we would visit our favorite spot known as "Azalea Allee. "Right now, however, the crowning piece of the whole secret arboretum is in full bloom: the Rose Garden. We love the combination of amazing colors and smells as you walk through garden after garden, rosebush after rosebush.

I'm not a rose gardener, but I love watching how they grow. Roses grow like vines, and some of them are quite covered with thorns, with as much as 20 thorns in an inch of vine. Just like any other plant, roses have to compete with other plants for all of the natural elements they need for survival, their thorny bases curling sometimes for several yards before producing the beautiful and fragrant blossoms for which they are so beloved. They stand dormant most of the year, fighting for sun and for life, choking out all of the other plants in their competition for survival, then for a short time, they produce these beautiful, heart-wrenching, color-filled, aroma-laden flowers.

Roses are parallel to human life; those nasty thorns are as much a natural protection as a reminder to us of how tough life really is. Sometimes survival is downright difficult, while the twisting and turning of the vines remind us that life isn't always going where we expect it to be. In fact, we spend most of our lives twisting and turning, surviving, growing, competing for resources, and very little time in full bloom. Yet for a brief time every year, we are showing our best colors, we can smell and taste the fruit of our own labors, we glory in the goodness of life.

To take the analogy further, the amount of beauty that comes out of a rose is totally dependent on the Gardener. Wild roses grow, but without a caretaker are limited to the vicissitudes and whims of their own environment. For those that are watched, however, sometimes the Gardener has to do things that may truncate the beauty, like prune the blossoms, so that the flowers will be better in the future. Sometimes the Gardener has to change the direction of the plant, or spread poison that may kill nasty bugs.

I would think that the roses rarely understand the actions of the Gardener. It never feels good when we are pruned, changed in direction, or poisoned, but somehow, when the roses come out, the Gardener's way seemed to make sense in the end.

Since I'm speaking about roses, let me share a timely example that has to do with love.

First we look at it from a human viewpoint: the pruning. I was removed from my job, my girlfriend, and my church in Grand Rapids to fight a disease. I moved five hours away to be with my family while I tackle this illness. My girlfriend Mary could not stand to see me fight the battle from afar, so she obtained a leave of absence from her work to move in with my family for the summer. Now both of our lives are interrupted, and we can't spend any time working on productive things, like the ministries that our lives once were.

But now that the roses have bloomed, we have started to see things a little differently. First of all, Mary is able to go through the tough times with me. Secondly, during the good times, we have a lot of time to spend with each other. This is not the pressured, time-confined seeing each other, either. God has allowed us a lot of long hours for talking, walking, going places, joyful long hours of just being together, laughing or silent, not having to worry about normal-life pressures, locked in accompanying each other through one great struggle. What a gift! No worries about jobs, very few schedule constraints, and each day to spend together discovering God's mercies in our lives.

It is amazing to look back and see how the Gardener allowed our rose vines to twist together at just the perfect moment. Neither of us wanted me to get cancer and move away; we didn't like the painful twists and turns that were made without our control. But now the only question we have is, "Why did we even question the Gardener in the first place?"

I have no problem questioning the Gardner, I thought as I read. *Couldn't He have given them time to walk and talk and be together under more positive circumstances? It doesn't seem like a loving thing to cause a young, godly couple to suffer so much just so they can have more time together. God, why did you do this?* Stuffing my anger at God, I read on.

I struggled to find a good Biblical example of a spiritual couple, but I think Ruth and Boaz paint an amazing picture of another two roses that the Gardener intertwined through lots of pruning and change of direction.

First of all, Ruth was a Moabite widowed daughter-in-law of the Israelite Naomi who had taken refuge in Moab due to a famine in her hometown of Bethlehem. When Naomi, also a widow, decided to return impoverished, struggling and bitter to her homeland, Ruth declared her allegiance to her mother-in-law, including to her God. This is significant because Ruth was a foreigner to Israel, and because Naomi herself was bitter towards her own God. So Ruth declares her allegiance to Naomi and they return to Bethlehem in Israel.

From God's command in Leviticus 23, Israelites were required to leave the corners of their fields ungleaned by harvesters so that poor folks and foreigners could get what they needed to eat. It was humiliating work for those who chose it, but Ruth had few alternatives for making ends meet, so she began working in the fields of an Israelite named Boaz.

The situation looked bleak for Naomi and Ruth, and then suddenly, the roses bloomed and the Gardener's work started to show its beauty. Boaz, who was related to Naomi, took notice of Ruth because her commitment to Naomi impressed him greatly. He overlooked the fact that she was a foreigner, respected her integrity, and made sure she had enough to eat from his fields. Then, through the wonderful and intricate kinsman redeemer process, Boaz married Ruth, making the quality of life for Ruth and Naomi suddenly a lot better. Ruth even had the honor of becoming the great grandmother of David, the great king of Israel.

Through Ruth's faithfulness to a Gardener she didn't know, her, Naomi and Boaz were brought to see the faithful work of the Gardener.

I feel like Mary and I are in a similar situation to Ruth and Boaz because God has pruned and twisted us, and even poisoned me. But through it all, just like Ruth and Boaz, we see the hands of the Gardener. Romans 8:28 says that God works through everything for the good of those who love him, and right now we can testify that in this situation, he certainly has kept his promise.

MEDICAL UPDATE

The Bleomycin treatment on Monday was better than usual, perhaps because they gave me some different countering drugs, and the side effects were less than usual. We have a catscan of the tumor region on Friday morning to determine the effectiveness of the chemotherapy. Needless to say, this is a pretty big thing. On Monday we will discuss the results and other tumor markers (indications of what and how the tumor is doing, such as chemicals in my blood that are produced by or in reaction to the tumor) with my doctor, and we will receive the final Bleomycin treatment in this cycle.

I have recovered from the hospital treatments. I feel pretty good and strong right now. I will be enjoying a crew of visitors this weekend. My appetite is very good. I am enjoying being somewhat productive with my days, and of course, spending lots of time with Mary.

This is a good time to pray for the wisdom of the doctors as they determine what all that these signs are saying. Please pray for a good, accurate catscan on Friday morning. Please pray that I will drink the barium solution for it with relatively no problems (I hate that stuff). Please pray for our Doctor's appointment on Monday. I will probably give a brief medical update that night, just to let people know how it went. Pray that we will see the tumor well, or even that we will not see it at all (meaning it has been completely destroyed.)This is brave, but we can pray for it anyways. Pray for the last bleomycin treatment on Monday after the appointment, that it will be effective and the side effects minimal. Please pray for Mary and I, that our love continues to blossom.

Thank you all for your prayers, emails, snail mail, and thoughts. We are convinced, thoroughly, that prayer made a huge difference in how I held up under the chemotherapy of this cycle. There is just no other good explanation, except that God's people are praying effectively and frequently and for the right things. Again, I'm sorry if I can't keep up with all the correspondence, but every word of it means a lot to me.

Love,
Andy Schrier

Andy's thoughts about roses reminded me of the time he had taken me to the rose garden, just to spend time with his little sister. I had been in high school, maybe my junior or senior year. Like a dutiful big brother, he asked about my latest boyfriend and my relationship with God. He reminded me to be careful who I dated and to be sure to look for guys who truly loved God. Now he was that guy for Mary. Every day I watched them walk together, leading one another closer to God and her supporting him as he battled this evil disease. As I placed pictures and captions in my scrapbook, I prayed silently for Andy and Mary.

God, let them have many years on this journey together. Make the tumors disappear so he can be himself again and she won't have to take care of him like this anymore. Help him continue to be the spiritual leader in the home that they will establish. Let them make it to that point, God! As I prayed, a picture landed in a crooked position on the page, a stubborn piece of photo tape holding it there. I struggled to unstick it without marring the decorative paper or ripping the precious picture of Shaun and me. The scuffle shifted my focus fully to the problematic picture. I studied its contents for a moment and there, looking back at me, was the man I had fallen in love with.

The all too familiar knot started to tighten in my stomach again. Ignoring it, I forced my brain to move on to planning the few short days of Shaun's visit. Of course, I would have to take him to the rose garden. A visit to the quaint little ice cream shop in which I had worked for so many summers was also a necessity. He would be in town long enough to attend the church I had grown up in and meet some of my oldest friends.

Finally winning my wrestling match with the photo, I marveled that anyone could enjoy such a thing as scrapbooking. I was artistic enough. I could draw a bit and didn't mind doing crafty things, but this was obnoxious. I was thrilled with the pages I had completed, though, and I continued my work, anxious to see Shaun's face when I finally gave it to him. *When should I hand it over*, I wondered. *I don't want to tell him what the last page says until he says those three little words to me. How will he do that? I know he's meticulously planning exactly how he wants to say it. That's just who he is. Ooooh, I cannot wait!*

Eventually I gave up trying to imagine the upcoming event. Too much daydreaming could spoil the joy when the time finally came. I retired that evening, hopeful that the times of trial were soon behind us and our tired family would soon have the joy of welcoming Mary and then Shaun officially into the fold—and Daddy would be well for all of it.

Chapter 11

AFTER AN OPTIMISTIC WEEKEND, both Daddy and Andy came home on Monday with disturbing news. Daddy's back pain was due, just as he had suspected, to blockages in his kidneys. He was dangerously close to kidney failure and would need exploratory surgery on Thursday to help the kidneys drain properly.

Andy's news was not as bleak, but we had been certain he would report that the tumors were gone, so we were somewhat disappointed to hear that the shrinkage of the tumors had been much less than we or the doctors expected. They were in fact shrinking, but not like the doctors had seen liver cancer do in the past, particularly in response to this specific chemotherapy regimen. For the first time since I'd come home, I saw Andy's spirits sink. I knew he had fully expected there to be no sign of the tumors at all. He had wanted so badly to be able to tell the doctors and the thousands reading his emails that God had healed his cancer. I watched his face carefully as he chose to wear a positive expression, as purposefully as though he were choosing an outfit to wear. An uncharacteristically short email sent the next morning was evidence of his internal struggle.

> 6-25-02
> Dear Friends,
> I'm sorry I didn't write last night; my treatment had me feeling quite sick, so I went to bed early. We did have our meeting with our Doctor yesterday, with the results of the catscan. I have to say that at first we were rather disappointed with the news. It appears that the tumors are smaller, with some of the smallest ones even disappearing. However, there is also a 6cm mass in the liver that decreased only by a half centimeter. Overall, we were not impressed by the rate of tumor destruction. At that rate, we could be here a long time.

However, if we choose to look at the bright side of things, the tumors are stopped in their growth, and there is decrease in size. They are in check for the time being. I also gained 4 pounds during this cycle, which is no small task. I have been eating like a horse, and I feel great. My tumor pain has been gone since we first started chemotherapy. So things are mixed. It is taking some time for us to process this last bit of information.

Mary and I have to remind ourselves that God is still in control, and that only he can conduct the healing. We are trusting him for it still. We have dedicated ourselves to more earnest prayer for complete healing. I will send out my normal update at the end of this week. Please pray that God will strengthen our faith throughout this week to deal with this news.

Thanks for your prayers and thoughts.

Love,
Andy Schrier

God, this is ridiculous! I have no doubt You can heal both Daddy and Andy, but You don't do it! Why? The glory would be only for You.

As if beating a dead horse, a third emotional blow came with a call from Grandma later that day. She explained that Grandpa's routine visit to his oncologist to assess the status of his chronic leukemia had not been positive. It seemed his cancer had become quite aggressive since his last visit and he would have to succumb to chemo treatments himself. No longer could we assume he would outlive fragile little Grandma with all of her heart issues. Still, he was eighty-four; sixty years Andy's senior. Instinctively, I felt that Grandpa's illness was sad; Daddy's was devastating; Andy's was tragic.

It was not so easy for Mom. After all, it was her husband, her son, and her father who were under attack from this despicable disease. Anyone who did not fall apart at this news would be unfeeling at best.

"I can't do this!" she sobbed into Daddy's lap. I sat on the couch on her other side and rubbed her back. Mary and Andy sat on the adjacent couch looking helpless. It seemed they were still reeling from yesterday's doctor visit and Daddy was in so much pain that his reputable brain was not able to properly function to find the words Mom needed. The burden fell to me to be the strong one and I had a sense of foreboding that it would not be the last time.

"It's ok, Mom," I crooned. "We are all going to do it together. That's why Mary and I are here—to help you. You don't have to do it alone. We will get through this." After what seemed a very long time, she finally sat up, squared her shoulders and drew a deep breath. Her delicate features were red, wet, and swollen and the sound of her sobs seemed to linger, each one a dagger to my heart. Through her brokenness, determination seemed to win out. She must have decided that she had no other option but to move forward. That was certainly the conclusion I had come to, as much as I wished I could wave a magic wand and make it all go away.

Wednesday morning, Daddy went to work as usual. At dinner that evening, he related how frustrated he had been attempting to reach the doctor who would be performing his surgery. After several attempts at calling the doctor's pager number, which he himself had provided, Daddy had finally called Dr. K., his urologist, to get a different number.

"It's inexcusable to treat patients that way!" he fumed. His temper did not often appear, but when it did it was best to stay clear of the fiery inferno which was sure to ensue. "He should have his license revoked. What if I'd had an emergency and needed to get ahold of him? My blood would have been on his hands if something had happened!"

Thursday came and Mom and Daddy headed off for the hospital for Daddy's surgery. For them, a disappointing week quickly turned into a nightmare as issue after issue arose. Of course, I did not learn of any of it until after the fact. I was at home, this time with Andy and Mary. We were all expectantly awaiting the news that Daddy was out of a successful surgery—that Mom would be home in a few hours. She did not return home that evening, however. He needed her to stay with him. Friday evening they arrived at the house in time for dinner, exhausted and angry. Mom recounted the ordeal.

"When we got to the hospital, we waited for—what was it, Honey? Over an hour?" He nodded grimly and she continued. "I finally asked what was going on, and it turns out the orders for the surgery had never been sent. So we were told to go to the city and have the procedure done there. We were waiting for over two hours there. Apparently they were looking for a bed for after the procedure. Why they needed it ahead of time, who knows. So they finally took him to the operating room, but then, after the surgery, they left him in a holding area and no one was there. I was able to be with him then—thank goodness—because he started going into sepsis!"

"What does that mean? How did you know?" I interrupted her.

"Well, he looked green and he was very hot and thirsty. I knew something was wrong, but I couldn't find anyone. Then he projectile vomited all over the bed, the wall, himself—everything—and he started shaking.

Just violently shaking." She held up her hands and demonstrated a ferocious trembling motion. "Finally a technician came through the area. Not a doctor or a nurse, mind you, a technician. She was able to see there was a problem and tried to page the surgeon, but once again, he didn't answer. They eventually got your dad into a room but then realized there were no orders for follow-up care. It was another two hours before a resident ordered antibiotics and pain meds." By the time she finished her story, Mom was riled. Andy, Mary, and I stared at her and Daddy in disbelief. Despite his extreme fatigue and obvious pain, it was clear by the sheer indignation on Daddy's face that every word of it was the truth.

"That's about four separate lawsuits right there," I said, in an attempt to move the conversation forward. Daddy piped up to add one last offense.

"Not to mention that housekeeping hadn't cleaned the room they finally put me in. There was all kinds of leftover filth from the last patient, including a jar of urine. What if they'd had an infectious disease?"

"Well, I'm so glad you're home and okay, Daddy. You must be exhausted." I stood from my chair and wrapped my arms around his shoulders from behind. In typical fashion, he patted my hand, truly appreciative of the gesture, but perhaps a little uncomfortable with my closeness. I began to clear the dinner dishes and bring them into the kitchen. Mom followed suit, but knowing how weary she was, I dismissed her and offered to do it myself. I did not turn down Mary's and Andy's help, however, and between the three of us, the task was done in just a few minutes. None of us had very somber personalities, yet we didn't talk much as we loaded the dishwasher, washed, dried and put away the pots and pans, and wiped all the counters and the table.

While we worked, music wafted in from the living room. Mom had begun her usual stress reducing activity—playing old hymns on the baby grand piano. The notes came in angry clunks at first. When we finished the dishes, I made my way into the living room and stood behind her to sing along. Hymn after hymn, page after page we sang, savoring each word.

When peace like a river attendeth my way,
When sorrows like sea billows roll,
Whatever my lot, thou hast taught me to say,
"It is well, it is well with my soul." (Spafford)

The tears began to flow, first down Mom's cheeks, then mine as I witnessed her pain. Was all well with me? My once steadfast faith seemed to be struggling more than I'd ever imagined possible. I could speak the words with confidence, but deep down in the core of my soul, they stung. The sorrows that had become my family's lot had certainly felt like wave after wave of hardship. Why wasn't God calming these storms? They seemed too rough to bear. And yet, where else could I turn for comfort and stability except to God? With these thoughts, we were on to the next hymn.

> *Nearer still nearer,*
> *Close to thy heart,*
> *Draw me my Savior,*
> *So precious thou art.*
> *Fold me, oh fold me,*
> *Close to thy breast.*
> *Shelter me safe in that haven of rest!*
> *Shelter me safe in that haven of rest! (Morris)*

The words mimicked my thoughts and became a pleading prayer. Only close to the heart of Christ would I find the safety I so desperately needed. I was still clinging to this hope the next day when I read Andy's next email.

6-29-02
Dear Friends,
    It has been a difficult week for my family, one where our faith has been tested very strongly. At the risk of sounding too dramatic about our own problems, I want to let you know what we are going through this week.
    As some of you may know, or I may have mentioned, cancer has hit our family on three generations. My maternal grandfather has chronic leukemia, my father is in remission from cancer in his bladder wall, and then there is me. This week we had a slim range of disappointing to disturbing news on all three of us. First, my father is suffering from hydronephrosis, or failure of the kidneys to drain properly, probably due to his surgery over a year ago to combat the cancer. He is currently recovering from surgery that he underwent on Thursday to correct this problem. Secondly, as I reported on Tuesday, we were disappointed about the lack of destruction of my tumors as reported in my latest catscan. Finally, my grandfather's leukemia, it was discovered on Tuesday, has taken a more aggressive form and is now through-

out his body. He will receive a more aggressive chemotherapy to combat this beginning on Monday. Needless to say, my mother and the rest of us have felt very assaulted this week. Our faith has been called into question almost openly. How we respond to such a week, such dire circumstances when the situation wasn't exactly favorable to begin with, is as crucial as it is challenging.

I can tell you how I felt like responding on Monday and Tuesday. Better yet, I can illustrate it with a Bible story. My favorite Bible passage is I Kings 19. It involves Elijah the prophet after his encounter with Ahab on Mt. Carmel and the destruction of the prophets of Baal. After such a victorious experience, Elijah feels overwhelmed by the pressure from Jezebel, flees into the desert, lies down under a tiny shade tree and prays to die. He then falls asleep, is attended by an angel, and continues into the desert for forty days to the mountain of God. When God speaks to Elijah, it is in the voice of whisper, not in earthquake or fire, and Elijah tells God basically that he is tired and overwhelmed. God then tells him to go back where he came and get back to work.

For me that is always the punch line of the story. How often that you tell a near-suicidal person to go back to whatever it was that caused them to be near suicidal? Elijah didn't get some miracle sympathy from God in completing his task. He didn't talk God into ending Jezebel and Ahab with a wave of his hand and restoring the nation to fearing him. He didn't erase all of the danger for Elijah so that he could return to Israel without fear of harm.

Instead: Go back the way you came. God simply said get back to the task at hand, restoring God's kingdom and standing up to those that opposed him. He gave Elijah instructions and a new helper in Elisha and sent him back to work. God must have known that Elijah wasn't yet at the end of his faith rope, and so he sent him back to it to climb some more.

After the news on Monday I wanted to quit the chemo. I wanted to switch to something more aggressive. After all the news about my other family members, I'm sure we all felt like we didn't want to keep fighting. We felt like running into the desert. The mess was too overwhelming for us and too tough for us to face alone. All humans, no matter how tough their faith, and no matter how strong their resolve, will be at least tempted in such moments to question their faith. Some will give in to that temptation, some will give it up, and others will resist. But the temptation is very real in such moments.

Tears streamed down my cheeks as Andy's words seemed to come straight from my own heart.

> And to me, God very gently said, "Go back the way you came." In other words, get back to work, get back to your chemotherapy, maintain a positive attitude about your family members, and believe MORE in my healing power for all three of you.
>
> I've always struggled with regularity in my prayer life, but I felt very strongly this week as though God wants Mary and me to spend more time in prayer. We have committed ourselves to that goal.
>
> So, through the fire, we have gained in strength and faith. We have learned that we aren't even close to near the end of our faith ropes, but that we have a lot more mileage left. And it's a good thing, because all three situations, plus other things going on, require a lot of earnest, true faith-wrought, child-like, standing firm kind of prayer.
>
> One last thing: in my last update from last week, I said that God poisoned me. Someone thought that I meant He gave me cancer. Not at all what I was trying to say. I simply was making a small reference to chemotherapy, as I think of it as poison. I can understand the confusion, but I want to make it clear that I don't think God "gave" me the cancer.
>
> Thanks for everything,
>
> > Love,
> > Andy Schrier

After reading each word carefully, some of them twice, I stepped away from the computer with a stronger resolve. I was going to pray harder and trust more. I would resist the temptation to walk away from my faith. God was in even this and He had a job for me to do. I could not walk away from my family in their time of need and I would not be able to continue in this role of caregiver without divine strength.

I felt somehow duplicitous to be drawing strength from the very person whose illness was causing me to flounder in the first place. I envied

Andy for his steadfastness. He was such a young man to be fighting for his life, so much of which he had not yet lived. He had no wife or children, no fame, no glory, no fortune, but he had so much to offer the world. He was so passionate about giving impoverished teenagers a chance at a college education. He wanted nothing more than to end the cycle of poverty, one child at a time. He was passionate about introducing people to the God he served and loved. Surely with all of this potential, God would not allow him to die before he reached his prime. Would He?

Chapter 12

OVER THE NEXT FEW DAYS, we expected Daddy to start feeling better. When he did not feel well enough to go to church on Sunday, we were not alarmed, thinking he just needed more recovery time. Besides, our minds were distracted by Mary's and Andy's departure for his next round of chemo. On Sunday evening Mary called us to report that Andy's blood counts were too low to proceed with the chemo and they would try the next day.

On Monday, I was a little surprised that Daddy did not go to work. But he had only been out of the hospital for a couple of days. To most people, it would be out of the ordinary for someone to go to work that soon after a major surgical procedure. For Daddy, however, it was unusual that he was not able to power through. When he chose to do some work from home on Tuesday, but could only manage a few hours, I could not push aside my heightening concern. He did attempt to go to work for a few hours at a time for the rest of the week, but he was not himself. His back pain had him hunched over and he was not eating much because of nausea. He made an appointment for a kidney x-ray with Dr. K. for the next Wednesday, July 9.

In the meantime, Grandpa started his chemo treatments with Grandma at his side. Andy and Mary came back home from the hospital on Friday, a day later than we'd anticipated because of their late start on the chemo. Too exhausted to pontificate a lengthy email, Andy penned a brief explanation, promising a more typical email when his strength returned. The brief note lacked proper punctuation or capitalization. It struck me that Andy, who had previously published a history textbook for the city of Grand Rapids, must have been experiencing an unrivaled level of exhaustion to not have had the energy to tend to these details. His chemo was affecting him more and more strongly with each treatment. Everything he did was approached with an overwhelming amount of energy and enthusiasm. Alarmed, I began to watch him closely for the next few days. He was certainly right that chemo was poison. In addition to his bald head, his face had begun to swell and his normally ruddy complexion had paled, despite the summer sun. His contagious laugh was becoming less frequent, and when it did emerge, it was strained.

To make matters worse, Andy's compromised immune system had allowed him to develop a summer cold. His body struggled to fight it off, rendering him quite lethargic despite himself. Thanks to his previously healthy lifestyle, he managed to recover from the worst of it after a few days.

By Monday, Daddy was able to get back to work for longer hours. He tried to hide it, but I knew him well enough to know he was still suffering a great deal of pain. He struggled to stand upright and I often spotted him with one hand supporting his lower back, much the way a very pregnant woman does. He suddenly looked years older to me. His hair had been a silvery grey for as long as I'd been around, but his face now looked tired— not the kind of tired you get from not sleeping well for a couple of nights, but the kind of tired which comes from too many energy sapping life experiences. But at least he was physically capable to again go through the motions of going to work.

On Wednesday morning, Andy was feeling well enough to send a more typical email update.

> 7-9-02
> Dear Friends,
> Sometimes my will power has to be put in serious check. Every problem that I've ever needed to solve before, with some notable exceptions of course, I've been able to just stir up the creative juices, the resources, the physical power, or just the sheer willpower to overcome. I'm not trying to brag, but it's just how we do things, isn't it? We muster up the willpower and we get things done.
> Yet this battle to me is like no other problem I've ever had. No matter how much willpower, diligence, resources, physical, or mental strength I have, it matters not at all to this cancer. In short, I can't do any more than I am already doing. No matter how much of my natural resources I command, I can't will the cancer to go away any more effectively. Nothing I do, aside from praying and keeping a strong positive mental attitude, will make any difference in the amount of tumor destruction that occurs.

This is perhaps the hardest thing for me to face. I've always been able to do something more to take care of the problem. Now, I cannot. And it is very frustrating.

I can relate to that feeling, I mused cynically. *I would give anything to have the ability to cure cancer right now. It stinks that all I can do to help is manage the house and be an encourager to Mom and Mary.*

One thing that does comfort me is a passage in Luke 18 that tells me I can pray a lot more. It must be a little known passage (I've never heard it preached on) about a widow and a judge. The judge in this particular town does not fear God or have any respect for other humans. Yet a widow in this town comes to bother the judge every day for justice against her adversary. The judge admits that he neither fears God nor has respect for other humans, but decides to rule justly in regard to the widow simply so that she will leave him alone. Otherwise, he says, she might drive him nuts with her pestering. So even in the case of this judge, the widow is granted justice. Jesus goes on to comment on the illustration that we can bring our requests to God the same way. The difference is apparent that because he cares about us, justice will be granted even quicker on our behalf. Luke even mentions that the reason Jesus told the story in the first place was to encourage the disciples not to give up and to keep praying.

It does seem kind of weird at first, to pray to God about something so much that he is pestered by our prayers. This passage enlightens us a great deal about prayer. I find it more revealing than a lot of scripture.

Of all the passages on prayer, we don't know how God really receives it. Does it come in bags to his office like letters, or has he switched over to a more efficient email-like system lately? Does he have to spend three days a week answering reading mail, and four days on a really busy week? Does he tally up requests for certain things? Do certain prayers "weigh" more because of who sent them on into heaven or because they may have been more heartfelt and less selfish than most? And how long does it take him to make decisions on really tough matters that have accumulated thousands of prayers?

Scripture doesn't answer a lot of these questions for us, and it probably doesn't need to. We probably don't need to know all those things. But in Luke 18 we learn a couple really basic things about prayer that I find very reassuring. First of all, aside from the fact that we don't have an understandable metaphor for how, God does receive our prayers. Secondly, the passage strongly indicates, at least by analogy to the judge, that God is interrupted or distracted by our prayers.

I think that is significant. That means a bit more to me than that he hears our prayers. I like the image that whatever God is doing, I can distract or interrupt him by sending up a prayer about something. I also like the idea that I can distract him for long periods of time. And not because I like to distract God, but because just like anyone else, I dislike bad listeners. I hate it when I say something and wonder if it got heard. I like knowing that God heard what I said. I like knowing that if I ask for healing 30 times a day, every time I asked for it God turned around stopped what he was doing to listen and mark the request for justice to be restored to my body. And not just anybody, but God himself. Jesus told this analogy at the risk of being associated with a judge that didn't care about people or God, but made it clear that he was not that kind of ruler. In fact, he is so much more benevolent and caring about us than any earthly judge could be, and that is what makes the analogy so powerful. We ARE in good hands, and are requests DO matter, no matter how many times we log them in his book.

This passage gives me a great deal of hope. One of the points behind my email updates is to focus our prayers so that we pray for the same things, and I think that helps out when it comes to asking God about things in unison.

Sadly, one of the things we forget to do most is pray. We hear about situations, talk about them to our companions, think about them a bit, and then forget to pray. At least I fall guilty of this way too much. This passage makes me want to capture every thought when I think about healing and turn it into a prayer.

I like the idea that I can "pester" God. I like the idea that each one of us matters to him enough that he cares about our needs that much. Especially in a world of cold injustice that doesn't care about how things turn out. We have someone to fight for us. I'm sure you can imagine how comforting that is to me when I want so badly to be healed and to return to normal life.

Thank you to everyone for keeping up with me this long. I know this is a tedious, enduring, patience-demanding struggle without immediate results, but I am thankful for every single person who stays updated on my condition, thinks and prays for my family and me. I eagerly anticipate the day when I can victoriously thank you all for participating in this prayer struggle. I praise God for your faithfulness.

                                    Love,

                                    Andy Schrier

If his last long email had left me feeling motivated to pray more, this one made me want to never stop praying until I saw the desired results—a family with no traces of cancer. Although my waking thought each morning for the last few months had been a desperate prayer for healing, I resolved to start to create my own pile on God's proverbial prayer desk. As I went about my chores and my routine at the house, I muttered under my breath or repeated silently in my mind, *God please heal Daddy, Andy, and Grandpa from this cancer. God please heal Daddy, Andy, and Grandpa from this cancer.* Over and over I prayed this simple prayer. As the words flowed from me, I imagined them written on small sheets of paper, forming a small pile, then a large stack which threatened to topple. I was doing my part. Maybe now God would listen!

I continued in this determination until Daddy returned from his x-ray, clearly distraught.

"One of the stents is in the wrong place," Mom explained, while Daddy gingerly lowered himself onto the couch and then wrestled with the cushions, trying to find the least painful position.

"Dr. K. is going to have to go back into the kidney to move it." She said this as sort of a sigh. She looked the same kind of tired as Daddy. I felt like a balloon when it is blown up to full capacity and then let go of before it is tied off. The sound of all the air rushing through the small opening was nearly audible, sending the balloon flying erratically through the air. All those prayers piled on God's desk were being blown away in its wake. Maybe I was too.

Chapter 13

IT WAS MISERABLE to watch Daddy have to wait six whole days to have the stent moved. The poor man was struggling desperately to function in the midst of his pain. He kept going to work for shortened days when he could. Watching him get out of the car after several hours at work and an hour of driving each way made me cringe. The man who was normally robust and springy had to move so gingerly to change the position in which he'd been forced to sit. When he finally did get out, it took him quite a while to straighten up all the way. He tried to put on a game face but I knew him better.

Finally his day came and he and Mom went to the hospital for the outpatient procedure. I thought he'd be able to return to his old self after a few days of recuperating under Mom's excellent care. But he didn't snap back. Not after two days, three, four . . .

Meanwhile, Andy had recovered well from his cold and his previous round of chemo. He and Mary were back to exploring the surrounding area and his laugh became more natural. His birthday was a few days after Daddy's procedure. He and Mary disappeared to the rose garden that day and didn't return until after the rest of us had finished dinner and I was cleaning up the dishes. I saw them pull into the driveway from the kitchen window. They burst into the house full of laughter and excitement. Mary, who was much quieter and more reserved, was glowing and giddy.

Curious, I set aside my rag and joined the hubbub to find out what was going on. We all convened in the sunroom where Daddy was trying to relax. In her excitement, Mary lost no time shoving her left hand in front of us. On her ring finger sparkled a brand new diamond ring. Of course Mom and Daddy and I had known Andy was planning to propose, but we hadn't known when. His birthday seemed like the perfect day. All too quickly the thrill of the moment quieted down. For Daddy's sake our loud celebrating turned to more subdued planning.

The next day, Daddy visited our family doctor who diagnosed a kidney infection and put him on oral antibiotics. We were scheduled to meet Jen's family for a beach vacation in two weeks, so we were all praying this would put an end to his pain, enabling him to enjoy a much needed vacation.

In the meantime, Mom had yet another worry on her mind. Katie's third child was due imminently. It was her tradition and her joy to spend a week or so with her daughters after the birth of a new grandbaby. Our vacation at the Outer Banks, North Carolina, was scheduled to take us to within a few hours of their home in Charlotte, but she couldn't ask Daddy to drive her there. Should she plan to fly out for a few days and leave Daddy in this state by himself? It was clear she was unable to decide what to do.

"I can handle it Mom," I tried to reassure her. In truth, I wasn't sure if I could, but she needed to be able to have a break from this insanity. Andy had Mary to take care of him so all I needed to do was make sure Daddy got fed. I could do that, couldn't I? But what if he got worse? I had visions of rushing him to the emergency room and needing to call Mom to come back home. My resolve stuck. She needed this break. Katie was always a calming presence for Mom, exactly the rock she needed right now. Besides, Mom would regret it if she did not go, even for a day or two.

"Anyway, let's cross that bridge when we get there, ok?" I suggested. This at least got her to set the matter aside for a while.

BEFORE ANDY AND MARY headed to the hospital for the next cycle, he sent another email.

> 7-22-02
> Dear Friends,
> I've gotten a lot of feedback on the emails I've written so far, mostly the spiritual nature of them. I guess I just want to say that the inspiration for these writings has come only from God. How do I know this? Well, if it were just me writing them, I could produce them any time I wanted, and I can't. I've learned over time that I have to wait on God to give me the inspiration for a writing. Thus I truly believe that God deserves all the credit for anything that was of value in my emails.
> I feel it is important to acknowledge this for two reasons. First of all, it is always important to give God the credit for anything he does. He doesn't like people stealing his glory. Secondly, I

hope it can be an encouragement to you as friends and prayer warriors. I hope it shows that his hand has been in this situation from the beginning, working in my faith to ready me for this battle. I hope this proves his presence, confirms his intentions to do something positive out of this mess, and gives you all the more reason to continue in this prayer marathon.

If there is anything I have learned so far in this process, it is that trusting in God for the long term during a battle is very difficult. I've learned that it is one thing to stand up in front of others and declare your faith as you start the battle, even going on the strength of that for a while, and another thing to keep trusting in the Lord as the battle drags on through its everyday twists, turns, ups and downs. Because we are humans and we have free will, our inner enemies of doubt, discouragement, depression, and worry take their toll as time goes on and the music and encouragement [of] others fades. Eventually, you find yourself alone and the questions in your head start to ask whether you can live up to the claim that you staked yourself to from the beginning. To use a cliché, this is where the rubber meets the road.

There is a biblical example for this phenomenon in the life of Asa, King of Judah, in II Chronicles 14-16. In Chapter 14, when Judah is attacked by a large army, Asa goes to God first for protection, relying on him for strength to defeat the attackers. God fights for Judah, destroying the army. In Chapter 15, Asa loudly and publicly renewed a covenant with the Lord, declaring his intentions to seek God with all their hearts. That was in the 15th year of Asa's reign.

But something happened in Asa's heart by the 36th year when the King of Israel attacked Judah. Asa turned to the military strength of another nation to save Judah from this peril. So hard was his heart by this time that he even put in prison Hanani the prophet who delivered the message that Asa had done wrong. Three years later, Asa was struck with a minor foot disease. He refused to turn to the Lord for relief, but relied on physicians to cure his condition. He died two years later.

I think God used the life of Asa in this passage to prove a major point: that relying on God for deliverance through tough times is usually a marathon and not a sprint. It is easy to verbalize strong declarations about one's faith in God, but a lot tougher to live it out in the long run. Asa started out well, but for one reason or another, he couldn't finish strong. As a result, he seems to have lost what started out as a very neat faith.

It is difficult to march through the everyday parts of the battle and still really, truly trust in the Lord for victory. Some days are more difficult than others. I think Asa is a warning to us to keep this in mind through our battles. Doubt, depression, discouragement, and worry are powerful and devastating, but perhaps not so much as apathy. I have a hunch, though no biblical proof, that this is what killed Asa's faith over the years.

It is difficult to stay focused on God throughout the endurance of our trials. I guess that is why James wrote about perseverance.

Please pray for healing for grandpa and Dad. Please pray that this cycle will result in lots of tumor destruction. Please pray that the hospital stay will be tolerable and go quickly. Please pray that my blood counts will be high enough to start chemotherapy on Tuesday. Please pray that Mary and I will continue to pray and keep a positive attitude everyday during the hospital. Please pray for our relationships with doctors, nurses, and other hospital folk.

Thank you all for your prayers and support.

Love,

Andy Schrier

Once again, Andy had done it. He'd written just the words needed to inspire strength and determination in me. *I refuse to allow this hardship to turn me into Asa. I will persevere through this nonsense! God help me to cling to my faith.* It seemed I was falling off a cliff of doubt, but a vague sense of God's hand holding onto me gave me an ounce of courage to cling to Him.

I would need that courage to face the next few days. Andy and Mary's joyful voices disappeared with them as they traveled to the hospital. Daddy's pain sapped any excess energy he might have had for conversation of any kind. Mom tried to help in any way she could, but nothing she did seemed to make him comfortable. He finally found that sitting in one of the wingback chairs was more bearable than the couch. With the pillows arranged in a particular fashion he could bear to sit for periods of time. Standing, walking, sleeping, or anything else were nearly impossible for him. But he continued to follow as close to a normal routine as possible anyway. He made his way to the table for meals, although the wooden chairs were excruciating, and he still travelled to work several times in the next two weeks. Numbness became my only emotion. It was all I could handle.

I busied myself with emails and phone calls to Melody about our living arrangements for the next semester, as well as phone calls to Shaun, planning for family vacation and Shaun's visit, and finishing my scrapbook. I needed to have it completed before we left for North Carolina because Shaun would be here a week after we got back home. The photos were all in their proper places and I had completed most of the captions, but I needed to finish the last artistic details to make it just right. Once satisfied that it was done, I was quite pleased with myself as I flipped through the pages. The finished product conveyed exactly the message I wanted it to.

As had become the norm, however, I had little time to revel in my accomplishment before yet another blow came our way. Andy and Mary arrived home early from the hospital with frustrating news. Andy's oncologist had conferred with a colleague in Indiana and was no longer confident in her original diagnosis. She wanted to perform another CT scan before deciding how to proceed. The good news was they had given Andy a growth factor to boost his immune system so he and Mary could come on vacation with us.

To that point I had only caught glimpses of Andy being discouraged. He always found a way to quickly regain his hopeful, cheerful demeanor, even if it was forced. This time, the depth of his struggle was palpable as his unusual quiet brooding lingered.

Meanwhile, Daddy was still not rebounding. He spent the majority of his time in his wing-back chair in the sunroom, reading books or napping because his pain made it impossible for him to sleep effectively at night.

Grandpa was also feeling quite ill. His energy was nonexistent, and he was stricken with nausea from the chemotherapy. He had reluctantly allowed Andy to buzz off the hair he combed across his head to hide the bald patches which had appeared.

"Now you get to look like me!" Andy joked, as chunks of black hair fell to the floor.

"Just what I always wanted," Grandpa shot back. Grandpa's Native American heritage had blessed him with a striking head of hair, long after most people's would have been completely grey.

"I bet Grandma likes your new look, Grandpa."

"Pretty sexy, isn't it?" He shimmied his shoulders in jest, but a frown showed his true feelings as he watched the pile on the floor grow bigger.

"Oh, Harold," Grandma scolded, her cheeks filling with color.

THAT SAME WEEK, Mary had a surprise for me.

"I need help going dress shopping. Want to come?"

She and Andy had set their wedding date for the weekend after Christmas, just five months away. That meant they needed to start planning right away. Many things were impossible for Mary to do until she was back in Michigan where the wedding would take place, but this was one thing she could not wait to get a head start on. I could not have been more flattered. So, on one of those miserable days, we hopped in Andy's car and drove to a local bridal boutique.

I could not help but picture myself as the bride as I helped Mary sift through aisle after aisle of white satin. Some gowns we pulled out because of their elegance, and others we decided she needed to try because we were so desperately in need of a good laugh.

"Well, at least it looks better on you than it did on the rack," we would chuckle.

"Do you like this one?" I asked, as I held up one I found to be particularly elegant.

"You should try it on! It won't be long before you'll need to look for yourself anyway. Pick a couple." I hesitated only a moment, then giggled as I pulled a few I'd spotted earlier and handed them to the attendant to take to a second dressing room. I pulled a heavy satin gown over my head and stepped up onto the platform in front of the wall of mirrors. I was sobered and speechless as I looked at myself in that white gown.

"You need a veil to get the full effect," the attendant cooed and hurried off. She returned a moment later with a tiara and veil and gently placed them in my hair. Suddenly I missed Shaun terribly and wished the two weeks until his visit would grow wings. *I just want to look into his eyes and tell him how much I love him*, I thought. *He is one of the only good things in my life right now. When will it be our turn to plan our wedding?*

When Mary and I finally called it a day, we were exhausted, but our hearts were full of thoughts of the men we loved. Our girlish giggle fest had served two purposes—it was oddly therapeutic and it solidified a unique sisterly bond between us.

Chapter 14

"His name is Micah Kenneth." Mom seemed touched that Kate and Jake had chosen their third child's middle name to match Daddy's. She relayed all of the usual statistics and we shared reserved smiles. News of his arrival brought joy, but not the level of excitement that normally accompanies such an event. It could not overshadow our growing concern. Andy was still melancholy from the news he'd received a week before. He had an uncharacteristic sulk in his demeanor. Mary, though fitting the profile of a blushing bride occasionally, was working hard to encourage Andy, and, at the same time, fight with the insurance company and plan their wedding. The stress showed in the decrease of her usual cheerful giggle and constant smile.

Daddy was still not bouncing back. If anything, his pain was worse. I overheard him making a phone call to one doctor or another later that day.

"I've nearly used the full course of the antibiotic and it seems to be ineffective," he reported, almost as though he was conferring with her about another patient and not himself. "I am still experiencing the back pain and I have developed a swollen lymph node in my neck and acute swelling in my leg." After some back-and-forth on the phone, he hung up and told us what she'd said.

"I'm to check in at the hospital tomorrow morning. She is sending the orders for IV antibiotics to be delivered over a two-day stay." Was that a slight twinge of relief I heard in his voice? He limped gingerly back to the only chair he could comfortably sit in, his lips curling almost intangibly in a hopeful smile.

Panic set into Mom's face. She was trying to keep it together for the sake of everyone else in the house, but now, on top of Daddy's pain, Andy's depression, and the plans for the vacation, she had to make a decision about going to Katie's.

"Katie will need me. But how can I leave you like this? What if these antibiotics don't help either? What about our vacation?" Her emotions were clearly torn between the needs of her husband and those of her daughter, not to mention the joy of holding her new grandson.

I was never so grateful for Daddy's ability to speak logically into a situation, and the hope of some pain relief rendered him more lucid than he'd been in several weeks. My brain functioned on emotions just like Mom's and I could not make a rational decision anymore than she could.

"Why don't you go after our vacation, Honey." Daddy said it as a statement, not a question. "We can meet them somewhere on our way back from the Outer Banks and you can fly home. That will give me a whole week for the new antibiotics to kick in and I should be feeling much better. Abby will be fine to take care of the house and food and anything else I might need. Don't forget, we've got Tim and Leslie just a few minutes away, too."

Mom relented and with all of this settled, she and Daddy prepared for their hospital stay.

"I left you a list of things to take care of and a grocery list," Mom informed me before they left the next morning. She fussed over each item on the list and I listened carefully. Much of the preparation for vacation was falling on me. I didn't mind a bit. "If you can get the towels and sheets and non-perishable groceries packed up, that would really help me."

I felt very useful as I took a careful inventory of the kitchen, washed and packed beach towels and sheets, and went to the grocery store for other items. Making sure the dog was fed, plants watered, laundry washed and folded, and dinner prepared were welcome responsibilities, especially since my scrapbook was done. The tedium of it all gave me a tangible way to feel as though I was making a difference in a dismal circumstance and served to pass the two and a half days more quickly. Additionally, it gave me a chance to prove to Mom—and myself—that I could handle things while she went to see the baby.

Mom and Daddy returned home to a clean house and bags packed for the beach. My chest puffed with pride as I saw Daddy's blue Town Car pull into the driveway. I anticipated a decent amount of praise for a job well done, but my spirits sank as they walked in from the garage looking defeated and exhausted. Daddy went immediately to the bedroom to lie down, but for the brief moments our paths crossed, I noticed how hunched over and ashen he appeared. He looked at least five years older than his true age. I turned to look at Mom for an explanation but she didn't look much better than Daddy.

She let out a sigh which seemed to sap what little energy she had, then gave a brief summary, "They said not to worry about the back pain and the swollen leg. The infection should be under control with the antibiotics and the pain and swelling is probably caused by renal colic from the stents. Nothing they can do. I'm going to bring him some medicine." She sighed again and rummaged through the medicine cabinet for his Oxycodone before disappearing into their bedroom.

What do I do now? I wondered. *I guess I need to keep taking care of things. They'll be hungry later. I should figure out what there is for dinner.* I checked the fridge and pantry and discovered there were ingredients for a cheeseburger pie and salad. I pulled the meat out to defrost, but it was only mid-afternoon and much too early to start cooking. I decided to sit out by the pool instead. The heat hit me like a wall after having been in the air conditioned house for most of the day. It felt more suitable to my current mood. I opened the gate and plopped down in one of the cushioned lounge chairs. I leaned back and closed my eyes against the mid-afternoon sunlight. I was so lost in my thoughts I didn't hear the dog come galloping over to be near me. Suddenly a giant, white, slobbery, furry head was nudging its way under my arm.

"Hi Zacc." I stroked the velvety ears which were nearly as large as my hand. Pleased with the attention, he sat down right on top of my feet, shifted his entire body a few inches closer to me, and leaned his head against my arm. Big, black, beautiful eyes gazed up at me and I imagined I sensed some concern in them.

"Oh, Zacc! It's not fair!" I began to sob. Zacc just pressed his head harder against me. I buried my face in his fuzzy mane. A mouthful of fur made me immediately regret that move. Taking time to spit the fur out of my mouth interrupted my tears long enough that I was able to refocus my thoughts. *This poor animal is probably feeling really neglected.* I tried to stand up to run around the yard with him, but he pushed his powerful body against me, forcing me back into my seat. *Poor thing thinks I'm going to leave him all alone out here.*

"Hey, Zacc, c'mon! Let me up! Let's play! Wanna play?" I set my tone high so he would sense my intentions. He let me up and I leaped out of my chair into a slight crouch. I gently batted at one of his ears and then turned and ran a few paces away, knowing he would follow me. Running backwards, I shouted, "Come and get me!" Thrilled with the attention, he bounded towards me. Suddenly, I lunged towards him and playfully pushed on his shoulder. He knew what was coming and planted his feet firmly, barely budging, though I was using all my strength. Using my other hand to push his opposite side, I caught him off guard and he gave way just a bit.

Again I ran backwards and again he followed me. I pushed him backwards with both hands on his shoulders and thus our game continued around the yard.

After half an hour, he became too hot and didn't plant his feet, sinking to the ground with my next push. He was done. I lay down next to him, sweaty and exhausted. Propping myself up on one arm, I began scratching his ear again.

"Thanks, Buddy. I needed that!" As I stood up to leave, he leaped up and trotted along beside me to the gate. "What, you wanna go for a walk?" His tail whapped loudly against the chain link fence in his anticipation, so I went to the pool shed for his leash. The usual spring in my step was replaced by a more melancholy plod as I led him down the driveway and through the neighborhood. He had an excited bounce for a little while until the heat trapped under his thick coat got the better of him. Eventually, I ended up practically dragging the giant dog back home. We were both exhausted but happy to have had some much needed positive interaction. Releasing him back into his enclosure, I watched him take long laps of water from his bucket before disappearing into the shade of the trees. *Poor Zacc. He's been so neglected. He has no idea what's going on, but he has to suffer because of it just like the rest of us.*

Feeling hot and exhausted myself, I retreated back into the house. The air conditioning shocked my legs and arms where my skin was bare. *Cold,* I thought. *Like reality. I don't even really want to go to the beach. What fun is it going to be anyway, with everyone this sick? And the car ride will be downright miserable. I guess maybe it will help get everyone's minds off of stupid cancer.*

Chapter 15

8-2-02
Dear Friends,

My eyes are closed. It is dark anyways. I stumble around with palms outstretched feeling for sensation and feedback. There is a sense of danger here, as though I may be walking into a trap. But, alas, it is just more trees, leading nowhere. I wonder how many times I have touched that tree, looking for my way out, and passed it by, hoping that by touching it, I gained some ground.

When your eyes are closed on a moonlit night, you can still have a general sense of where the moon is. You can't tell how close or how far away it is, or where it is in relationship to anything significant, but you can tell that it is there, beating down on you from the general direction in which it comes. And so, in blind hope, a person in such a predicament will continue to feel around in the general direction of the moon because it is the only reference point they have.

Well I still feel like I'm wandering around in the wardrobe, following a lamppost that faintly glimmers in the eyes-closed perception of my mind, always representing a faint hope that my mad journey will one day end.

As the characters in Narnia also did, I have lost all sense of time in this new world. My perception of the other world that I came from comes only in faint memories, sometimes distorted and very far away. I've been hobbling around in here for so long that I fear what it will be like when I actually return. How will I act, what will I do, what will I say, how will I be different? I'm afraid of returning to my other world, yet I still seek it. Indeed, my only hope is bent on reaching it as soon as possible.

How will I ever describe this world to anybody? Will they believe I was here? Will they care? Yet I want out of this wardrobe more than anything I can imagine. There is also a sense of shock and amazement. I still can't believe I'm here. Every once in a while I pinch myself. Is it really true?

There are some days that are very frustrating. What possible good does it do to have me walking around aimlessly in this thing anyways? And I sure can't step out whenever I want to. Nope, I'm trapped here, until the lamppost leads me out. This could be days, weeks, months. So everyday I wake up, not knowing how many more days it will be until I can leave the wardrobe and this world behind, returning to "normal" life. Somedays I wonder how much more I can take, or if I can take any more at all. But that thought isn't relevant, because I can't control the results of that anyways. I don't have any choice. I can't be anywhere but where I am. There are two comforts that get me through every day. The first is that I actually have that day to live. The second is that the lamppost really is in charge and could miraculously end this whole journey at any point.

It is both amazing and exhausting to believe in a miracle for one's everyday hope and sense of direction. I don't know that I can say much more about it than that. My greatest fear is that I will somehow get stuck in this wardrobe, that I will never be able to come out.

Andy's description of being stuck inside C. S. Lewis' famous wardrobe frightened me. I disliked the dark as much as the next person, but it wasn't the metaphor, but rather, what it stood for which was concerning. Andy's words served as confirmation of what I'd thought I was observing in him over the last few days—for the first time since his diagnosis, he was consumed by fear.

Since the results of the last catscan, I have been unable to place my faith for healing in chemotherapy or medicine. At the beginning of the last hospital stay, our doctor informed us that she had consulted with a germ cell tumor expert at the University of Indiana regarding my case. Together they determined that they don't believe that I have germ cell cancer. They now think I have some sort of hepatocellular, or gland-based tumor. The next catscan will reveal what tumor damage has been caused during these last two cycles, and based on these results, they will determine whether to continue with my current form of germ cell treatment, or whether to switch to a treatment that is more geared against a hepatocellular tumor.

The next catscan will take place on August 12th, with a conference with the doctor to take place the following day. On August 13th, in that conference, we will review the catscan and decide our next medical moves.

Needless to say, this is disappointing news to us. It is very hard not to know what we are dealing with exactly. It is much harder to be placed under a mystery category than under a category where the doctors know exactly what to do and follow a prescribed regimen for your health.

It is also very hard to wait for news on the catscan. Do we hope and trust that all is simply healed, or should we be more realistic and prepare ourselves for the option that we have more cycles to go? That option seems unbearable. Is it weak faith on our part not to expect a miracle?

Finally, it is difficult to anticipate a possible change of chemotherapy. Although we don't love the treatments I am receiving now, we are used to them. There is a comfort in that which could change when my body is introduced to new drugs and new treatment schedules.

Last, but not least, the doctor is letting me go on vacation with my family this week. Every year we take a trip to the beach in North Carolina. This year I had ruled out the possibility of being able to go, due to the cancer, but they have canceled the Bleomycin treatments for the rest of this cycle due to the switch of diagnosis. Therefore, I don't have any treatments until the week of the 13th. They gave me a growth factor shot that will keep my immune system in good shape while I am gone. This is encouraging. It will give me a whole week to feel normal and [have] fun with my family.

I know the tone of this writing has been considerably more dismal than my others, but I'm trying to be realistic about my feelings. I'm not trying to win sympathy points as much as trying to understand myself and convey my feelings to others. I do this because I know most of you care, and maybe it will help you pray for me. I am well aware that this has become the hardest fight of my life, harder than anything I've endured before. The constant mental battle is ever there, never leaving and sometimes better than others, sometimes worse.

Please pray for the final destruction of tumors during these last few days of the fourth cycle. Please pray for a good and accurate catscan and conference with the oncologist. Please pray for a good vacation. Please pray for our spirits to be rejuvenated. Please pray for my father's pain and my grandfather's chemotherapy.

Thanks to all of you,
Andy Schrier

I read Andy's words just before we left for the beach. My thoughts were still fresh in my mind as we started to drive, so I was grateful Andy and Mary were driving separately. It would give me time to think. The plan was to go halfway today and meet at a hotel for the night before completing the journey tomorrow. So I sat quietly in the back seat of Daddy's car and let my mind go where it would.

Andy's mood scares me. How far is that leap from despair to just plain giving up? Is it true that a person's will to live directly impacts their biological ability to do so? Surely Andy still has a strong will to live: he has so much to look forward to. He's getting married in just a few months. He and Mary will make incredible parents some day. And he's making such a difference in the lives of so many impoverished kids. He dreams of doing so much more for them. He cannot lose sight of these dreams!

Tears threatened to spill over and that was the last thing I wanted my parents to see. They needed me to be unwavering. I focused my attention on Shaun. I wished he could be with me on this vacation. The joy and comfort of his nearness would have made it so much more pleasant. But Daddy's rule was we could not bring significant others unless we were engaged or married to them. Besides, with Shaun's illness earlier in the summer, he needed to work as much as possible so he could earn money for books and food for the coming school year.

Unable to read in the car because of carsickness, I opted to close my eyes for a bit. Within just a few short minutes, I was immersed in a sweet dream about Shaun expressing his intense emotions of love for me. Subconsciously aware of Mom and Daddy speaking to each other in low tones, I was eventually awakened by Mom suggesting they listen to a lecture Andy had given them on ancient Jewish holidays. I had previously enjoyed some of the other lectures in the series. My foggy brain snapped to attention, excited for a distraction to help pass the time.

The lectures were about ninety minutes long. Part of the way into the second tape, Daddy began to squirm, gingerly repositioning his cushion every few minutes. Mom noticed too.

"Bruce, would you like me to drive? You could put the seat back and close your eyes for a little while."

"No, no." He was so stubborn. "It's only another hour or so. I'm fine." The strain in his voice said otherwise, but he made an obvious effort to appear more comfortable, sitting straighter in his seat and fidgeting less. Causing Mom to worry about him must have given him more emotional pain than the physical pain he was actually experiencing. Or maybe he hated to appear weak.

Sure enough, Daddy rallied enough to reach the hotel about an hour later. After collecting the key at the front desk, he purposefully arranged some pillows on the bed closest to the window and dozed in a half-seated position. Mom and I began to carry in our overnight things. Andy and Mary arrived just a few minutes later and brought their things in. We had reserved two rooms next to each other so the five of us converged in the second room where Mary and I would be staying. Much to my surprise, Mom got out a bottle of wine and began unwrapping the plastic cups provided by the hotel.

I had never seen my mother have a glass of wine. In fact, she usually chastised Grandpa whenever he poured himself a scotch or a whiskey in front of any of her children. I watched in surprise as she filled three cups about halfway.

"Abby, would you like some?" She reached for a fourth cup. My jaw nearly fell off, it dropped so quickly.

"Um, I, uh . . . Mom, I'm not 21." I assumed that in her mental state, she had merely forgotten my age. I was wrong.

"You will be in a few months," she stated. "I'm your mother and I'm offering you some. Didn't you drink in Ireland anyway?" My mother had the ability to surprise me unlike anyone I knew. Usually so straight-laced, she chose to be a rebel at the most unexpected times. I had intentionally failed to mention that I had indeed partaken in a drink or two most of the nights I'd been in Ireland. In spite of the fact that we'd been told by the President of the college that the school rule was to abide by the legal drinking age of the hosting country, which I was well over, I assumed Mom and Daddy still wouldn't have approved.

"Besides, who's checking?" Andy chimed in, taking a long sip from his own cup.

"Ok, sure."

Chapter 16

I HUSTLED AROUND *my house gathering up my three young children and piling them all into the car. I had a short list of groceries to purchase and I needed to get gas. As I strapped the baby into her seat, I habitually dialed Darrell's mother to let her know I was heading out.*

"Hello?" her nervous voice answered before the first ring ended.

"Hi, Mom. I'm just heading to the grocery store."

"Are you taking the children?"

"Yes, I have all three of them." No, I'm going to leave them at home unattended, *I thought in annoyance.*

"Darrell's at work?"

"Uh huh." Of course he's at work. He called you at 7:20 to tell you he was leaving and probably again at 7:35 to tell you he got there. *"Listen, I've got to go, the baby's crying. It should only take me an hour."* The baby wasn't really crying. She was happily pulling her socks off of her pudgy little feet, but I knew the clock had already started ticking down.

"Ok. Call me as soon as you get home."

"Of course." I was relieved that she couldn't detect the resentment in my voice. I quickly drove the three blocks to the grocery store, hauled the children out of the car, and rushed into the store. Bustling through the aisles, I checked my watch as often as I checked my list and broke up fights between the two boys. The long check-out lines caused a groan to subconsciously escape my lips. Would the extra fifteen minutes I'd allotted be enough? I still needed to get gas. The light had come on while driving here. I couldn't risk running out, Darrell would be furious if he discovered I'd driven it that low with the kids in the car. It was not an option to tell him I'd been afraid of being late calling his mom back. I'd made that mistake before and he had accused me of trying to destroy his family. Oh how I wanted a glass of wine to calm my nerves. But alas, this too was forbidden. Still, it was right next door. Perhaps I could hide it. Darrell wasn't smart enough to figure it out. But if he did find out, he'd be sleeping at*

his mom's again and it would be as if I didn't exist to him or his family. No. No wine for me.

Finally, I finished paying for the groceries. I still had ten minutes to get gas and get home. Just as we reached the car, the older brother punched the younger for something he'd said. He was still much too little to do any real damage, but his brother broke into sobs anyway. I managed to calm him, punish his brother by taking his favorite toy car and headed down the street to the gas station. The skirmish had cost me valuable time and now my heart was pounding. As a security measure, I pulled out my phone and dialed my mother-in-law again.

"I'll be home soon. I just stopped at the gas station. I didn't want you to worry."

"How can you call from the gas station? Don't you know you could cause an explosion that way!"

I SAT STRAIGHT UP in the bed, drenched in sweat and grasping for any clue as to my location. Glancing around the dark room, I noticed Mary sleeping in the bed next to mine, unfamiliar furniture and decorations becoming evident as my eyes gathered information in the dark. The hotel. Reality began to settle in as one nightmare faded into another. I stood and groped my way to the bathroom before going back to bed and struggling to get more sleep.

One look at Mom's face in the morning told me it had been a difficult night in their room as well.

"What's the matter, Mom?"

"Andy was up all night throwing up," was the weary response. Daddy's face displayed an alarming level of concern, too. Andy's face was a grotesque shade of grey and his eyes were bloodshot.

My own stomach seemed to do an awkward somersault. The lightest fare from the hotel's complimentary breakfast didn't alleviate it and neither did four more hours in the car, mostly napping. At least once we were at our beach house, I could help unpack, shop for groceries, plan the week's activities, and actually do things that were constructive, rather than just sitting helplessly in a car.

UNFORTUNATELY, our week at the beach was anything but a vacation. A few of us settled in to watch the movie *The Perfect Storm* one evening because the weather was too uncooperative to be outside. I thought perhaps that perfect storm was reoccurring just a few miles off the coast from where we were located. The gentle beach breeze I loved so much was replaced by terrible howling winds and an almost constant downpour.

But the weather was the least stressful factor. In fact, the few moments that the climate was pleasant, the sun seemed almost to mock us. The rain seemed a more appropriate reflection of everyone's moods. Andy didn't snap out of his depression as I'd expected him to. Mary and I kept him occupied with puzzles, games, jokes, movies, and books to try to steer his mind clear of his physical ailments. Nothing seemed to help. His swollen, bald face was eerily dark and sunken.

Meanwhile, Daddy and Mom had mounting concerns of their own. Daddy's leg was so swollen that the compression hose Dr. K. had recommended were not even helping. Furthermore, his pain had become so debilitating that his doctor prescribed him a narcotic over the phone. He couldn't sleep much so he spent the days dozing off in one location or another until the pain awakened him and he had to find another spot. He barely ate and was unable to engage in conversation with anyone or enjoy Jen's children as he normally did.

By the final day of our vacation, the deep, yellowish circles under Mom's eyes had turned grey. Worry lines streaked her forehead and the corners of her mouth and eyes. *She doesn't want to leave him at home to go see Katie and the baby,* I realized. *She has to go. She must get away from this for a few days and get some sleep. She needs a reason to be joyful.* I needn't have been so worried. Daddy wouldn't hear of her not going.

"It's already been arranged. Your ticket can't be refunded," he reminded her.

"It's just money, Bruce. You can't be alone like this."

"I won't be alone. Abby will be there. She is a young woman, Shirley; she's not a child anymore. She can cook and clean and take care of me if she needs to. Andy and Mary will be there, too. Tim is just a couple of miles away. I have an appointment with Dr. L. on Tuesday. I'll be okay." I was shocked that he was able to speak so clearly through his delirious fog. I was also thrilled that he recognized me as an adult and put so much stock in my ability to take care of the affairs of the house. Mostly, his words made me nervous though. *What if I can't help him? What if something happens while she's gone and I panic? He's the voice of reason. What if he passes out and can't tell me what to do? Will I be able to keep it together?* My heart thumped incessantly in my ears and chest. I hoped he would look reassuringly at me, needing him to tell me it was okay. Instead he bore holes into Mom's eyes.

It was she who needed his unwavering steadiness right now, not me. I took a deep breath and mustered all the strength I could. *I have to be able to keep it together. There is no other option. God will help me.*

"We will be fine, Mom," I managed to utter, hoping the words didn't sound too forced. Her face turned from Daddy to me, her look of pain and fear softening slightly at my voice.

"Of course you will, Honey." She sounded apologetic. She thought she'd hurt my feelings. She could not know how scared I truly was. The clock on the wall indicated that it was 9 p.m., presenting a perfect excuse to get out of this most awkward of moments.

"I'm going to go call Shaun!" I tried to sound excited, as though I had no idea how serious Daddy's health issues really were. Maybe my feigned naivete would give them the hope they needed.

"Hi, Babe. It's me," I opened the conversation when Shaun answered the phone. Mental exhaustion must have dripped from my vocal chords.

"What's up, Hon?" His voice was filled with concern.

"Daddy's really not doing well." Tears began to form unbidden in the corners of my eyes. But I could not cry here. Although I was alone for the moment, the only phone in the beach house was in the kitchen and open to the main living area. Cell phones were still new technology and we didn't have them. Tomorrow I could tell him everything from the phone in my bedroom, but tonight's conversation must be frustratingly superficial. "I'll fill you in tomorrow when I'm home," I told him and then changed the topic to something less pressing. We chatted about surface things for awhile. Finally, feeling drained, I began to close the conversation.

"I'm falling asleep, Babe, and tomorrow's going to be a really long day. I think I'm going to go read my book for a little while and go to bed."

"Okay, Sweetie. Eight more days and I'll be with you!" There were those tears again. I choked them back before managing to reply.

"I absolutely cannot wait!"

"Those three little words," he said softly. A crack in his voice belied the effort it took for him not to say the words he really felt and I had to work to reign in my response as well.

"Those three little words." I had to practically whisper the salutation so he didn't hear my voice breaking up. I hung up the phone and quickly dabbed my eyes again before retreating into the living room, intending to lose myself in my book. I read a few pages, but retained very little of their content. The truth was, Shaun's visit was terrifying to me. Oh, I couldn't wait to see him, to tell him I loved him and to hear him say those words to me for real. But it was the only event I had planned between now and my return to school, which meant I would no longer be useful in this battle against Andy's and Daddy's illnesses.

Giving up on the book, I retreated to my bed. Closed eyes didn't prevent racing thoughts, however, and my sleep proved to be quite restless. The next day's long drive to drop Mom off with Katie and then continue home was a welcome opportunity to rest.

That evening, in the privacy of my bedroom, I conveyed the latest details to Shaun. Tears rolled freely now and he listened quietly. For a man of little emotion, he handled mine with a huge measure of kindness and patience.

"I'm so sorry, Babe," he scrambled for words. "I don't know what else to say."

"It's okay. Thank you for just listening. That really helps, actually." He skillfully changed the subject and got me laughing before we hung up. I collapsed into my bed. It really would be phenomenal to be in his arms in just one week.

Chapter 17

I WOKE UP AND THERE were only six days before Shaun was to arrive. It was Sunday, so Daddy, Andy, Mary and I went to our conservative little country church together. It was one of those everyone-knows-everyone-else's-business type of congregations. Typically, we had to dodge remarks such as, "You aren't praying hard enough if you haven't been healed yet," or "What sins are you hiding? God must be punishing you for something!" Andy always responded with a joke.

"I must be kneeling on the wrong side of the bed," he would reply and then chuckle as though there was nothing offensive in these accusations.

Daddy would quote Scripture back to them, reminding them of Job's suffering despite his righteousness and how his friends wrongfully accused him of sinning. Really, only a few people made these ignorant comments; most had either learned not to or were sympathetic and offered their prayers and comfort on a regular basis, as they had no clue what else to say or do. Even these comments got old though. I wished people would talk about something else, but our family's situation was news due to its extreme nature.

The birth of Micah was a relief because it gave people something more positive to discuss on this particular Sunday. Still, I was glad when it was time to leave. Our afternoon consisted of a hot lunch which I prepared and naps for everyone. Once again, I found myself out by the pool with Zacc, alternately dozing in the warm sun, petting the big teddy bear, and chasing him around the yard.

Monday marked five days of waiting for Shaun. Andy had a CT scan to help determine the next course of action. Seeing as how it was over an hour's drive to the hospital, he and Mary left mid-morning and would be gone most of the day. Daddy walked past the study as I sat in front of the computer to check my email. He stepped in for a second to squeeze my shoulders and plant a kiss on the top of my head.

"I'm going to go to work for a little bit," he informed me. "Will you be ok?"

"Yeah. Mom asked me to get some groceries and I was going to go shopping for a new outfit for Saturday." I saw Daddy flinch a bit. Was it the pain or was he really dreading meeting Shaun that badly? I chose to believe it was the pain. He'd like Shaun once he got to know him. "Would you like me to make you a sandwich or something?"

"That's okay. I have some soup at work and I don't think I'll stay long." That was code for *I'm in an incredible amount of pain, but I have so much work to catch up on because of our vacation that I can't stay home.* I knew he'd be more miserable staying at home and feeling useless so I didn't try to talk him out of it.

As I began to plan my day, I called Grandma and asked if they'd like some company for lunch. Every mall was about an hour away, but one was only a few minutes from their house. It had been quite a while since I'd seen them. I'd stop by the mall before heading home and hit the grocery store on the way.

"Thank you for coming!" Grandma exclaimed when I arrived. "How is Shaun?" She blushed at her own forwardness.

"He's fine. Excited about coming." I couldn't hide my smile, but felt I didn't really need to with Grandma. I snuck back to Grandpa's office where I found him sleeping on the couch. Waking him with a gentle kiss on the forehead, I asked him what he'd like to drink before letting him get back to his nap. I headed into the kitchen where Grandma had already started setting out lunch items. We chatted about Shaun and about how tired Grandpa always was while we arranged open-faced sandwiches.

"It's such a beautiful day. Can we sit on the patio?" I asked.

"Sure. Let me give you a rag and you can clean off the table." I soaked in the soft sunshine of their shaded patio. As I child I had hated doing chores like this, but the warm wet rag in my hand and the warm sunshine flooded my mind with joyful childhood memories. Grandma and Grandpa's home was where I had learned to ride a bike with Grandpa's black dress socks tied around my knees. This is where I had spent many summer days wasting time in front of the TV. This is where I had savored cantaloupe for breakfast and a Klondike bar before bed, because Grandma knew they were my favorites.

After cleaning the tables and chairs, I helped Grandma set the lunch plates and drinks out, along with a bowl of fruit. We called Grandpa to the table and basked in the summer air. It wasn't long before the topic of Shaun came up again.

"Are you going to get your MRS degree out of this one?" Grandpa asked. I had to pause for a moment to think about what he was asking. MRS degree? I would graduate in two years with BA in music, but an MRS? When it finally hit me that he was asking me if I was going to marry Shaun, I must have turned thirty shades of purple.

"Um, I don't know," I stammered. "I think so. I hope so." I looked at the uneaten half of my sandwich, too embarrassed to look at either of my grandparents. Curiosity got the better of me, though, and I cautiously glanced up at Grandpa to observe his response. What a relief to see him smiling.

"Oh, good!" he chuckled.

"He's so much better for you than that other boy. What was his name?" Grandma asked.

"Darrell. Yeah, not sure what I was thinking with that one," I replied. After a relaxing lunch and some light chatter, I said goodbye and headed over to the mall, but not before Grandpa could slip some cash into my hand.

"Buy yourself something pretty." He winked at me mischievously as he whispered his instruction. In his tired, dark eyes, I could still sense a twinkle of adventure. He really wanted Shaun to be the one. I knew arguing with him about the money would be fruitless, so I thanked him and hopped into my Oldsmobile.

I arrived home a few hours later with a couple of new outfits and groceries for the family. I felt so grown up putting the groceries away in their proper places and then cooking dinner for Daddy, Andy, Mary and myself. Mary helped me out when she and Andy got home. Andy went to the study to work on his next email. Daddy was already home but was resting in his bedroom. When dinner was ready, I cautiously walked down the hallway and knocked on his door.

"Dinner's ready, Daddy," I called.

"Okay. I'm coming," came his groggy response. After a quiet, uneventful dinner, Mary and I cleaned up and I took a turn at the computer. A brief email from Shaun and something from Melody regarding our housing arrangement for our junior year gave me the courage to open the one Andy had sent just before dinner. I'd been dreading the follow-up to the last email. I was surprised by the general positivity of its contents.

8-12-02

Dear Friends,

A friend of mine once sent me a quote by C.S. Lewis. I don't know the origin of the quote, but it has since intrigued me and I've never forgotten it. The quote reads: "I believe in God as I believe in the sun; not because I can see it, but because by it I can see all things."

I think this quote intrigues me because I've questioned the existence of God before. I've struggled with doubts about the tangible whereabouts of a being that I can't physically see, yet in which so many people place their faith. I've struggled with the uncertainty that this stirs in my soul, and I've wrestled my way back to a faith in that being, a faith that is totally mine and not reliant on anyone else's.

Throughout this process I've learned the truth of this quote by C.S. Lewis. For some of us it takes believing in the Lord to see his work in our lives. That's not to say that he doesn't work in our lives if we don't believe in him, but that some of us don't have a perspective that will allow our belief system to accept that it is in fact God working within us. In other words, if someone doesn't know the work of a particular artist, one will never recognize the artist's touch that distinguishes that person's art from other paintings. Or, if one doesn't believe in the wind, one can't believe that the wind was responsible for blowing down a tree.

This last week, Mary and I both witnessed tangible evidence of the Lord working in our lives in a powerful way. To us, it was a miracle that we will never forget. The power of the moment was not in being able to physically see God, but to see the things he showed us and to witness his work in our lives in an amazing way.

Last Friday, we journeyed with my family down to the outer banks of North Carolina and sat on a beach for a week. When we left, I was at a pretty bad point. I was sick of being a cancer patient and battling a situational depression that was growing stronger and nastier. It was getting hard for me to be joyful about anything, and I really didn't think I could handle any more cycles of chemotherapy. I felt trapped.

We took two days to travel to the beach. When we arrived at our cottage on Saturday night, Mary and I went for a walk on the beach. We both felt "at the end of our ropes," and that the depression on top of everything else was just too much to deal with. We cried about it for a while and then we prayed. I told God that we needed to hear from him and that we felt as though we couldn't go on. It was a bold prayer, but one that we were compelled to pray. There are few times in my life where a prayer was uttered with such desperation and sincerity of need. And I've never wanted to have God give a booming response so badly in my life.

And it didn't take long to feel, not hear, God's response. On Sunday, the effects of the depression began to melt with the sun and wash away with the waves. I felt much better, and the laughter and conversation of my family helped to pull me out of the slide I had been in. As my mental health improved, and Mary saw positive changes, we both increased in our joy.

Was he on a different vacation than me? When was there sunshine? Why did it seem to me as though his depression never lifted throughout the week? Did my concern for him cloud my vision of the entire vacation?

As if that wasn't enough, God wanted to make sure we got the message. On Sunday evening, I received an unexpected phone call from my good friend and prayer partner in Grand Rapids. He had felt God's presence urgently directing him to cry and pray for Mary and me as he drove to church that evening. When he got to church he gathered others and led them in prayer for us, and also brought us up as a concern during the service.

After the service, he felt that he had to let us know. So he tracked down our phone number and called to let us know that he didn't know exactly what our needs were or why he had been struck by the notion to pray for us, but that we had been prayed for. I listened as chills ran down my spine. In my entire life, I had never experienced such a profound answer to prayer in such a desperate time of need.

Mary and I experienced a deep wave of awe. God cared enough about us to let us know he had heard our prayer.

But he wasn't done yet. He continued to work on us as the week went on.

The source of my depression was an overwhelming sense of

uselessness and boredom. I had been ripped away from my job and many other things I loved, and there was no telling how long it would be until I could resume normal life. My sense of purpose and joy had been eroded by the long months of chemotherapy.

Throughout the week, God spoke to us through a series of messages, including conversations between us and my parents, our own conversations, and our daily devotional time. He reminded us we had been set aside for this time in our lives for a purpose. That purpose, he revealed, was to take lots of time to spend with him everyday, to get to know him in a completely different way. As we brainstormed about it, we realized that this was, in fact, a gift.

How often in my busy, "normal" life have I wished for an extended period of quiet time for reading and reflection? How often in my life have I craved to really take meaningful time for such things as prayer and scripture memorization, but been too busy to actually follow through?

How often have I desired to bury myself in good books, not worrying about the busyness of life to keep me from finishing them?

By the time Friday of the vacation arrived, Mary and I were actually excited about how we would spend our time with God when we returned. We are still excited to see what he will teach us as we spend time everyday in prayer, scripture memorization, singing praises, and thinking about his goodness.

My joy has returned. Only God can wipe away depression in a week. Only God can rejuvenate me and give us strength in the midst of a great battle. And only God will see us through.

I rejoice and thank him for all of these things.

Tomorrow (Tuesday, August 13) is a huge day. Today I had a catscan which we will find out the results of tomorrow in a meeting with our oncologist. Based on the results of that scan, we will determine which chemotherapy to pursue. I will then be admitted to the hospital later in the afternoon for five days. So, I will be in the hospital until Saturday, and out of communication on email until then. I will probably have my sister write a quick email tomorrow containing any medical information that we learn.

I thank you all for your prayers, especially in response to my last email. I hope that you can take encouragement from the miracle that God has worked in our lives this last week. I think God intentionally used praying people as part of this miracle to encourage us that prayer is important and that it works. So please don't give up.

Love,
Andy Schrier

I didn't have much time to percolate on Andy's thoughts before I knew Shaun was to call, so I tucked them into the back of my mind and said a brief, silent prayer of thanks for Andy's and Mary's improved moods and asked again for healing. They certainly had seemed more like themselves at dinner tonight, even if they were tired from their day and a little anxious about tomorrow.

After a long, lighthearted chat with Shaun, I decided to head to bed. I was planning to go to the hospital after Andy was settled and had started his treatment and would need a good night's sleep to safely navigate the construction and traffic on the highways. I found Daddy reading in his chair in the sunroom.

"Goodnight, Daddy." I kissed the top of his head and he squeezed my hand.

"Goodnight Sweetheart." He glanced up at me with his familiar green eyes.

"Don't stay up too late." He sometimes had a habit of reading well into the night, especially when his pain was at its worst. He promised me he wouldn't and I went to bed. With Andy's joy returned, and a sweet chat with Shaun, I slept peacefully.

TUESDAY. Four more days. There was a scurry of activity. Daddy was going to work, so I packed him a lunch, carefully wrapping his sandwich and two cookies in wax paper, just the way Mom did. Mary and Andy were packing up Andy's car for their extended stay at the hospital. I would leave after lunch to join them and see how I could help. Soon I was alone in the house again, but I didn't have much time to be bored. I watered the plants, cleaned up the breakfast dishes, and wiped the counters and table. Then I took Zacc for a long walk before it got too hot. After giving him food and water, I went out to the vegetable garden and picked the last of the green beans. They'd be great for Daddy's and my dinner tonight. By the time I'd finished, I was drenched in sweat. The air conditioning was a welcome relief. I sat in the sunroom with a glass of lemonade and a handful of potato chips and then got in the shower. Before I knew it, the morning was gone and it was time to eat lunch and make the trek to the hospital.

The mixed tape Andy had made me the year before kept me company on the hour drive. As I listened, I recalled the trivia Andy had told me when we listened to it together for the first time—facts about the musicians he'd chosen to highlight. I loved his choices in music as much as I loved his heart for people. Each song he had carefully selected for this tape had deep personal meaning for the artist who had written it, and he knew every story.

I arrived at the hospital and was able to find a parking spot with little trouble, although I did have quite a bit of anxiety about it. I inquired about Andy and was given directions to his room. I passed a variety of patients, doctors, and nurses, all with their own stories. *What song would they write, given the opportunity*, I wondered.

Lost in contemplating song lyrics, I had forgotten the circumstances which brought me to the hospital. I was taken aback to enter Andy's room and see him sitting in a hospital bed, wearing a sterile, patterned gown. I'd grown accustomed to his baldness and his swollen face, but in this setting, they were jarring. Suddenly he looked like all the rest of the patients I had just passed in the hallways. He looked ill.

Mary stood next to the bed, leaning against the window sill on the opposite wall. They were discussing something serious and didn't notice my entrance. I was grateful that I had an extra moment to hide my horrified expression.

"Knock, knock!" I tapped the open door and smiled fakely. Andy turned in his bed, careful not to hit his I.V. stand. He smiled genuinely, but could not hide his weariness.

"Hey Abs," he replied. I suspected his greeting was more cheerful than he felt. "Did you have any trouble?"

"Nope! Did great! More importantly, how are you guys?"

"Good!" He looked positive enough, but there were worry lines by Mary's eyes and mouth. "The tumors are shrinking. Maybe not as quickly as we'd like, but they are shrinking. The oncologist is happy and wants to keep going with treatment. So here we are." He turned to look affectionately at Mary when he said "we." "So, can you send an email for me tonight?" He wrote down some instructions for me and I tucked them safely in my purse. I had always wondered why his emails said "Great Cloud" in the "to" field. He explained that Great Cloud was the name he'd given the group of recipients. All I'd have to do was type in "Great Cloud" and it would send the email to everyone in the group.

"Why 'Great Cloud?'" I asked.

"It's from Hebrews 12:1. 'Therefore, since we are surrounded by so great a cloud of witnesses, let us also lay aside every weight, and sin which clings so closely, and let us run with endurance the race that is set before us.' It's a reminder to me that my words need to represent Christ to everyone who reads my emails."

For an hour or so, the three of us chatted about nothing memorable and then I had to head back home. Time to make sure there was dinner for Daddy.

After dinner was eaten and cleaned up, I found Andy's instructions and penned the following email to his contact group.

> 8-14-02
>
> Hello all. This is Andy's sister, Abby. Andy asked me to write an update for him. He had a catscan on Monday and got the results yesterday. Basically the cisplatin etoposide is still doing some damage to the tumors, although not a lot. His oncologist was encouraged by this and decided to keep giving him the same treatment. So Andy and Mary are now in the hospital receiving the fifth treatment. They are no longer going to be receiving the bleomycen. Please pray that the cisplatin continues to work and that the tumors will be completely killed. Pray for Andy and all of us who are with him for mental stability and spiritual growth. Thanks to all of you for your prayers and support. I have no doubt prayer has the power to heal, we just need to keep praying. God bless.
>
> ~Abby Schrier~

Wednesday. Three days of waiting. It was a frustratingly uneventful day. Andy and Mary were at the hospital and Daddy went to work, albeit for shortened hours. Amidst caring for Daddy and my usual chores, I spent the day mentally preparing for Shaun's visit. It was so soon that I felt somehow giddy and terrified simultaneously. *What am I going to wear?* I ran to my closet and tried on outfit after outfit. Suddenly nothing seemed suitable, even the new clothes I had just purchased. I put on one of the new outfits and glared into the full-length mirror on the back of my door.

"I'm ridiculous," I chided myself out loud. "Shaun loves me. He's not going to care what I'm wearing." Hearing those words spoken aloud, even from my own mouth, gave me chills. "He loves me," I whispered, half expecting a different result. The same chill traveled down my spine and I shivered it away. All at once the clothes didn't matter. A grin spread across my face. I could not have stopped smiling if I tried. I changed back into my original outfit and cheerfully folded and put away the pile of clothes that I'd discarded onto the closet floor.

I hummed through the rest of the day. Praise songs, hymns, love songs, whatever came to mind. It didn't matter. Shaun loved me and I couldn't stop singing. Even when Daddy came home, too exhausted and too weary from pain to manage much of a smile, my mood was unaffected. I felt as though I could face any challenge this life could offer as long as I knew Shaun loved me.

Thursday—two days. The somber news of the day didn't dampen my mood much. Daddy went to see Dr. L. who suspected Daddy's inflamed lymph node in his neck was a tumor. He was told to wait for two more weeks before more tests could be done. I was discouraged, of course, but I somehow avoided my normal spiral of despair and questioning.

Friday—last day of waiting! Mom was coming home and Daddy insisted on picking her up at the airport by himself. I busied myself with making sure the house was completely clean, the laundry done and folded and the plants and dog all cared for. Mom didn't need anything to worry about except for Daddy. When they finally arrived home, I greeted them in the garage. They were in their new normal state of exhausted worry. It was clear they had talked the entire way home about Daddy's health and no longer had the mental or emotional capacity to feign happiness or interest in anything.

"Hi Sweetheart. Thank you for taking care of things," Mom almost whispered as she hugged me weakly. That was all she could muster. I wanted to ask her about the baby, to talk with her about my excitement to see Shaun, but I refrained. She was too tired.

"Why don't I make dinner while you guys go rest for a little bit," I offered as I grabbed Mom's heaviest bag out of the trunk. They seemed happy to accept this suggestion and I began to search for some simple ingredients. An accomplished chef I was not, and while Daddy was just happy to have food in front of him, Mom was a very good cook and I didn't want to disappoint her after such a trying day.

I don't remember what I managed to make, but no one complained about it. I took that as a good sign and cleared the dishes. Mom mustered the energy to help clean up.

"Are you excited to see Shaun tomorrow?" she asked, her hands immersed in a sink full of suds. I beamed and blushed, but couldn't find words. Simply saying yes wasn't enough, but I didn't want to gush, given all of her stress. She didn't need me to form an answer—she could read it in my giddy silence.

"He's a really nice boy, Abby. I really like him." She knew. This was what made Mom so special. She'd watched me fall in and out of infatuation with many boys. She'd laughed with me when things were going well, offered advice, and held me when my heart was broken. She knew Shaun was different without me having to say it.

"Do you think Daddy will like him?" I was truly concerned about this. After bringing Darrell home last summer, I didn't think my father would ever trust my taste in boys again. He certainly must know how I felt if Mom did. Even if he couldn't sense it, she would have told him by now—prepared him.

"He will come around," she replied with a wink.

I hoped she was right.

I lay awake that night imagining how the next day might play out. When sleep eventually came, fitful images of Shaun, Daddy, and Darrell mingled in my dreams. Warm sun through the window awakened me late the next morning. Unhindered by my lack of rest, I hopped excitedly out of bed. This was the day I'd been waiting for! He was coming!

Chapter 18

HOURS UPON AGONIZING HOURS I waited. I finally took up waiting on the steps which led to the front door, knowing how miserable this decision would make me, but not caring. I wanted to be the first thing Shaun saw when he pulled into the driveway. I sat there, picking at the corroding mortar between the bricks, trying to contain my overflowing emotions.

Oh man! Just my luck! I thought, realizing that I really needed to use the bathroom. *He's going to get here the moment I go inside!* And so I waited. Before long, however, the tell-tale dance began and I finally had to give in. Sure enough, as I walked back toward the front door, I noticed Shaun's car outside one of the windows. I was in time to run out the door before he got out of his car. And all at once, I was in his arms—my favorite place to be.

After what seemed like half an hour, I pulled back and looked up at Shaun's face. I was tired of waiting to hear him say what I was dying to say myself. It was there in his eyes, but he did not speak it. Instead he lifted my chin in his hand and kissed me, gently at first, then his arm dropped to my waist and he pulled me closer, kissing me with all the angst which had built up from two and a half months apart. My arms wrapped themselves around his neck and my feet stretched up on tiptoe to savor this long awaited kiss. In his arms I could finally forget the battles raging around me, if only for a moment. Reality would have to wait—I was in paradise.

All moments come to an end, however. After all, we couldn't stand in my parents' driveway kissing forever, so I eventually pulled away.

"Let's go meet everyone!" I suggested, hoping I didn't sound nervous. I started to walk away, but Shaun still had one of my hands in his and he pulled me back towards him for another kiss. I laughed, but the bubble of joy had floated away re-exposing me to the real world. As I pulled away a second time, he held a bouquet out toward me.

"These are for you!" Red roses. Of course. He thought of everything.

Always. A smile of admiration filled my face and I stood on my tiptoes to peck his cheek.

"Thank you." I led him into the house. We found Mom in the kitchen starting on dinner. She immediately turned a welcoming smile on him and hugged him like an old friend.

"It's good to see you again, Shaun. How was your drive?"

"Oh, not too bad, not too bad."

"How long did it take you?" Mom asked.

"I think it was about eight hours. I left around 9 this morning and had to make a couple of stops." He looked down at me, then put his arm around my waist in a side hug. "But she's worth it," he clarified.

"Yes she is." Mom smiled at him and then turned back to her dinner preparations. "Dinner will be ready in about half an hour, so why don't you show Shaun around, Abby. Then could you please set the table?"

"Of course, Mom." I gave her an excited kiss on the cheek before taking Shaun into the sunroom where Daddy sat in his chair reading the paper.

"Hello, young man." Daddy stood as quickly as he was able, trying to hide his pain and appear normal. He looked Shaun up and down, clearly drawing some conclusions about him from his appearance.

"Hello, sir," Shaun replied awkwardly. I'd never seen him nervous before, but Daddy's forthright manner, large stature, and thick beard intimidated most people, even in his frail state.

"Daddy, this is Shaun. Shaun, this is my dad." Formal introductions now aside, it was time to make small talk, something at which neither Daddy nor Shaun were particularly gifted.

"This is a very nice home you have," Shaun broke the silence first.

"Thank you. Tell me about yourself. You live on Long Island with your parents?" At least Daddy was being civil.

"Just my mom and my brothers," Shaun replied. I could feel rather than see Daddy cringe. "My parents got divorced when I was really little. She was remarried and had two sons from that marriage."

"You didn't mention your step-father living with you?"

"No, they were just divorced. He has a lot of psychological issues."

"But you lived with him most of your life?"

"Yeah. I also spent a lot of time with my dad's parents." Fortunately, Andy and Mary arrived home from a visit to the rose garden at that precise moment. Shaun didn't seem to notice Daddy's inability to mask his disapproval.

"There's Andy and Mary! Come and meet them and then I should set the table." I took Shaun by the hand and pulled him back into the kitchen. Andy could be best friends with a spork if you gave him five minutes, and I knew Mary was excited to meet him, so I was certain this would be a better interaction. After introducing Shaun, a witty banter quickly ensued and I felt comfortable excusing myself.

"How many Mom? Are Tim and Leslie coming?"

"No. They will be here tomorrow for dinner and so will Dave."

"Okay, so just six."

"Yes, I think so."

I set six places around the big pedestal table in the sunroom and helped Mom finish carrying out the dinner. Everyone sat down and Daddy made his way painfully to the head of the table. He bowed his head and thanked God for our blessings and for Shaun's safe arrival, although I wasn't sure I believed he was truly grateful for his presence. Of course, once we started eating, Andy got Shaun talking about himself comfortably. After dinner, everyone disappeared to do their own thing. Shaun and I were left alone in the sunroom by ourselves.

As we chatted about nothing in particular, I considered going to get the scrapbook to give to him, but I stuck to my resolve to wait until I heard the words from Shaun's mouth. I lost myself in our conversation and before I knew it, the windows all around us had grown dark.

"Can we go sit outside?" Shaun asked, a bit abruptly.

"Sure." Wordlessly, I led him outside and we sat down near the pool. My insides began their familiar churning. *Was this the moment I'd been waiting for all summer?* I could feel my heart rate rocketing as Shaun moved a chair so he could sit across from me. He reached for my hands and leaned forward to be closer to me. Looking sweetly into my eyes, he began, "Abby Schrier, I am having so much fun dating you." Before he could continue, however, a big fluffy white head wedged its way between our hands. We both erupted into laughter and welcomed Zacc into our intimate conversation. Holding my hand with one of his and rubbing Zacc's ear with the other, Shaun continued.

"The last five months have been the happiest of my life. It's been torture to be away from you; to not be able to hold you or kiss you. My arms ache when I'm not with you. I don't ever want to be away from you for this long again. I want to spend my life with you. Abby, I've never been in love before, but I am one hundred percent certain I am in love now. And I'm in love with you."

For years I had dreamed of the day I'd hear these words. I'd imagined being at the top of the Eiffel Tower or on a mountain hike somewhere. But here, with Shaun, with Zacc snuggled between us, there was no need for a more romantic environment. I reached for his face with both hands.

"And I am so in love with you." It was all I knew to say in response. Hoping he could see reflected in my eyes all I didn't know how to say, I held his gaze for a moment before kissing him. Suddenly I remembered exactly how to show him what I felt.

"I made you something. Let's go into the sunroom and I will go get it." I led him back into the sunroom where I left him for a moment. I bounded as quickly as possible up the stairs, got the scrapbook out of my bedroom and brought it down to where he sat waiting on the couch.

"Come sit at the table. It will be easier to look at together." He sat down in a chair next to me and I pushed the scrapbook in front of him. We giggled like children as we looked carefully through each page. His eyes overflowed with joy and I knew it had been a good investment of my time that summer. As we got closer to the back page, my palms began to sweat. Several times I had to wipe them on my pants before I could touch a page. Finally, he turned the final page over and smiled at the picture of the green bear he had gotten me in Dublin. Below the picture was a quote from Moulin Rouge, a movie which we enjoyed watching together, "The greatest thing you'll ever learn is just to love and be loved in return." Above the picture I had carefully written in calligraphy the Gaelic for "I love you."

"Do you know what it says?" I asked, pointing to the fancy Gaelic words.

"No," he replied, attempting an awkward pronunciation. I had found a phonetic pronunciation of it online and gave it my best shot.

"It means 'I love you.'" He smiled deeply and it seemed as though his eyes were glistening just a little bit.

"Thank you, Honey. I love the scrapbook and I love you. I can tell you spent a lot of time working on this. It really means a lot to me." I had successfully encapsulated my feelings for him within just a few simple pages. It had been worth every moment and every penny I had spent. No—he was worth it, and so much more.

Chapter 19

SHAUN'S VISIT was much too short. Perhaps we packed it too full and therefore didn't have time to just relax and be together, or perhaps we just never wanted to be separated again. The days were packed with a visit to the ice cream shop and rose garden, church, dinner with friends, meeting Tim, Leslie, and Dave, and going to Grandma and Grandpa's. All too soon it was time for Shaun to go back to Long Island. It was clear my circumstances had toughened me because I did not cry as I kissed him goodbye and watched him pull away. Instead, I leashed Zacc and went for a long walk, taking my sadness out on the pavement with each pounding step.

When I returned home, I busied myself with beginning to organize and pack what I would need for my year at college. Things being what they were, my excitement over the house Melody had found for us to live in had been overshadowed. Now I forced all my energy into getting ready and made the happy discovery that I really was looking forward to living there. We had discussed who would bring which items since we would need dishes, silverware, pots and pans, cleaning supplies, etc. Over the next several days, I made lists of what I still needed, used the little money I had to purchase the necessary items at WalMart and the Dollar Store, registered for my classes, and did other menial tasks to make the time move more quickly.

On one particularly hot day, Mom took me out to shop for some clothes and to visit Grandma and Grandpa one last time before I left. We climbed into her baby blue Accord and started off. Mom was quiet at first, but the set of her jaw showed me that she was thinking deeply about something. Finally she spoke into the silence.

"Daddy won't be well enough to drive you to school." I felt utterly foolish for not thinking of this ahead of time. Images of the first time they'd dropped me off flashed before me. I wished I'd taken those goodbyes more seriously. "Are you okay with me asking Gail to come with us so I don't have to drive alone?"

"Of course, Mom. That will be fun!" Wanting to focus her attention on the positive, I continued, "Remember when we used to drive to the school together to get Katie and Gail's daughter Emily? We can have girl time in the car and then make dinner together at my new house before you have to go." I made sure to sound more excited than I was.

"Will Shaun already be there?"

"Yeah, he's moving into an off-campus apartment this week."

"Do you want to see if he'd like to join us for dinner? Maybe he could bring a dessert? We'll go to the grocery store when we get there."

"That sounds great. I'll ask him when I talk to him tonight."

A COUPLE OF DAYS LATER, Mom, her friend Gail and I were on our way in Grandma and Grandpa's minivan, which we'd swapped for Mom's sedan on that last visit. It was not a fun trip, but rather somber instead. I had known this would be the case, but didn't want Mom to be worried. Gail was always pleasant and talkative, so it was very helpful to have her happy presence. Even her company didn't brighten Mom's mood, however. I wanted to sleep, but realized the butterflies that fluttered in my belly every time I was going to see Shaun were much too active. Guilt stung my conscience a little at the thought of Mom's melancholy mood. But I could not stop the butterflies long enough to find ways to engage her in conversations which would interest her.

Fortunately, thanks to Gail's cheerful banter, the six-hour car ride went as quickly as possible. Before I knew it, we were pulling up to the big stone house in which I was to live for that year. Before the ignition was shut off, Melody ran out the front door to embrace me. She had a way of making uncomfortably long hugs seem perfectly natural and I marveled at this gift for a moment. I'd had my fill of sorrowful hugs, consoling arm squeezes and sympathetic pats on the back. This was no more and no less than a hug of joy to be in my presence and I welcomed it.

"I missed you!" she crooned and kissed my cheek. This was crossing the awkwardness line for me and I pulled away from her.

"I missed you, too. It's going to be so much fun to see everyone tomorrow."

"Is Shaun coming over tonight?"

"Yeah, he'll be here for dinner. We have to go grocery shopping after we get everything unpacked. Wanna show us around? This house looks awesome! I love the balcony!"

Melody helped Mom, Gail and me unload my things and gave us a tour of the house. I could tell that, even in Mom's anxious state, she was enjoying the architecture of the old home. Our voices bounced off the high ceilings, wide planked wood floors and open archways.

"Oh Abby, I'm so glad this is where you'll be living!" I knew she meant she was thrilled I'd have a beautiful, restful place to stay which aligned so closely with her design tastes. I was too. It reminded me of the farmhouse in Maryland. I think Mom somehow felt the similarities would make her feel as though I was a little closer to home. That was certainly my hope.

After moving my few items into what would be my bedroom, we gathered in the kitchen to make a grocery list.

"Of course you'll want eggs and milk and bread. Peanut butter and jelly?" Mom asked, writing everything on a piece of paper she'd borrowed from Melody. "Some fruit and vegetables; we'll just see what looks good." Her list grew and I felt a twinge of guilt each time a new item was added. But she didn't stop until she was sure I'd be well provided for for a couple of weeks.

"You go ahead and fix up your room. Gail and I will go to the store. Just remind me how to get there." I gave her some simple directions and they were off. Melody and I headed upstairs to start unpacking my things and catch up. She turned some music on from her computer in her room next door and sat on my bed while I sorted through my stuff.

"How was your summer?" I asked her, pulling out books to put on the shelf the school had provided.

"It was so good! Jesse wrote me a song. I'll have to play it for you!" Practically before I realized she was gone she'd gone to grab her portable keyboard from her room, turning off her music in the process. She skillfully plunked out some folksy chords and sang a beautiful ballad. Her soprano voice was strong, but soft and slightly raspy. I always loved hearing her sing, even if it did fill me with no small amount of jealousy at her natural talents. Music was something I loved but it didn't come to me naturally, I had to work at it. For Melody, it was like breathing and that is what her voice sounded like. She breathed, she sang.

"Do you like it?" she asked when she was finished. "We were sitting on a blanket under the tree in my front yard when he played it for me. It was so sweet." It certainly seemed sweet for Melody, but I pitied poor Jesse. Melody had never fully gotten over her last boyfriend, Ryan. I was afraid things would not end well for Jesse.

"But how was your summer?" She suddenly changed the subject, perhaps not wanting to know my true thoughts. "Did Shaun visit?"

"He said it!" I blurted, before answering either of her questions. "He said he loves me!" Suddenly I couldn't think or move; I could only stand there, a pile of shirts in my hands, waiting to be placed in a drawer. I fell dramatically backwards onto my bed, my feet hanging over the edge where I'd been standing. Melody assumed the same position next to me and nestled her head against mine. We lay there quietly for a moment, sharing my joy. I didn't need to look at her. I knew she was smiling for me. After reveling in the moment together, she squeezed my hand and sat up quickly.

"How did he say it? Tell me all about it!" I slowly sat up next to her and told her about the scrapbook and the roses. I told her how impatient I'd been even though I knew he must have planned the perfect moment and every word. I told her about Zacc's welcome interruption and repeated Shaun's words verbatim. Goose bumps sprung up all over me as I realized that his words, the touch of his hand, the look on his face were all etched permanently in my memory. I didn't know how I knew, but I was certain I'd never forget every detail of that night.

Downstairs, we heard the door open and Gail's voice carried through the echoey house. "We're back!"

We ran down the wooden stairs and met them in the kitchen.

"We'll go unload," I volunteered, giving them both an excited hug before running out the door to the van. Melody followed close behind. When all the groceries were inside and the four of us were finished putting the groceries away, Mom started on dinner.

"I'll make company casserole and I'll make two of them. That way there will be leftovers for you for a couple of days."

"Ooo, yum! Company casserole is the best!" Recognizing Melody's look of confusion, I did my best to explain the family favorite, "It's sort of like a less complicated lasagna."

"That sounds delicious."

"Would you girls work on a salad and then set the table, please? Gail, could you help me mix up the filling?" As we worked, Mom asked Melody about her summer and her family. Before we were finished with the dinner preparations, however, I glanced out the window to see Shaun walking towards the house. My stomach proceeded to do its signature flip flop as I ran out the door to greet him.

"Will it ever stop?" I asked him as I slipped my hand into his.

"Will what ever stop?" He leaned over sideways to kiss me. His free hand held a delicious looking cheesecake.

"The butterflies. Every time I see you, I feel like I'm a little kid."

He grinned. "Yeah, I know what you mean. I hope they never stop. But they'll probably fade with time, as we become more comfortable." He was so practical. And sometimes a bit unromantic. I just shook my head, not allowing myself to be bothered by his realism.

"Like my house?" I asked.

"It's amazing! I'm jealous!"

"Well, maybe we can buy it someday." Our private conversation was interrupted by Mom as we stepped inside.

"Hello Shaun!" She hugged him warmly and kissed his cheek as I set the cheesecake in the fridge.

"Hi Shaun. It's good to see you again." Gail hugged Shaun and then Melody gave him an exuberant squeeze.

The butterflies were so intense that I don't really remember eating dinner. My excitement to see Shaun overshadowed even saying goodbye to Mom. Did she and Gail spend the night in the house before driving home? There certainly was room since our other roommates wouldn't be coming for a few more days. Maybe they got a hotel.

The next morning, we had rehearsal at 8:00. It would be a long day, but I would be with Shaun and so many of my friends. It was like a new beginning for me. Time to relax and enjoy college. Time to put some space between me and my problems.

Chapter 20

FOR A FEW WEEKS, the distance really did renew my joy for life. Classes, studying, rehearsals, dates with Shaun, plays and movies took my mind off of the trouble at home. I began to feel like a normal college student for the first time. I was loving school, loving my friends, loving my house, and loving being in love. It was like freedom. An uplifting email from Andy solidified this feeling.

> 9-7-02
> Dear Friends,
>
> When in the course of human life, Christians endure suffering, they often turn to the Biblical example of Job for comfort and direction. Job's refusal to turn his back on God, despite the remarkably depressing circumstances of his life, are a shining paradigm to us all. In fact, even most folks who don't profess faith in Jesus Christ know of Job and his trials, and many take comfort and strength from his ordeal. Suffering is a human phenomenon, and misery loves company, so to associate ourselves with others who go through suffering is a natural human response and coping mechanism.
>
> While I love and respect the story of Job, I've come to appreciate another Biblical example of suffering much more. Genesis chapters 37 and 39 through 50 tell us about Joseph, a promising and extremely talented young man, the youngest and favorite son of the patriarch Israel.
>
> Joseph's hardships began at the young age of 17 when his brothers sold him into slavery; they despised him because their father favored him, and because he had dreams that indicated that one day he would rule over [them]. Joseph ended up in Egypt, far from his homeland, while his brothers convinced their father that his youngest son had been killed by a wild animal.

Alone, as a slave in a foreign country, Joseph surely was tempted to give up on life, slip into a depression, blame God, be angry at his brothers, or waste his life away as in servitude, living in a shell of bitterness and hatred. Instead, there is no indication that Joseph gave into any of these temptations; in fact, he made up his mind to make the best of the situation and let God use him. It must have taken a great deal of positive mental energy and a great faith in God to believe that God could indeed have a purpose for Joseph in such a tragic circumstance, especially for a teenager (I guess we don't know for sure that Joseph was still a teenager when he arrived in Egypt, but, for me at least, the strong possibility that he was somehow adds to the story). It is exactly this spirit of Joseph's that I find inspiring.

Like a flower that refuses to wilt, Joseph maintained a positive attitude and worked diligently, allowing all of his talents to be used, and God blessed him. His owner, Potiphar, rewarded Joseph's trustworthiness and abilities by placing Joseph, even as a foreigner, in charge of his entire household.

Tragedy struck again for Joseph, however, when Potiphar's wife falsely accused him of making advances towards her. Potiphar banished his Hebrew slave to prison.

Even after this tragedy, and even in prison, Joseph refused to bow to the lure of discouragement. In a prison that was full of former leaders from Pharaoh's court, Joseph's talents and leadership abilities caught the prison warden's eye. The warden placed Joseph in a position of immense responsibility and authority in the prison. So great was his trust in Joseph that the warden did not pay attention to the decisions and responsibilities that were under Joseph's authority.

It was in prison that God provided deliverance for Joseph. Joseph correctly interpreted the prophetic dreams of two inmates, the former royal cupbearer and chief baker. According to Joseph's interpretation, the cupbearer was restored his position at Pharaoh's side, while the baker was hanged. After two years, Pharaoh had two dreams which none of his advisors could unravel. The cupbearer remembered Joseph and recommended him to Pharaoh. When called before the monarch, Joseph reported that the dreams predicted seven years of prosperity followed by seven years of famine. He then advised that Pharaoh place someone in charge of storing up food during the years of plenty so that there would be food during the years of scarcity. Pharaoh, immediately impressed by Joseph's wisdom, placed Joseph in the very position he had recommended; he became second in command to Pharaoh himself.

In the years that followed, to make the long story short, Joseph stored up enough food during the plentiful years that other nations came to Egypt to buy food during the years of famine. During that time, Joseph's own brothers came to Egypt looking for food, and through that process, the family was reconciled and moved to Egypt, restoring Joseph to his beloved father. Thus, through the tragedy of Joseph being sold into slavery, God provided salvation for all of the Hebrew people from the severe famine.

So why do I prefer the story of Joseph to that of Job? Because I'm amazed by Joseph's courage and strength in the face of his suffering and tragic circumstances. I'm sure Joseph went through moments of doubt, worry, fear, and discouragement, but his perseverance through times of trial enabled him to make the most of his life, and allowed God to work through his life.

Throughout my struggle with cancer, I have found it hard not to give in to feelings of despair, doubting God's faithfulness, fear and discouragement. At times, it has proved difficult to engage in the very things that give me joy and hope, and to cherish the very things that make life worth living. God has challenged me through the story of Joseph to not just persevere through suffering, but also to maintain a positive attitude, take joy in life, and above all, to trust in him for deliverance.

Tomorrow, Saturday September 7th, I will go into the hospital for my sixth round of chemotherapy. We are continuing Cisplatin and Etoposide treatments. As reported by my sister Abby, my last catscan showed very little tumor destruction. However, my tumor marker was down significantly again. The tumor marker is a protein in my bloodstream that is produced by the tumors. Compared to what it was when we started the first cycle, it is approaching zero. This is a very good sign because it means that there is significantly less tumor activity.

Mary and I have decided to move back to Grand Rapids in mid-October whether I am in remission or not, mainly because we don't want her employer to hold her job open indefinitely. Also, since I have energy most of the time, I would like to find a job. Needless to say, we are very excited about this move. It places us near Mary's family, a wonderful church home, a job that Mary loves, and a huge and wonderful support group of loving friends that we were forced to leave. Above all, it will allow us to get on with our lives in as normal a fashion as possible. This is important because we didn't expect that this would take this long, and there is no telling how long the disease and treatments will drag on.

As usual, I will be out of email contact for five days until Wednesday. Thank you all for your prayers, contacts and thoughts.

Love,
Andy Schrier

Andy's thoughts seemed to confirm exactly what I was feeling. We must persevere, making the most out of what appeared to be a desperate situation. It was because of that email I was shocked to receive a desperate call from Mom just two weeks later.

"It's Andy," she sobbed. Thinking the worst, I held my breath until she continued. "He left Mary." Relief flooded over me for a moment but was quickly followed by confusion. *What can she mean?* She was still talking between sobs, but I couldn't make out was she was saying.

"Mom. I can't understand you. What? What do you mean he left Mary?"

"He got in his car and left. He said he doesn't love her and he's going back to Michigan by himself. And he says he doesn't believe in God anymore." I sat on the front porch of my house in silence for a moment, listening to my mom sob on the other side of the phone. I was stunned. *He was just saying he was feeling so positive. I don't get it!* But I really did get it. I remembered all too well the state he would be in each time he returned from treatment. *It must just be too much suffering for so little gain. Oh God, why can't You just crush those stupid tumors?* My thoughts were interrupted by Mom's voice, barely audible through her tears.

"Just pray, Abby. Just pray. Tim and Dave are going to Michigan to get him and bring him back. Pray they can convince him . . ." her voice trailed off.

"I will Mom. I love you." I hung up and retreated to my room.

I did pray. All night. I lay in the dark quiet of my room and whispered my pleas to God. I imagined myself as Jesus in the garden of Gethsemane, sweating drops of blood because He was praying so hard.

"Why, God? Why are You allowing this? Just bring him back home. Make him trust in You." I whispered these words into the night, but they were met with only darkness and space. Where had my trust gone? Did God really have control? Perhaps He just didn't want to heal Andy. I chose to pray past all of my own doubts.

Give Mary strength. Let her know it is only the depression and the chemo talking. Andy does love her. I saw it. Help Mom and Daddy. Help them have peace and get some sleep tonight. Keep Tim and Dave safe and give them the right words. Let Andy listen and be encouraged.

Over and over, I prayed the same prayers, more out of desperation than belief. Sometime in the wee hours of the morning, I drifted into a fitful sleep. Vaguely I heard my housemates' footsteps as each of them rose to get ready for their classes. I buried my head deeper under my pillow and faded in and out of consciousness. I could not face the world. Not today.

Around noon, hunger awakened me. I stumbled down to the kitchen to make some coffee and get a bowl of cereal. I could feel the puffiness of my eyelids. My sides ached from sobbing. Surely my hair was a comical mass of frizz. I carried my breakfast up to my room so I could email my professors the reason for missing my morning classes, but the words just would not formulate. *How do you explain this?* I wondered, before finally settling on "a family crisis" as my reasoning.

As I finished the last email, the phone rang. It was Mom.

"He's coming back." There was so much emotion packed into those three words, and I knew instantly she hadn't slept. Daddy probably hadn't either.

"Oh good. Now we can all get some rest."

"Abby?"

"Yeah, Mom?"

"If you feel like you need to be on an antidepressant, I can talk to our family practitioner and get you a prescription."

"No, Mom, I'm fine, really."

"Okay. Let me know if you change your mind."

"I will. Love you." *What was that all about? Why does she think I'm depressed? I'm not depressed. She's just worried I guess.*

Thinking a hot shower would put Mom's awkward question out of my mind, I began to get ready for what remained of my day. Two afternoon classes and Concert Choir rehearsal later, I was still thinking about what she had said. I sat in the cafeteria staring at my dinner, wondering if she was right.

"Abby, he's going to be alright." Shaun put a hand around me and squeezed reassuringly. I hadn't told him about Mom's question, so he assumed my quietness was due to worry over Andy. *I can't be depressed. I'm too strong for that. My faith is too strong. Isn't it?* I smiled synthetically at him.

"You're right. He's probably home now. He'll be fine." This satisfied Shaun and I tried hard for the rest of the evening to keep my mind on other things. I had a fair bit of homework to do, but no motivation to actually do it. Instead, Shaun and I sat in his apartment and watched TV.

"Want a mudslide?" I had heard Shaun's roommate using the blender, but didn't think much about it. He was often drinking. He held out a blue plastic cup full of chocolatey goodness.

"I won't be 21 for another two months. Are you sure you want to offer me alcohol?"

"Who's gonna know?" He was right. Who would know? Who would care? I took the drink and sipped slowly, savoring the cold chocolate concoction. You really couldn't even tell there was alcohol in it. I sat there comfortably in Shaun's arms, watching TV and sipping my drink. Suddenly nothing seemed like a big deal anymore. Andy was fine. Daddy would be fine. Homework? Who cared? I could stay right where I was and not care if I ever moved. As our show ended, I tipped my cup high to drain the last drops. I was vaguely aware I needed to use the bathroom and struggled to stand.

"Ted, how much rum did you put in that?" I practically yelled the question even though Ted was in the very next room and there was no door. He emerged from the kitchen with a grin. He didn't answer my question but took my empty cup from me as I stumbled to the bathroom.

"That was pretty strong," I commented to Shaun when I had finished.

"Or you're not used to drinking. Come on. I need to get you home."

"Oh, really? We could watch something else," I begged him.

"No, I'm tired and you need to go to bed, too. Remember to drink lots of water when you get home." He held my arm as he led me outside and helped me into his car. We were quiet on the two-minute drive back to my house. I could feel the alcohol starting to wear off and the anxiety beginning to take its place. The assignments still left to do for tomorrow's classes loomed in my mind. Embarrassment washed over me at my lack of self-control. I said goodnight to Shaun but kept my thoughts to myself and he drove away unaware of my internal struggles.

As Shaun's car pulled out of the driveway, I grabbed a glass of water and a handful of chips on my way to my room. My bed lay unmade, inviting me to forget unfinished journal reflections and studying for the music history listening test. But I had slacked off enough for one day, so I plopped into my chair in front of my computer and began to check assignments off of my to do list.

Chapter 21

I MADE IT to all my classes the next day. And I heard from my mother that Andy was home and Tim and Dave had used the travel time to talk him into a much better emotional place. The last round of chemo had left him in a very dark frame of mind, but its effects were wearing off now. I felt better for a little while. But only a few days later, discouraging news trumped this slight positive swing. Daddy's pain was only getting worse. They were scheduling more tests, but I didn't have much faith in tests or in God anymore. It seemed as though my faith tank was like a well which had been close to overflowing before I'd witnessed the horrors of cancer. Now, with little to replenish it, it had been drained till it was nearly dry. Without it, I felt much like a zombie, half-dead, stumbling through the world, desperately trying to find something to fill me.

There were moments of joy with Shaun which sustained me, kept my sanity. Even those were wearing off though, or perhaps becoming too commonplace to be as exciting as they had once been. When I felt as though I couldn't bear it anymore, there always seemed to be Ted, offering me a mudslide or a screwdriver or a margarita. The alcohol helped, or so I let myself think. For an hour or two, it made it seem as though nothing mattered. But the temporary buzz blinded me to the fact that it was only causing me more pain and stress. Now, I not only had family members whose health was deteriorating, but I also had the guilt of my own poor choices looming over me. Some days, I made it to my classes, but more and more frequently, I didn't have the emotional strength to make myself go, mostly because I didn't want to see anyone. Eventually, assignments also started getting ignored or altogether forgotten.

One crisp fall morning in late September, I was feeling less melancholy than normal and managed to get to an interesting course entitled African-American Women in the Church. I had the current assignment and two outstanding assignments ready to hand in. When I was able to attend, I always found this class quite compelling. Today was no exception, but when class was over, I gathered my things extra slowly, waiting for everyone else to file out. I'd gotten in this habit to avoid having to talk to anyone, but today, the plan backfired. To my horror, the professor made her way to where I dawdled.

"Abby? Would you be able to meet with me in my office for a few minutes?" *How can I say no?*

"Uh, sure."

"It's just upstairs." I followed her awkwardly, against the flow of countless students who were heading to the cafeteria for a quick lunch between classes. But I was too numb to care about them or about how uncomfortable this conversation was going to be. I knew I wasn't doing well in this class—or any of my classes for that matter. I just wasn't sure any of it mattered. She had every right to be angry with me. Her class just wasn't as important to me as my father and brother dying.

"Have a seat, Abby." She motioned to a chair which faced her desk as she closed the door. She sat professionally straight in the swivel chair behind the desk. Wordlessly, I propped my backpack on the side of the chair as I slumped into it, not daring to look at her.

"Tell me what's going on, Abby." Even through her odd, squeaky voice I detected a high level of compassion and concern. Surprised and a little suspicious, I glanced up, daring to search her face. I found the proof I needed—she was not angry at all. She truly cared for me, a student, whom she barely knew, and who was likely flunking her class. The unfettered, unconditional love in her eyes undid me and I began to weep as I had never wept before.

"I can tell you're smart—a good student. I've never had you in class before, but I'm sure it's not typical for you to fail classes."

"My dad . . . he's sick . . . cancer. My brother, too." I choked over every word. They must have been nearly imperceptible over my sobbing. The professor waited a moment before speaking again, letting me cry it out.

"Your father and your brother both have cancer?" she finally asked. I nodded my confirmation. "Oh you poor dear. How are you handling this?" Her question surprised me. *Doesn't she know the answer already? Isn't it obvious?*

"I'm not," I muttered, hanging my head again. Hearing the words from my own mouth made them real. *Perhaps that's why she asked the question.*

"Are you depressed?" There was the flood again.

All I could do was nod and squeak, "Yes."

"You don't have to go through this alone, you know. There are counselors who work at the school. They are here for people like you. They can help."

"But my mom . . . she doesn't need my depression on top of everything else. If I go to counseling, she'll know."

"I think your mother would rather find out from you now rather than some other way later. Don't you?" Nod. "I will call the counselors at the Health Center and let them know you'll be coming. Will you make an appointment?" Nod. "Okay. I'll see you in class on Thursday."

I grabbed my backpack and quickly left the professor's office. It had suddenly become very claustrophobic in that room. Slowing my pace as I turned a corner in the hallway, I began to ponder what I had just agreed to do. *Do I really need counseling? Daddy and Andy will get better and it will all be okay. I can power through this. I just need to be tougher. No more drinking, no more sleeping in. I'll just get up and go to class, do my homework, do my practicing. I can do this.*

As I exited the building, I looked to the right where the Health Center was. Several students passed between it and me and I turned instead to the left, towards the cafeteria. Then, realizing the red and puffy state of my face, I turned slightly more to the left to head past the library toward my house. I would find something to eat there and put on some fresh make up before heading to my next class.

I was relieved to find my house hauntingly empty. With four other girls living there, it was usually echoing with voices, music from someone's computer, a TV, or a million other cheerful noises—noises representing life. Feeling less than alive, the silence was welcome. Sauntering into the kitchen, I downed a peanut butter sandwich, a glass of chocolate milk, way too many chips, a bowl of cereal, some cookies, and anything else I could find until my stomach simply could not hold anymore. Despite the fullness of my insides, the emptiness in my soul seemed deeper than ever. Still, I forced myself through the day, attending two more classes and Concert Choir rehearsal. Then I sat with Shaun and Melody and all my friends in the cafeteria and filled my stomach to overflowing again, attempting desperately to fill the void and put on my happy face. I didn't tell Shaun or Melody about my encounter with my professor. I was not ready to admit defeat.

For two days, I continued this behavior, almost ritualistically doing what I had to do to get by, faking every move and avoiding any conversation that involved any depth. Then, Thursday night I received a call.

"Hi Abby." The familiar strained voice on the other end sounded more weary than ever.

"Hi Mom." I had stopped asking about her well-being a long time ago and simply waited for her to update me with whatever news there was. She followed tonight's pause with dreadful words.

"Daddy's in the hospital. His pain has gotten much worse and his nodes are very swollen. He'll probably be here for several days. They want to run some more tests. Probably some CT scans and MRIs along with more blood work and urine samples."

"Can I talk to him?"

"He's sleeping right now. They gave him some morphine. I'll call you tomorrow when he's a little more alert."

"Can I come see him?" What I really meant was, "*Should I come see him before it's too late?*" Mom knew perfectly well what I meant.

"Abby, how can you do that?"

"I can do whatever I need to do for my family, Mom. I can leave tonight if you need me to."

"Oh, I don't think you need to do that."

"Well, I think I'd still like to come for the weekend. Maybe Shaun can bring me first thing Saturday morning. We don't have any concerts or anything this weekend."

"We would like that."

"Okay. I will call you after I talk to Shaun. Tell Daddy I love him. And I love you, Mom."

"Love you, too." I called Shaun and he agreed a visit was in order. He'd pick me up first thing in the morning on Saturday and we'd drive to Ohio together. I confirmed with Mom, then ran a load of laundry and finished up my homework before going to bed.

Friday seemed to drag, but I still forced myself to go to every class, if only to make the time go more quickly. Shaun and I had dinner together but parted ways early in the evening. We needed to finish our homework since we'd be spending much of the weekend in the car and arriving back to school quite late on Sunday. After a fitful night of sleep, I found myself in the passenger seat of Shaun's hunter green Buick heading west on the Pennsylvania Turnpike. At first we chatted jovially, keeping the focus off of the purpose of our spontaneous road trip. After a few hours, however, we began to run out of idle conversation starters and the closer we came to our destination, the closer the reality of my father's dire situation seemed to loom.

"Thank you for bringing me home, Babe." The tears which had been kept successfully in check for a few days now spilled over. Shaun glanced lovingly at me and squeezed the limp hand that rested in my lap.

"Of course, Sweetie. You need to see your dad. I'm more than happy to bring you to see him." Silence filled the car for a moment as our thoughts drifted in different directions. *Poor Daddy. Stuck in a hospital bed, forced to be away from the comforts of his own home.* I stared out the window, tears silently streaming down my cheeks. *Is he really going to die? What if I'm not here for him?* Awkward throat clearing interrupted my thoughts. Shaun had something uncomfortable to say.

"So, I've been thinking. . . . Um. . . . What should I say to him?" I couldn't comprehend what he was getting at and my face must have shown my confusion, even through my tears. He glanced at me, then at the road, then back at my blank, questioning face. His eyes begged me not to force him to say anymore, but I had not followed him down his thought path.

"What do you mean?"

"Well," he attempted to clarify, "do you think I should tell him I'm going to take good care of you?" The words hit me like a slap in the face, confirming the questions I'd just been asking of myself and was unwilling to answer. Shaun thought Daddy was going to die. Imminently.

I'm not ready for that! I wanted to scream at Shaun. My misplaced anger helped minimize the reality that he was probably right. All I could manage to say in response was, "I don't know." I shrugged and turned back to the window. I hoped he could read my mind well enough to know not to tell Daddy that.

I was too in love to stay angry for long. Shaun gave me a moment and then changed the subject to something much lighter, I don't remember what. He kept my mind on topics of music or theology or history for the remainder of the trip and I nearly forgot about his question.

Finally the long drive ended. We stepped inside the big white house which had been my home for so many years and a sense of gloom enveloped me like a cloud. There was no one who was excited to greet us. There was no fragrance of a meal or fresh baked goods wafting through the house. In fact, no one was to be found. Mom's purse and lunch were sitting on the counter in anticipation of her heading to the hospital, but I couldn't see or hear her anywhere in the house. Stepping into the sunroom, I noticed the gate to the pool area was open. She wouldn't have gone for an impromptu walk with Zacc and left her things on the counter, so he must have gotten out somehow. He was really good at that when he felt neglected and I'm sure the chaos of the last month didn't leave him much time for one on one attention.

Sure enough, a moment later, Mom emerged from the backyard looking aggravated. She marched in the back door, and upon spotting us, gave a weak smile and hurried hugs.

"Zacc got out again," she explained what I had already surmised. "Could you guys go get him? He went into the woods behind the neighbor's house, down by the creek. I told your dad I'd be at the hospital this morning to keep him company, and if I don't get there soon, it won't be morning anymore. He's in room 326—the local hospital. I'll write it down for you. You know how to get there, right?"

"Um, I think so." I hesitated a moment, trying to visualize the route in my mind. I could get to the big city hospital, an hour away with a blindfold on, but the local hospital was not so familiar.

"I'll write down directions. Please get Zacc before he gets hit by a car."

"We're on it." I hugged her before Shaun and I hurried out the back door. As we trekked out behind the pool enclosure, and past the big barn to the top of the hill, we spotted the white furball in the distance. He meandered happily through the trees, just where Mom had directed us.

"If we run towards him, he'll think it's a game and go the other way," I told Shaun in a half whisper. "We have to try to get as close as possible without him seeing us." We made our way down the steep, grassy hill and into the woods, being careful not to step on branches or piles of dried leaves. Shaun, whose Long Island upbringing had not sent him on many excursions through the woods, was stepping more heavily than I preferred.

"Walk on the sides of your feet," I whispered, "and roll them from back to front. You'll make less noise." He didn't balk at being given instructions. On the contrary, he seemed to get a kick out of my outdoorsiness. Either way, he walked much more quietly and we were able to follow the stream to within ten or fifteen feet of Zacc. Then, the dog's head spun towards us in a movement that seemed too quick for a beast his size. He seemed to smile at us before he crouched down, floppy ears cocked just enough to be perceptible, paused a moment, then bounded the other way. Shaun and I broke into a run after him, taking consolation only in that he was running away from the road. After twenty yards or so, Zacc jumped around with surprising agility and faced us, taking on the same obnoxiously playful stance as before, then again, bounded away with glee. Four or five times he did this before we got smart.

"You're faster but I'm stronger," Shaun shouted to me, just as I was formulating the same plan in my head. "You run up around and behind him and send him back towards me. Then I'll grab him." In this way, we finally managed to capture the incorrigible animal, Shaun tackling him like he was a quarterback with the ball. I clipped the leash to his collar and we were headed back to the house, sweaty despite the fall chill, and covered in leaves.

After getting Zacc safely into the pool enclosure, I prepared us a quick lunch and we left for the hospital, Mom's note with directions and room number in hand. As we found the elevator to the third floor and made our way down the endless hallway that smelled as white as its walls, my chest thumped and constricted. My hands became increasingly sweaty and I self-consciously pulled my right hand away from Shaun's left, wiped both hands on my jeans and shoved them into my pockets. Ever the perceptive one, he wrapped his arm around my shoulder and held me firmly as we walked, the room numbers on the white door frames increasing.

There it was. 326. I took a deep breath and stepped through the open door. Mom sat just inside the doorway, her blue shirt and jeans standing out awkwardly against the sterile room. Everything in here was a strangling shade of white; the curtain separating Daddy's bed from the one by the window, the sheets and pillows, the blinding floor tiles, the cabinets behind Mom. And propped on the white pillows was Daddy's silver hair, surrounding his pale, tired face, blending in with the environment. He smiled weakly at the sight of me. Then his eyes fell on Shaun and there was an expression I couldn't comprehend. It was not a happy one. Shaun's hand let go of my shoulder. He saw it too.

Stepping close to Daddy's bed, I hugged him tightly, not wanting to let go. With surprising strength, he held onto me, too. Subconsciously I was aware of what I would not allow myself to think; there would not be many more hugs from this saintly man I called Daddy. *Be strong. Don't cry. DON'T CRY,* was all I could think for the brief moments the hug lasted. There was nothing to say, so I whispered, "I love you Daddy," kissed the top of his head, and stepped away. Shaun stepped forward to shake Daddy's hand.

"It's good to see you again, Sir."

"Thank you for bringing Abby," my father replied, a little coldly.

"Did you get Zacc back in okay?" Mom asked, clearly feeling the need to steer the conversation carefully away from anything regarding Shaun and me. We described our pursuit of Zacc in detail and Daddy's demeanor gradually changed. I told him all about Concert Choir and Singers, but avoided talking about my classes. I didn't want either of my parents—or Shaun for that matter—to know how much I was struggling.

After a time, a nurse popped her head in.

"I'll be coming back in about five minutes to give Bruce medicine. You can stay," she motioned to Mom, "but I'll need you two to let him rest." I looked over at Daddy whose typically stoic face appeared particularly pained, either physically or emotionally. Fiery tears burned my eyes, but I refused to let them come.

"I'll take good care of her." The words came like daggers out of Shaun's mouth. The threatening tears seemed irresistible, but Daddy squared his shoulders, lifted his head and took on a look of utter determination.

"Oh, I'm not ready for that!" he declared. Internally I cheered. *He still has fight left! He could still beat this!* Suddenly I was not angry with Shaun for failing to read my mind. His willingness to fill Daddy's shoes had given Daddy an extra measure of strength, and had given me what I'd lost somewhere along the way—hope.

The drive back to school the next day was much more upbeat than the one the day before.

Chapter 22

THE NAME ABIGAIL literally means "joy of the Father." As a child, I had loved my name. Daddy would frequently quote Psalm 127:3-5a, "Behold, children are a heritage from the LORD, the fruit of the womb a reward. Like arrows in the hand of a warrior are the children of one's youth. Blessed is the man who fills his quiver with them!" Then he'd remind us all that "in Bible times, a quiver was considered full when it held seven arrows." I always felt special to have been the last arrow to complete his collection, and my name seemed symbolic of my position in the family.

Over the summer, I had felt particularly close to Daddy, being the only one of his children who was in a position to live at home to help care for him. Before visiting him in the hospital, however, the geographic distance, coupled with his physical decline, had caused me to feel as though I were failing at living up to my name. If he knew how depressed I'd become, how I'd let my classes become an afterthought, how I'd been drinking to try to quiet my racing thoughts, he would not have found much joy in me, I was certain.

But, standing beside his hospital bed, seeing how seriously he took his responsibility to care for me, put all of that aside. It was not my actions which brought him joy, but my person, my need for him. My spirit was rejuvenated in knowing this. Joy and hope carried me through my daily activities. I felt a renewed boldness to pray for Daddy's healing. Depression at bay, I felt free to be myself and get back to the responsibilities school afforded.

A few days after our visit to Ohio, Andy sent a new email. I read it with rose-colored glasses, believing with renewed fervor that Andy and Daddy and Grandpa would all still be healed and we would return to a more normal existence.

10-6-02

Dear Friends,

    I know it has been a long time since I have written an update, and I'm sorry. I've been struggling a lot lately, mentally and emotionally, and I haven't written or talked to many people.

    During the last few weeks, I have encountered a huge flare up of anxiety and depression due to the mental stress of my situation and my family's struggles. But God has been faithful in leading me through this situation through the love of Mary, my family and friends, and through professional and medical help. I am now seeing the light at the end of the tunnel and I am starting to feel like myself again.

    Mary and I are happy to be moving back to Grand Rapids this coming weekend (Oct. 11th). We are not completely satisfied with leaving my father and grandfather during their struggles, but we are glad to try to get on with our lives again. We are excited to rejoin our church family, wonderful friends, and Mary's parents. Mary will return to her job, while I will hopefully find a job soon.

    Medically, my tumors are under control, but not gone. Catscans have shown very little tumor deterioration, but no progression either. After seeking a second opinion from a national expert on germ cell tumors in Indianapolis, we have learned that my cancer is almost certainly not germ cell, but either pancreatic or liver cancer. Knowing this makes me feel lucky to be alive, as this diagnosis is much less favorable than a germ cell diagnosis.

    We have also decided that my body needs a rest after six cycles of chemotherapy. I may resume a different regimen of chemo if and when the disease flares up again, but for now, I am trying to get enrolled in a clinical trial at Wayne State University in Detroit. The trial involves a new drug taken orally every day with very few side effects. It would allow me to rest my body, grow my hair back, live pretty close to normal life, and yet still be doing something about the disease. I hope to secure an appointment at Wayne State this week to see if I qualify for the trial. I have also nailed down an appointment with a new oncologist in Grand Rapids.

    While my Grandfather is doing relatively well under new chemo treatments, my Father is really struggling with back pain, kidney function, nausea, and other complications. It is very difficult to watch him suffer through this time, waiting for doctors to find out what is wrong with him.

Please pray for my Father, for a decrease in pain and an elimination of these complicating health factors. Please pray for my Grandfather, that his chemotherapy will be effective and minimal in side effects. Please pray for my anxiety and depression to completely disappear. Please pray for Mary and I as we move to Grand Rapids. Please pray for me to qualify for the clinical trial at Wayne State. Please pray for me to find a decent job.

A special thanks to all of you for your continued support, cards, emails, gifts, visits, prayers, thoughts and phone calls throughout this long battle. Thanks especially to those who we leave behind in Ohio, and we look forward to seeing those of you in Grand Rapids.

Love,
Andy Schrier

Although the general tone of Andy's email was somewhat grim, and was void of its usual devotional nature, it strengthened my hope and resolve. Andy was moving on with his life, unhindered by the cancer still in his body. I needed to follow his lead and go on with life, too. These signs of hope gave me strength to rebound from my own depression for a few weeks. The Abby who had skipped classes and ignored assignments was a person from a dark past. In her place was a confident young woman who was determined to conquer depression, school, and cancer.

When another email came from Andy two weeks later, I read it eagerly, soaking in my brother's wisdom and drawing strength from him.

10-21-02
Dear Friends,

Almost everyone of a Christian background has memorized Psalm 23, verse 4, which says, "Yea, though I walk through the valley of the shadow of death, I will fear no evil." As a young, imaginative kid, I often wondered what King David meant by "the valley of the shadow of death." Was it some nasty place in the writer's homeland where hungry predators roamed, waiting to kill and eat humans?

As I've grown up, I've studied a bit about the land of Israel, including an intense month-long visit four years ago. I've also listened extensively to a series of lectures by Ray Vander Laan, an expert on Jewish background to the Bible. I've even had the privilege to visit the "valley" where David fought with Goliath. In Israel, I learned, a valley is almost always a dry riverbed, called a wadi, that flows out of the central mountain ridge of the country, channeling water either west towards the Mediterranean Sea or East to the Jordan rift valley. These wadis remain dry, harmless and quiet throughout most of the year. But the rainy season or an isolated storm in the mountains can cause a flash flood that cascades without warning down the wadi, destroying everything in its path, and likely killing any animals or humans unlucky enough to be caught unawares at the bottom of the wadi.

When sheep roam through the desert land of Israel, searching for water, they may be inclined to drink from pools of water left at the bottoms of the wadis. What the sheep doesn't know is that drinking from those pools could get them swept away by a flash flood. Therefore, shepherds guide their flocks away from the bottom of the wadi, searching for living water, or still water: water that won't get them killed.

A skilled shepherd may even take his flock of sheep into the wadi if the shepherd knows it is safe, and that no flash floods are coming. As long as the skilled shepherd is with the flocks, keeping an eye out for signs of flooding, the sheep will be safe in the wadi.

In the 23rd Psalm, David clearly compares himself to a sheep and the Lord to his shepherd. In my opinion, "the valley of the shadow of death" is David's reference to the walking along the bottom of the wadi. At any moment his life could be snuffed out by a flash flood, but because he knows that the shepherd is watching, he has no fear.

As sheep in His flock, God sometimes has us walking on the high, safe banks of the wadi, looking for water that is still, quiet, or living. Other times, he will lead us directly into the bottom of the wadi, into the valley of the shadow of death, where, if He were not in charge, we would be washed away.

I've certainly lived most of my life on what I perceive are the comfortable, relatively safe banks of the riverbed. What I have come to realize is that there is a considerable risk in always walking on the banks where death is not imminent. The danger is that of losing perspective, of not realizing one's need for the shepherd.

I've also realized that when you walk in the valley of the shadow of death, at the very bottom of the wadi, you depend on the shepherd for the peace and safety of every moment. Only with the shepherd's guidance can you live without fear and anxiety of turmoil and death.

Right now, God is leading me through a valley where the shadow of death is long, dark, and menacing. Several tumors sit dormant in my liver, threatening at any time to attack again. No one knows when or how. And no one can tell whether or not further treatments will be effective in containing these killers. The prognosis for liver cancer is not good. In fact, I'm glad I don't know what the doctors say the percentages for living should be. The fact is, I don't depend on the limitations that medicine or its percentages might place on my life.

Because I know the shepherd, because I know he leads me through this valley, because I know he controls the real percentages of whether and when I live or die, I have peace. My cup overflows. And most certainly, goodness and love will pursue me with reckless abandon for every day of my life that I have left, be it two months or two hundred years, and I anticipate the rich feast of living with Him in His dwelling for the rest of eternity.

MEDICAL UPDATE

Mary and I have moved back to Grand Rapids. It is wonderful to be back in our church and near our large group of friends and Mary's parents. Right now, I have a lot of energy, and I even played ultimate frisbee yesterday. It is nice to have this break from chemotherapy, and I am eagerly searching for a job. My hair has even started to grow back in the last week.

As I mentioned, I am taking no treatments at all right now. We have met with our new oncologist here in Grand Rapids, and he will keep an eye on the tumors. He also thinks that this trial at Wayne State University would be a great thing for me to be enrolled in.

Thank you all for your prayers, thoughts, and support.

Love,
Andy Schrier

Yes, I thought, *God is the one who alone controls the future, whether we live or die. His purposes are good and I must hold on to faith in that, whatever happens to Daddy and Andy and Grandpa.* I did not allow my mind to consider their deaths as a possibility. Instead, I placed all my trust in God leading them each safely out of their respective "wadis."

My determination to be positive lasted until I got a phone call from Mom just days after Andy's email. I was expecting her to call with the results of all of Daddy's tests, but I was not prepared for what I heard.

"The cancer is all through his body. There is nothing the doctors can do for him." I know we talked for a few minutes after that, but my shock rendered me incapable of comprehending anything else. I probably offered to call some of my siblings for Mom and she probably gratefully declined. I found myself sitting at my desk, which my roommates and I had moved to the family room while rearranging the bedrooms upstairs. I sat there idly checking my email and instant messaging random high school friends intermittently. Pointlessly. Wasting time, not thinking. But no matter how effectively I kept the thoughts from coming, I could not control the tears. They were two rivers flowing wildly down my face, soaking my turtleneck sweater.

"Abby? What's wrong?" I hadn't noticed my housemate Chrysta enter the room behind me, nor had I noticed that I was sobbing.

"My daddy's dying!" I blurted, without thinking. The truth of the words came like a sucker punch to my gut. Chrysta eyed me with a look of horror as I burst into uncontrolled weeping. We were merely roommates out of convenience, not because we knew one another intimately. Shame overcame me at the realization that I was being so vulnerable with someone I knew only at a surface level.

"I . . . I'm so sorry," she muttered, hugging me. But her pity was too painful and I retreated to my bed where I pulled my flannel comforter over my head and cried myself to sleep. I never heard Melody, with whom I now shared a room, come home. I heard her the next morning when her alarm went off and she rushed to shower and dry her hair. I heard Chrysta and our other two housemates up and moving, readying themselves for a normal day. But this was no normal day for me. This was a day straight from hell.

It's all my fault, I told myself, shocked by how vehemently I believed it. *Daddy is dying because I must have done something horrible and God is punishing me. Andy will probably die, too. And Grandpa.* Images of past mistakes—lies I'd told; boys I'd kissed with no intention of dating; friends I had hurt with unkind words; swear words I'd uttered just to impress someone I thought was cool; change I'd snuck from Mom's container to buy a cookie or ice cream from the high school cafeteria—all of these flooded my memory. Something must have been heinous enough to warrant the nightmare I was now living. *If only I could die instead, maybe they would be healed.* Sleep was my only escape, so I rolled over, put the pillow over my head and silently cried myself back to sleep.

Growling in the pit of my stomach woke me around one o'clock in the afternoon. I plodded down the stairs and into the kitchen in search of something to satiate the appetite which seemed to be the only part of me that had a will to keep living. Unthinking and unfeeling, I gathered any food item that looked comforting, not caring which of my housemates it belonged to. Working my way through the kitchen like the *Hungry Little Caterpillar*, I ate until my stomach ached, and then went back to my own personal cocoon. But one can only sleep so much, so an hour later, I schlepped into the bathroom. Perhaps a shower would make me feel more alive. I would have to go to Concert Choir in a little while anyway. Skipping Concert Choir without a doctor's note would mean failing, and that would mean I would have to scramble to meet the requirements of my major in order to graduate on time. Not graduating on time meant putting off marrying Shaun. That was the only reason I cared.

The water of the shower, as hot as I could stand it, washed over me, warming me from the outside, while thoughts of Shaun warmed me from the inside. He was the only person I wanted to talk to right now. I didn't even care to see Melody. I couldn't possibly talk to Mom in this state. It would destroy her to know how broken I felt. All I wanted to do was sink into Shaun's arms and sob while he held me and whispered that he'd be there for me no matter what.

One way or another, I faked it through rehearsal and through dinner in the cafeteria. Self-consciously clinging to Shaun's side when we were not singing, I was keenly aware of my swollen eyes and gloomy demeanor. I avoided as much interaction with anyone else as possible and smiled synthetically to anyone who approached me, trying not to make eye contact. I couldn't risk anyone asking, "How's your dad?" Finally alone in Shaun's apartment, I collapsed onto the couch and into his open arms. He asked no questions, only held me as my sobs shook both of us. Resting his cheek on the top of my head, he gently stroked my hair.

"It's okay. I'm here. I will always be here for you." He softly whispered exactly what I'd longed all day to hear. Unable to speak or even move, I marinated in the truth of his words. *Who is this man who knows exactly what to say, what to do? I don't deserve him. In all the things I've done, what good did I do to earn this angel whose love I cannot possibly justify or repay?*

"Thank you," I eventually managed to whisper into his warm chest.

"Of course, Darling. I love you. I love you so much." I felt his arms tighten around my back, easily enfolding all of me. "What's going on?" he queried, his eyes full of concern. His warmth calmed me a bit and, after another moment or so, I gathered the strength to sit up and offer an explanation.

"I got a call from Mom last night." My voice caught on the lump in my throat and the tears began right where they'd left off only a moment ago, but I took a deep breath and continued. "Daddy has cancer . . . everywhere . . ." The word cancer did me in and I had to choke out the rest between wracking sobs. "There's nothing . . . more they can do . . . it's only a matter of time."

Shaun pulled me back against him. "I'm so, so sorry."

I could no longer think. Saying those words out loud had sapped every ounce of energy I had earlier possessed. My mind went blank, my body numb. More tears than I'd ever imagined possible flowed freely from me.

Shaun shifted his weight and my face slid backward on his sweater, uncomfortably encountering an enormous wet spot where my tears and probably some snot had soaked into the fabric. Rather than moving my head, I pulled on the sweater so my cheek rested on a dry spot. Then, inexplicably and completely unexpectedly, I chuckled. Shaun's hands moved to my shoulders and pushed me to a sitting position. His eyes looked quizzically into mine, a tentative smile on his face.

"I'm sorry!" I said, placing a hand on the wet spot. "I got your sweater all wet!" Again I laughed and this time he joined me.

"I love you." His eyes searched mine for a sign that I believed him.

"I know. I love you, too. I don't deserve you, but I love you." I hugged him in an attempt to escape the intensity of the love in his eyes, but his hands on my shoulders refused to release me so easily.

"I'm the one who doesn't deserve you." He kissed me as if to prove his point. I did not have the strength to argue with him, but I knew I was the one with the upper hand on this topic.

"I need to go home and go to bed. I think I'll make an appointment with a counselor tomorrow. Maybe I'll talk to Mom about getting an antidepressant. I don't know if I can get through this if I don't." Nearly bowled over with the shock of my own words, I stood up from the couch and walked to the front door. Some sense of self-preservation must have taken over me because I refused to allow my thoughts to wander from these two goals. I would make the phone call to the Health Center at 8:00 tomorrow morning, before I could change my mind. I'd call Mom first and let her know what I was thinking. She'd be up and could call my doctor to get a prescription before going to be with Daddy.

Chapter 23

THE NEXT MORNING, I stuck to my resolve. At 7:30, I picked up the hallway phone and stretched the cord into my bedroom, shutting the door as best I could over it, attempting to gain as much privacy as possible. Taking a deep breath, I dialed home. When Mom's tired, anxious voice answered, I started right away before I could back out.

"Mom, I think I need you to get me an antidepressant. I'm going to try to get an appointment with a counselor, too."

"Okay, Honey. I'll call Dr. F. before I leave to visit Daddy this morning." I was relieved that she didn't ask me any questions and we hung up after an unusually short conversation. It was not yet 8:00, so I headed downstairs to get some breakfast. Then I again stretched the phone into my room to call the Health Center. A voice on the other end of the line caught me off guard. I hadn't planned far enough ahead to know what I would say.

"Health Center. Would you like to schedule an appointment?"

"Um, yes." I hesitated for a moment, feeling embarrassed. "Um, I think I need to . . . I mean, I need to schedule an appointment with a counselor . . . I guess."

"Okay, what's your presenting problem?" I froze. *Cancer. Cancer is my problem.* But I knew that wasn't what she was looking for.

"Depression," I finally blurted. Thankfully, the lady seemed not to notice my uncertainty. I could hear her typing something into her computer, presumably looking up the counselors' schedules.

"Okay, Mrs. N. can see you at 12:30 this afternoon. Would that work?"

"Yeah, that's fine."

"Please arrive fifteen minutes early to fill out your intake paperwork."

"Okay, thank you."

Inexplicably, my body was overcome with exhaustion again. My classes didn't matter. I hung up the phone and curled up on my bed, quickly setting my alarm for 11, but thinking there was no possible way I could sleep that much. Three hours later, my fingers found the snooze button and I rolled over for seven more minutes before finally hopping into the shower.

A little while later, Mrs. N. sat across from me in her spacious office, yellow notepad in one hand, pen scribbling away in the other. She leaned forward as my story poured out of my mouth, the tears from my eyes keeping pace.

"There are tissues on the table next to you," she indicated sympathetically. She did not move to hug me or touch me in any way. I was glad. It seemed like everyone I had ever had a moment's interchange with felt obligated to give me a pity hug. I grabbed a tissue and dabbed awkwardly at my face. "So your father, your brother, and your grandfather all have cancer?" She waited for me to nod in affirmation. "And now the doctors can no longer treat your father?" Again I nodded. "How are you managing your classes?" Blood rushed into my cheeks and I studied the pattern on the carpeted floor, afraid to answer.

"I . . . I'm really not going to them much. I've just been sleeping a lot. And crying a lot. I don't really know how someone can sleep so much and cry so much." At first I chuckled, then the tears rolled afresh. "What if I fail all my classes?" I wailed, then cried even harder, embarrassed that I was such an emotional basket case.

"Have you spoken to any of your professors about what's going on? I'm sure they would work with you if they knew what you are going through." *I hadn't thought of that. She is probably right, but it seems too little, too late. Most classes I've now missed several times and failed to complete more than a few assignments. How can I ask them for grace now?* The only professor I'd spoken to was the one who'd approached me first.

"Do you think that would help?" Mrs. N. asked.

"I don't know. I'm really behind."

"You're too embarrassed to ask. Would you like me to speak with them? I'd be happy to do that for you." Relief suddenly washed over me. Overcome by fresh tears, this time due to gratitude, all I could manage was a nod. "Okay. You'll have to follow up with them and see what they are willing to do, but I can make the initial contact and tell them what you're struggling with. Can you tell me their names?" I had to concentrate hard in order to answer her. I closed my eyes tightly to block out the fog which had taken over my brain recently. *Monday. What classes do I have Monday? At 9:30 I have Genesis. That's Professor G. At 11 there's Church History with Professor N. After lunch I have Songs, Hymns, and Spiritual Songs with Dr. R.* A month and a half into the semester, my schedule was not emblazoned onto my brain as it usually was by two or three weeks. It took me several minutes to come up with the names of all of my professors for Mrs. N.

"Great. I'll send an email before the end of the day. Now, I have some more questions I need to ask you, there's a survey I'd like you to take that will help me know a little more about your depression, and I have an assignment for you. Is that alright?" I nodded.

She began asking me questions about my family, history of mental illness, drug use, etc. The clinical nature of the interview helped me to calm down significantly.

"Do you drink alcohol?" Certain I would get into trouble if I answered honestly, I shook my head "no." Finally, she pulled a piece of white paper out from under her yellow notepad and handed it to me, along with a pen and a clipboard.

"This is the survey that will tell me a little bit more about how you're feeling. I'd like you to answer the questions as honestly as you can, but don't think too hard about them. Just go with your first reaction to each question." The survey had me rate various items like how much I slept, changes in my appetite, avoiding friends, difficulty completing tasks, how much I cried, and whether or not I had thoughts or intentions of committing suicide. At the end I had to add up my answers. I was surprised to see that my score indicated I had moderate to severe depression. Terror shot through me to think I had let myself get this bad before getting help. I handed Mrs. N. the sheet and she in turn gave me a book to start reading.

"I only ask that you read the introduction and the first chapter, but if you'd like to read more, you may. Our time today is through, but I'd like to pray with you before you go. Is that okay?" I nodded.

I walked back to my house slowly, book in hand, carefully studying the cover. Feeling overwhelmed, I searched the refrigerator and cupboards for something that sounded appealing. Grabbing a box of instant mashed potatoes, I turned to the introduction as I stirred the sticky mixture in a pot. Not even bothering to put a serving into a bowl, I carried the whole pan to the dining room table. I spooned mediocre mush into my mouth with one hand, and held the book with the other. An hour later, I had gotten up only to grab a pen and notepad, had devoured all of the mashed potatoes, and was two chapters into the book. *I can identify almost every concept in the book as something I'm struggling with, but I didn't know how to fix any of it. What is there to fix really?*

Feeling defeated and fat, I marched up the stairs and went back to bed.

Chapter 24

I SLEPT AND ATE my way through the leaves falling from the trees, my twenty-first birthday, and most of my classes. Thanksgiving was just around the corner. I had started the antidepressant, but all it seemed to accomplish was making me sick if I skipped a day. I continued to see Mrs. N. regularly, but I couldn't get through five minutes without breaking down into tears. The book she'd given me helped me identify some of the thoughts that were causing me to feel depressed, but identifying them and stopping them were on two very different playing fields. My coping mechanisms of food, sleep and alcohol were failing me and my guilt level was rising daily. To complicate matters, I got word that Grandpa was now getting sicker by the day from his treatments. The nature of the news was upsetting, but didn't alarm me. I'd come to expect the worst. In the meantime, Daddy had been moved home with Hospice Care coming in regularly to keep him as comfortable as possible and encourage Mom. And there was another, long awaited email from Andy. He'd been silent for over a month.

> 11-25-02
> Dear Friends,
>   The man named Shimei hurled rocks and insults at King David and his exiled party. He did no real physical harm to David and his men, but his diatribes were aimed a bit more accurately. "You are a man of blood!" he shouted at the King, amongst of tirade of other harmful words. If none of his other ill-intended remarks struck David, certainly this one caught him like a knife in the back.

I'd like to hurl rocks at God. He's a God of blood. My thoughts shocked me and I pushed them aside to continue reading.

Some time earlier in his reign, David had aspired to build a Temple in which God would reside. With great intentions in his heart, he probably began to form great ideas and visions about this wonderful temple and how all the world would...and then God told him, "no."

God told David—the shepherd-boy-become King, the man after God's own heart, mighty warrior against Israel's nemesis, the Philistines—God told David that he didn't want him to build a temple. Why? Because he had blood on his hands; he was a man of battle, a warrior, a man of blood.

Imagine saving up for and envisioning the perfect gift for your favorite person, a gift so well-intended that it would last forever. Then imagine that person telling you, "No. You are not to give me this gift because..." Whatever the reason given, you would be devastated.

In spite of God's rejection of David's gift, he delivered the message with a great deal of sensitivity. The Temple would be built, God promised him, by David's son Solomon, who would succeed him on the throne of Israel.

This was no small promise on God's part, and subsequently no small response on David's. If David's ego was hurt by God's statement about him as a "man of blood," he quickly let that hurt go in response to God's generosity. The promise to David insured that his son Solomon would reign, and that a temple would be built, keeping Israel focused on God for yet another generation. This pleased David immensely, and he humbled himself in gratitude to God.

Now we know—from a comfortable distance, when we aren't going through tough times—that God always keeps his promises, even though we may have to take a few significant detours to get there. But it is a little more difficult to trust God to fulfill his promise when the detours start going down treacherous cliffs, up steep mountains, across icy and frigid land, through deserts—anywhere but in the direction of the fulfillment of God's promise. The detours cause some of us to question if God really gave us that promise, or maybe that the terms aren't quite as we remember them. Some of us doubt that God ever spoke at all, or if He's real, or if He isn't just playing some kind of game, with humans as the pieces on the board.

God, am I nothing more than Your game piece? My family—all of us just trinkets You toy with to get some sick sense of satisfaction?

Although there doesn't seem to be record of it in the Bible, I would be willing to bet a sizable amount of change that David went through some of the mental anguish that I described in that last paragraph.

You see, God didn't just fulfill that promise right away for David; He took David—and Israel—on some significant detours before the details of the promise came true. And in those moments, David had to have wondered—any mortal would have to wonder—whether or not God was off His Throne-rocker, or if David was for listening to Him.

The trouble started with Absalom, one of David's many—and most beloved—sons. Before David's death, Absalom declared himself King of Israel, converted enough of David's old faithful followers, and acquired such a significant army that David and those loyal to him had to flee from Jerusalem rather than face death at the hands of the renegade King Absalom. They fled east, into the Judean wilderness where David had run from King Saul. During this flight, David and his men encountered the wrath of Shimei, a relative of the house of Saul.

If I were in David's shoes at the time, I would have seriously questioned God's promise about putting Solomon on the throne. I would have been angry, shaking my fist at God and crying out, "Why, God, won't you do what you promised? How can you fulfill your promise to have Solomon rule and build you a temple when Absalom has seized the throne and seeks the death of his own father?"

Enter Shimei: hurling stones and insults at David, kicking a man while he's down. That one line spoken by Shimei, "You are a man of blood," must have haunted David at the time. Not only was it a reminder of why God didn't want David to build the temple, it was a direct reminder of the promise to have Solomon on the throne and providing the Lord's residence—a promise that, at the time, seemed to crumble before David's very eyes. It's possible that Shimei's comment cut David even deeper; it could have said to David, "You're the king, but God doesn't want you building his house because you've fought too many wars; you're not even worthy of building God a house!" When we are down or depressed, statements like this resonate and echo within us, haunting us and reminding us of our failures and shortcomings. We forget the promises of God, and our inadequacies seem larger than His mighty power.

I don't know how David's attitude held up during this trying time: did he question God's promise? Did he doubt his abilities and blame himself? Did he feel weak, hopeless, and depressed?

It is likely that he did, because when Absalom's troops were defeated, and Absalom himself killed, David could think of nothing but the loss of his son. Joab, the commander of his army, delivered a sharp warning that David needed to shape up and take control of his kingdom before he lost it again.

So King David regrouped himself, and on his march back to Jerusalem to restore his kingdom, he even forgave Shimei. The kingdom was restored to David, and God's promise fulfilled as Solomon eventually succeeded his father and built the Temple.

Six months ago, my Dad received a message from God that we took as a promise for my healing. The promise came from 2 Chronicles 20, when several armies set out to attack Jerusalem. In humility and desperation, King Jehoshaphat gathered his people at the temple and cried out to God for deliverance. He then set out to fight the much larger invasion force, making the tactically suicidal blunder (if God isn't fighting for you, that is!) of placing a group of singing Levites at the front of the army. By the time the Israelites reached the enemy camp, they found that the invading armies had killed each other off, to a man.

My Dad, Mary and I took this as a promise for God's healing, that the invading armies of cancer cells would kill each other off, to a cell. I must admit that I have had trouble trusting God for the fulfillment of this promise through the detours, road blocks, man-eating potholes, and washed-out bridges of the road I've been on. Like King David, I've encountered some resistance, I've faced mountains that looked hopeless, and, like King David, I've need people along the way to challenge me to get back on the right track.

And there's still a bit of the story that isn't quite finished: the fulfillment of the promise. God is always faithful, and he always speaks the truth. Just because the road is tough, just because it may travel through a mine field, just because the road may appear to be going the wrong way—these things don't mean that the road isn't going where God intends.

Tears were flowing freely down my face as I read. My anger erupted at God and His seemingly unfulfilled promises. Could those verses really have been meant as a promise of Andy's healing or was it just wishful thinking and coincidence?

It is hard to focus on God for the fulfillment of this promise. It is sometimes difficult to muster up the mustard seed of faith needed to believe in His healing power and to wait on Him.

Yet, for the first time in my life, I find myself believing that promise more than ever, and wanting its fulfillment more than ever. As our wedding day "creeps" closer and closer, Mary and I thank God for the energy and strength we have had to focus on our wonderful relationship. But more than anything, we want to be able to stand before God, family, and friends on December 28th and proclaim without a doubt that God has healed me of cancer. It would be an amazing testimony to the Lord's power for Him to heal me while my body is free of anti-cancer drugs and treatments, to declare that though humans are still limited in knowledge, God's power never wanes.

Yeah, that would be a great way for God to prove His power, but will He? Is this all just a pipe dream? I just don't understand. Why is it so hard to believe? I have no mustard seed left.

Another Old Testament king, Hezekiah, knew the power of God's healing. When he learned he would die, he cried out to God. God healed him and granted him another 15 years of life.

Well I'm pleading to God for another 50 years of life. I want another 50 years to love my wife, my family and friends, and, above all, to praise God for healing me through whatever means of communication I can. I would like for everyone to join with me in this prayer, not for the glory of Mary and I, but for the glory of the Lord and his mighty power.

How many of us are empty and waiting for the Lord to show himself to us? How many of us are broken and need to see a miracle? How many of us wonder if God even works miracles anymore? I know that sometimes I wonder all of these things.

But now Mary and I approach the Throne of Grace with confidence, boldly asking God for healing before our wedding and before any more medicine is put into my body.

Anyone can pray this prayer; not just Christians and churchgoers, not just pastors and elders. God wants to reveal himself to everyone: broken people, hurting people, people who wonder if he exists, people who don't think they're worth anything, people who have no faith in anything, people who wrestle to understand God, people who have told God that he isn't worthy of their worship, people who are afraid to believe in something so amazing. The list could go on.

So no matter who you are or what your faith is, will you join Mary and I in our bold prayer? Will you pour your heart out for God to show His mighty power? Will you ask Him to reveal Himself in this situation? If you have any care for us, will you please ask him for another 50 years for me? Please join us, even if this is the only prayer you have ever dared pray in your life, and then see what the result is.

My medical update is short, thankfully. I'm still holding up well, looking well, and getting my hair back. We are enjoying ourselves very much and checking on the tumors every four weeks. We are still waiting to find out about the Wayne State trial.

Thank you all for your steadfast prayers, thoughts and support.

Love,
Andy Schrier

I can't pray—not really. Prayer doesn't seem to be working for Daddy or Grandpa and Andy's tumors aren't destroying each other like we'd asked. But if I don't pray it and Andy dies, how will I ever forgive myself?

I could no longer pray sincerely, but I was relieved that I could soon go home and help. I could use my hands to ease others' burdens, even if it was just for the five brief days of Thanksgiving break. So, welcoming the opportunity to finally do something tangible, I packed my bags, made my transportation arrangements and headed for home.

Nothing could have prepared me for what I saw when I arrived, however. Relief was not even on my radar when I walked into the large, heated sunroom, where Daddy lay in a hospital bed. Barely responsive, he cracked a weak smile when he saw me. I could only stare at the pale yellow skin hanging like a wet rag around his jaw, forehead, and cheekbones, his eyes protruding from hollow sockets. Under the thin sheet, his bony knees stuck up like knots on tree limbs. His pajamas hung loosely around his once solid chest. Now it was nearly concave in juxtaposition with his distended belly. In a brief month and a half, he had deteriorated so drastically.

"Hi Daddy," I croaked, tears falling unbidden.

"He would probably love it if you snuggled next to him on the bed," Mom encouraged, a hand on my elbow. She seemed to sense my shock. "Wouldn't you, Honey?" Daddy managed a smile again and I noticed how his cheekbones protruded from below his eyes. I had always admired his cheekbones. They seemed to capture his strong, stoic personality. But now, they made him look powerless, impotent against the disease whose name I didn't even want to think. Cancer. It had become a curse word.

I sat down as gently as I could on the bed and rested my head on Daddy's shoulder. It was too pokey, so I moved my head to his chest and pleaded with God for words, but none came. His arm around my back seemed stronger than I had expected and he rubbed his thumb slowly between my shoulder blades. "I love you Daddy." It was all I could think to say.

"I love you, too," he replied, in no more than a whisper. Then he was asleep, having spent all his energy on those four words.

Later that night, Mom and I sat at the sunroom table. Daddy snored softly on the bed next to us. "I have everything for Thanksgiving dinner tomorrow, I just don't know if we should have it. I don't have the energy," she sighed heavily. Her shoulders sagged in her chair. The circles under her eyes looked swollen and dark.

"I'll make it." The words were out before I could stop them. It's not like there would be a huge crowd. Everyone was coming to see Daddy at different times so as not to overwhelm him. It would only be Daddy, Mom and me, Tim and Leslie, who had moved in with Mom and Daddy a few weeks ago, and Grandma and Grandpa. Dave had taken an assignment in Hawaii for a year, so we had to wait until Andy's wedding to see him. Seven people for Thanksgiving dinner was miniscule to the gathering Mom usually fed. Yet, I had only ever watched Mom prepare the traditional meal and helped with things like polishing the silver and setting the table. But if Mom was too tired, I would do it. It might not be quite the spread she put out every year, but it would have to do.

"Just tell me what to do and I'll do it. I'll set the good china out here so we can be close to Daddy."

"I didn't polish the silver," Mom said, as her only protest. She was too exhausted to make any other argument.

"I'll get started now." Before I could panic about the commitment I had made, I got up and began counting out the silver we would need from the dining room buffet table. Mom helped me figure out which serving pieces we would need and then went to be with Daddy in the sunroom. Taking my anxiety out on the silver, I made each piece gleam like it was fresh out of the box. Engrossed in my task and in my melancholy mood, I was only minimally aware of the tears that were dripping slowly from my face. Suddenly a strange sound erupted from the sunroom, breaking through my gloom. I turned to see Tim, Leslie, Mom and Daddy, all in the sunroom laughing.

"What's going on in there?" I called, my hands elbow deep in soapy water.

"Mind your own business!" Daddy hollered back with his usual spunk. I could hear that there was a huge grin on his face. For a moment he looked almost healthy. I forgot the sting of being left out and went back to my preparations, overwhelmed with a forgotten emotion—something close to joy.

An obnoxious beeping awoke me the next morning in time to prepare the turkey. Once I was certain it was defrosted and well stuffed, and I had fed Zacc, I sat down at the table in the sunroom with a bowl of cereal and a cup of hot coffee. Mom sat on the couch, leaning close to Daddy and reading to him from Psalms. His eyes were closed, but I knew the look of deep concentration wrinkling his eyebrows and setting a slight smile to his mouth.

> Psalm 97
> [1] The Lord reigns, let the earth be glad;
>   let the distant shores rejoice.
> [2] Clouds and thick darkness surround him;
>   righteousness and justice are the foundation of his throne.
> [3] Fire goes before him
>   and consumes his foes on every side.

> ⁴ His lightning lights up the world;
>   the earth sees and trembles.
> ⁵ The mountains melt like wax before the LORD,
>   before the Lord of all the earth.
> ⁶ The heavens proclaim his righteousness,
>   and all peoples see his glory.
> ⁷ All who worship images are put to shame,
>   those who boast in idols—
>   worship him, all you gods!
> ⁸ Zion hears and rejoices
>   and the villages of Judah are glad
>   because of your judgments, LORD.
> ⁹ For you, LORD, are the Most High over all the earth;
>   you are exalted far above all gods.
> ¹⁰ Let those who love the LORD hate evil,
>   for he guards the lives of his faithful ones
>   and delivers them from the hand of the wicked.
> ¹¹ Light shines[a] on the righteous
>   and joy on the upright in heart.
> ¹² Rejoice in the LORD, you who are righteous,
>   and praise his holy name. (NIV)

These words to which I had once clung now stung right to my core. I could not believe them. But there was Daddy, basking in them, taking comfort from them, breathing in every syllable. *I'm glad he can find peace in this nonsense,* I thought. *Why can't I? Why am I so angry? It's not God's fault he's dying. It's probably mine. I must have really ticked Him off.* Mom glanced up from the page, and, noticing that my cereal was gone asked, "Would you like to come pray with us, Abby?" She patted the seat next to her. Daddy's eyes opened and he lifted his head to smile at me. Feeling duplicitous, I sat close to my mom so I could hold her hand and reach across to Daddy's also. Then Mom prayed for our day, for Andy and Mary in Michigan, for Grandpa, for each of her children, and finally asked for healing for Daddy.

"There is nothing more the doctors can do, Lord, but we know You can if it is Your will. Please make him well. Destroy every cancer cell in his body and grant him strength and years. But if it is not Your will, Lord, please give us precious times and memories in these last days."

Of course it isn't His will to heal him. I'm still here to make God angry. God, what did I do to deserve this? Forgive me, please! Suddenly the couch under my backside felt like hot coals. The moment Mom was finished, I hopped up and retreated, under the pretense of taking my dishes into the kitchen. Aware that a tear had snuck out of each eye, I wiped them awkwardly on my sleeves, hoping no one would notice. There was plenty of time before I needed to get started working on the dinner, so I took a long shower and then called Shaun to wish him and his family a happy Thanksgiving. Even in my melancholy mood it was reassuring to hear his voice.

Around noon, Grandma and Grandpa arrived. Grandpa's appearance was shocking, although not nearly as much as Daddy's had been the day before. Where thick, wavy black hair had always crowned Grandpa's dark, Native American face, bald skin now reflected the light. His face seemed swollen, his cheeks like a chipmunk hoarding nuts. His button-down shirt had extra fabric around the shoulders and waist and his pants sagged between the loops where his belt was cinched a notch or two tighter than normal.

Everything in me wanted to collapse to the floor in anguish, but instead I summoned every ounce of fortitude I could and hugged my grandparents, smiled and greeted them happily. Grandpa smiled. Then, without a word, he stepped into the sunroom to greet Daddy, sat down in an armchair and promptly fell asleep.

Turning to Grandma, but having no idea what to say, I asked, "Can I make you a sandwich, Grandma?" I wrapped an arm around her tiny shoulders and together we headed toward the fridge.

"Oh, thank you, dear. Do you have Lebanon bologna? I'm sure your grandfather would like a bite to eat, too." I began pulling lunch items out and setting them on the counter.

"Mom, what would you and Daddy like?"

"Oh, I'm sure your dad would like some of those peaches and maybe some Jell-O. I'll get it for him."

These surface conversations and simple tasks were the only way I could function. Anything regarding that cursed disease made my head spin. But cancer somehow permeated everything. I watched in horror as Mom scooped out meager portions to the man who'd always had a healthy appreciation for three square meals. The rest of us sat at the table just feet away, eating our sandwiches, pickles and fresh fruit, while Mom spoon-fed red putrescence into Daddy's mouth. My toasted turkey and Swiss on whole wheat with spicy mustard turned to cardboard in my mouth.

Somehow I had to go from chewing cardboard to putting a decent turkey dinner on the table for my family. It's what I had said I would do. It was the only way to keep putting one foot in front of the other. Grandpa and Daddy went back to sleeping while Mom ate the sandwich I had made for her. I started organizing what I would need to prepare. As I set items out, I noticed there were peaches and Jell-O on the counter that had gone uneaten. I wrapped them in plastic and stuck them in the fridge, dropping them on the shelf as though they were burning my fingers.

Okay, I forced the negativity out of my brain. *Potatoes need to be peeled and cut. The extra stuffing is ready and can go in later. Peas go on at the last minute. Rolls can go in the oven at the last minute, too. Grandma's Ambrosia Salad is in the fridge. I guess I need to start with the potatoes.*

"How can I help you, Dear?" Grandma interrupted my thoughts.

"I'm just going to start working on the potatoes."

She reached for a knife and pulled a dripping potato out of the sink. "How is Shaun?"

Small talk. Small talk is good, I thought before answering her question with too much enthusiasm. Potato peels began filling the trash can and I felt my heart rate slow. Thinking of Shaun always made me feel better and Grandma must have known it.

Miraculously, dinner made it to the table. The turkey was a little dry, the potatoes slightly gummy, and the peas were cold from being done well before everything else, but the table setting looked beautiful and no one went hungry. Daddy alternately watched us from his bed and dozed in the sunlight.

Anxiety faded ever so slightly throughout the remainder of the weekend with each helpful task I took on. Mom seemed to relax in Daddy's company when I did the dishes, made dinner, or did random household chores, so I kept myself busy. I don't remember any of the details, just that I felt useful. And I don't remember from whom I bummed a ride back to school, but somehow three hundred miles were once again put between me and my dying father.

Chapter 25

SLEEP. ESCAPE. Hide under the covers. It seemed like the only thing I did in the next two weeks. Although, I did manage to eat. Plenty. And see Shaun. And go to rehearsal. I had an appointment or two with Mrs. N. sometime in there. Rolling out of bed, throwing my hair in a ponytail and pulling on some sweats, I braved the bitter cold and walked nearly a mile across campus and back to sit in a puddle of tears in her office, able only to offer moans and non-verbal cues in answer to her questions. Then back to bed.

I must have gone to some classes, not because I was learning anything or doing any work outside of class, but sheerly out of guilt. *Mom and Daddy are paying a lot for me to go to such a nice school because I proved in high school I was able to apply myself. But that isn't really me. I was lucky. I'm not as smart as Jen or Dave or any of them. Tim's a much better musician than I am. I don't deserve to be here. I should be at home helping Mom. Even if I was at home, I'd probably screw things up. Like Thanksgiving dinner. Daddy's probably dying because of me anyway. God, what did I do to make You so angry? Are You going to take Andy, too? Oh God, don't take Andy! What if I sacrifice myself? I'm sure I could find enough pills in this house to kill myself. Would You spare them then?*

The respondent silence was deafening until sleep took over. The nightmares of sleep were nothing compared to those of my reality. Awake, that familiar line of thinking seemed the only way to make sense of the nightmares of actuality. Each time, the thought of suicide became more and more appealing. And then Mom would call or Shaun would stop by. I couldn't do that to them.

Two weeks after Thanksgiving, I had dragged myself out of bed in time to get to Songs, Hymns, and Spiritual Songs, a class which, under different circumstances I would have loved, and which was taught by one of my favorite professors. But today, the same cycle of thoughts had been playing in my mind for a dangerously long period of time. I sat at my desk, Dr. R.'s voice a vague whisper in comparison to the voice telling me that giving my life might spare Daddy's and Andy's. I took a sheet of paper from my notebook and robotically began to write.

> My Dearest Shaun,
> I need you to know that this is not your fault. You have loved me in a way I could never deserve and I thank you for that. You are an angel and you deserve so much more than this messed up little girl. I hope that when I am gone you will find someone who deserves all that you have to offer. I just can't take it anymore. It's all my fault and I have to make it stop. I have to try at least.
> Those three little words,
> Me

Then I began a second letter. Mom deserved a note, too. The pen touched the paper, but the words wouldn't come. Tears came instead, pouring, drenching my note to Shaun. Familiar faces sitting all around me had blurred into nothing, but now loomed like a hundred pointing fingers. I shoved my binder into my backpack, grabbed my things and fled for the bathroom before anyone could notice. The cold water from the bathroom sink could not stop the tears, so I ran all the way back to my house, hoping it would be empty.

I can't. I can't do it to Mom! But if I don't, they'll die! Oh God, what do You want from me? My own internal voices were far too overpowering to hear any answer from God. *Maybe . . . maybe if I just take enough to make me go to the hospital. Maybe a bottle of ibuprofen or something. Maybe then they'll send me home. But how do I know how much to take? And then Mom would have to take care of me, too.*

Utterly conflicted, hopeless and helpless, I flung open the back door of the house, ran into the dining room and picked up the phone. But who was I going to call? I couldn't call Mom. She could not know what was going on. Shaun, and practically everyone else I knew, was at class. Without thinking, I dialed the number for the Health Center.

"I need to talk to Mrs. N.," I managed through my sobs. The receptionist must have sensed my urgency, because Mrs. N.'s voice came through the line in a few short moments.

"Abby, are you alright?"

"Um, no, not really." I continued to bawl. But I didn't know what else to say.

"Can you come in right away?" *That's probably better than swallowing a bottle of pills.*

"Yes. I'll be right over." I retraced my steps back to the music building and beyond. It was bitterly cold, but I didn't mind—it seemed to be the same numbing temperature I felt internally. The warmth inside the Health Center was unsettling. It seemed undeserved. Sitting in front of Mrs. N., shame overcame me. The sea of tears somehow stopped, like someone had turned off a faucet inside my head. But my voice did not work.

"Tell me what's going on, Abby?" Mrs. N. inquired, kindly. My head hung low and I looked up at her without lifting it. I shrugged, unable to utter the despicable truth.

"Is your father getting worse?" I shook my head, keeping my eyes on the floor. She paused for a second.

"Your brother?" Again, a slight shake of the head was all she got.

"Were you thinking of hurting yourself?" An icicle shot straight into my chest and froze every part of me. My head shot up and my eyes met hers. *How did she know?*

"Would you feel better if you could go home? I could ask your professors to give you incompletes for now and you can catch up next semester."

"You can do that?" I didn't know I had spoken—didn't know I could speak. In a few minutes, it was all settled. I would ask Shaun to help me find a way home and Mrs. N. would contact my professors, giving me psychological leave for the rest of the semester. It was less than two weeks at this point, but a day longer was too dangerous for me to risk. I needed to go home and help take care of Daddy for whatever little time he had left. I practically skipped out of the Health Center to meet Shaun at the cafeteria for lunch. I told him what Mrs. N. and I had decided.

"So, I guess I'd better give you your Christmas present tonight, then." Shaun's eyes twinkled with excitement as he spoke the words. My stomach gurgled with nerves. My limited budget and inferior gift giving abilities had led me to purchase an Old Navy hoodie and pajama pants for Shaun's Christmas gift. In no way did these items convey what I wanted to say to him, but I didn't know what would. It was too late now anyway.

That evening, Shaun fidgeted in his seat across from me, hiding a package behind his back as I apologetically shoved the clothing box at him.

"I didn't know what to get you and I didn't have much money," I blubbered, wanting to crawl inside my own skin.

"Oh, awesome! I need these! Thank you!" He was too kind. But his thanks seemed genuine. Then, with the same excitement I'd seen at lunch, he revealed the gift bag he'd been concealing. The name of a well-known New York jeweler was on the box, and for a moment my heart fluttered inside my chest. *Did he get a ring? Is this going to be the moment every girl dreams of her whole life?* I looked around the room for a moment. I selfishly hoped he was more romantic than to offer an engagement ring as a Christmas gift and without any kind of flare. Daddy certainly wouldn't have given his approval and I hoped Shaun was sensible enough to know he must ask first. Guilty relief flooded me when I opened the small black box to reveal a pair of princess-cut diamond earrings. Even these were way too much.

EARLY THE NEXT MORNING, Shaun kissed me goodbye from the platform of the train station. I'd never taken more than a short train ride. The sense of adventure was strong enough to overcome the dread of what I would find when I finally arrived home.

"I'll see you at Andy's wedding," Shaun whispered, his arms still wrapped tightly around my waist. "Be careful." I knew his worry stemmed more from concern for my emotional well-being than for my physical safety. The train pulled up next to us and the doors opened. One or two people stepped out and Shaun grabbed my duffle bag. He hefted it into the train and up onto the luggage rack. Then he kissed me again and stepped off the train.

"I love you," I saw him mouth as the train slipped away. He was always so good to me. Too good. The note I'd written to him the day before loomed in my mind. The desire to end my life was gone, but the belief that he was much more than I deserved was never so real. Since hearing that I needed to go home, he had researched the best travel methods, narrowed down the best departure time, purchased the tickets, dropped me off at the train station, and given me a little cash he really could not afford to give up. I hadn't mustered the courage to tell him how severe the depression had become, but he wasn't dumb. He knew the school wouldn't allow me to go home without serious academic repercussions if it weren't for a very good reason.

I had the entire day on that bumpy train to ponder my relationship with Shaun. I fingered the diamond earrings in my ears frequently as I thought about the man I'd fallen in love with. *I'm not good enough for him. But it's way too late to walk away now. That would destroy both of us. What does he even see in me? I'm such a mess and nothing about my life is much fun right now. Who would blame him for giving up on me? But he never does. Why did You give him to me, God? Why?* This time an answer came.

Because I love you, My Child. My thoughts stilled. My soul felt calm. I knew it was authentic because He always used that salutation when He spoke to my heart.

The steady rocking of the train nudged me into a more peaceful sleep than I'd had in nearly two weeks. I'd spent countless hours in fitful, nightmarish sleep which seemed to only leave my body more exhausted than before, but this quality of rest had been elusive. Each time the train stopped, I stirred enough to hear that voice resonating somewhere in the recesses of my mind; *I gave him to you because I love you, My Child.*

Chapter 26

FINALLY, after many hours, I arrived at the train station in Ohio. By that time, I had marinated in God's assurance of love long enough that I had uncovered a small spark of joy. And I had a plan. I would be Daddy's joy for whatever time he had left. I would work for Mom, doing everything I could to make Daddy's remaining days more comfortable. Then, when Daddy was safe in God's arms, I would return to school and work harder than ever to catch up.

Mom's friend Gail entered the train station with open arms. She had agreed to drive the two-hour round trip to pick me up so Mom didn't have to miss a moment with Daddy.

"You had a rough time back at school, Honey?" *You have no idea*, I thought to myself as I sank into her familiar hug. She held me for an extra moment, in an effort to convey her sympathy. "Your parents are so happy you are coming home."

"I am too. I just want to help." That was all we needed to say. We climbed into Gail's warm car and I was never so grateful for how easy she was to talk to. There was not a moment of silence on the hour drive, because it was filled with Gail's bubbly chatter.

It was quite late when we pulled into my parents' driveway and Gail still had a twenty-minute drive home. She came in for a moment to say hello to Mom and to give Daddy—who barely moved—a quick hug and then she was gone. Then I was alone with them. Tim and Leslie must have already gone to bed. *What should I tell them about why I'm home?* I wondered. But they didn't ask for any further explanation for my early return. Daddy barely seemed to register that I was there. I chalked it up to the fact that it was well past his bedtime.

The morning did not make Daddy much more lucid, however. He awoke for only brief periods of time, once long enough to notice the diamonds decorating my ears.

"Where did those come from?" he asked indignantly.

"They were my Christmas present from Shaun," I replied, gently, trying to play it down.

"This boy is moving way too fast." I knew it would further upset him if I argued, and the energy he had already expended in getting irritated had clearly exhausted him. He shifted slightly on his bed and closed his eyes. Brushing a grey curl away from his forehead, I watched him drift back to sleep. His appearance in the daylight was more astonishing than ever. White flesh clung to his cheeks, arms and legs, and his belly was distended like the stereotypical African children in the TV commercials. His hair was uncharacteristically thin and his nails had started to turn yellow. I spent the next two days helping Mom bathe and feed him, do housework, and cook meals for Mom and me. The monotony was briefly interrupted by an upbeat, albeit long email from Andy. I plowed through the entire thing in one sitting, even reading portions of it over again, wrestling with its content.

> 12-14-02
> Dear Friends,
>
> Two years ago, God blessed me by sending me on a trip to New York City. I was there for a conference, but I remember more of the city than I do of the conference.
>
> One night, I was trailing my group down Broadway Avenue, seeing the sites and letting the best Chicken Parmesan dinner I had ever tasted settle in my stomach. As I moseyed past the B.B. King Blues Club, a tall man in a long trench coat walked directly out of the club, and straight towards me. I immediately recognized the face, but I was off in dreamland; with a big grin and a nod, the man spoke a friendly "hey" to me as I passed.
>
> "Hey," I said as I continued walking past, but staring back at his highly recognizable face. I was already a crucial 5 feet past him, and he was immediately mobbed by a throng of other admirers and picture-takers as he stepped towards his car. He graciously said a few words and smiled for a few shots before being driven away. Only then did it hit me who had just said "hey" to me: it was none other than Bill Cosby!
>
> I laughed at myself for being a daydreamer. If I had been more alert, all I would have had to do was stop when I first recognized him, put out my hand, and said hello to have met Bill Cosby, one of the coolest and funniest celebrities I could ever hope to run into.

Although the event was quite exciting, I mentally kicked myself a hundred times during the next several days. I had the chance to meet Bill Cosby, but because I had my head in the clouds, I missed my opportunity. It passed me by. The only thought I could console myself with was, "well, at least I know he's real."

That's kind of the attraction with seeing a celebrity; it's that exciting feeling of, "hey, I've seen them on TV," or, "I've listened to his music. That person really is real, in person, not just something the TV producers want me to believe in." To actually get to know that celebrity would be more of a rush, even if it is simply a "hey" or a handshake, or a question about Jello pudding commercials.

As a result of that incident, the rest of the weekend became a hunt for celebrities. We checked every face in hope that we might find a movie star or a musician and be the first annoying tourist to ask for their autograph. Then we would share our stories with other tourists at the conference who would say, "Oh yeah, well we saw Master P!" And then we'd reply, "Yeah, but BILL COSBY! Top that!" And they would sullenly realize that we were right, because everybody knows that nothing tops a Bill Cosby sighting. Except God himself.

Sometimes, in my spiritual life, I've felt like that New York weekend. I run around everywhere looking under rocks and behind every tree, talking to every person, listening to every sermon, looking for a chance sighting of God. Sometimes, after a long period of searching I get frustrated. I think of the U2 song, "I Still Haven't Found What I'm Looking For." I'll cry out to God, frustrated that I can't see him: "God can't you hear me? Where are you and why can't I see you? If you are so powerful, why can't you reveal yourself to me? Don't you want me to believe in you, after all? Don't you want to have a relationship? How can I believe in you if I can't see you or hear you?"

Often what I really want is just a glimpse of God: like Thomas, to see the nail piercings in his hands and feet, or like Moses, who saw a very small glimpse of God's glory as he passed by. Sometimes, ironically, I want to be struck blind, like Paul, and hear God's booming voice in such a way that my life is totally changed and I will never doubt God's presence again. I would bet that

98% of Christians would admit to feeling this way at some point in their lives, if not often, and the other 2% are probably liars or in denial. Yes, there are Christian liars, just as there are many non-Christian truth-tellers.

I'll admit, it is much harder to believe in God than it is to believe in Bill Cosby. But just as I missed my chance at getting to know Bill, some of us miss our chance at getting to know God. We are so busy hunting for God in the places where we expect him to show up that we miss where he has already shown himself. Can I get an Amen? Does anyone else feel that way? I know I sure do.

For example, I could have spent the last six months of my life praying for my Dad's healing from cancer, saying, "God show yourself by healing my Dad; if you really are who you say you are, then you will heal him. And if you don't, its going to be very tough for me to believe in you."

As I dodge the proverbial bolt of lightning for my irreverence, I realize that if I pray that prayer too doggedly, expecting God to only act one way (MY way), I will miss the other messages, the other sightings of God that may be going on. But once I quiet myself, I listen to my Dad's prayers, and I heard God through Dad's pain and suffering and his weak voice: "God, thank you for being Sovereign and in charge. Help us to honor you with this day. May your will be done in our lives."

"Your will be done," where have I heard that before? Oh, yeah, Jesus prayed that in the Garden of Gathsemane (Mark 14:36), when he was "overcome with sorrow to the point of death," (Mark 14:34) and when he sweat blood through his pores in agony (Luke 22:34). Did God have the power to heal him? Certainly; Jesus was God and probably could have healed himself of the anguish. Did God have the ability to stop the course of the Cross? Sure. But did God have a purpose for his son's suffering and death that no one who loved Jesus one earth would have understood at the time? Without a doubt! That is the very hope that our faith is based in.

Jesus . . . my Dad . . . Job . . . "Your will be done, not mine . . . "Though he slay me, yet I will hope in Him (Job 13:15)" When your body is racked with pain; when your mind falters; when everything you love in this world is right in front of your eyes but your sight is failing; when you might have to leave all of it behind; when your loved ones cry out for healing for you but don't get it; when you can't sleep at night because you wonder when you're going to die; when you watch the one you've committed your earthly life to dry up in your arms with your tears fresh on their face; when you watch bad things happen to good people; when six million of your people are slaughtered by a ruthless dictator; when you have to endure a death that will take on the sins of the world and separate you from the Father—How do you continue to believe in God? More so, How do you continue to love him and trust him? My father did it, Job did it, everybody in Hebrews 11 did it, Jesus Christ did it. How? Why?

Because they saw God in the rocks and trees and landscapes, in the human body, in the stars, in history, in the Bible, in the deep yearning within the deepest parts of their soul, in all the little things in their lives that seemed like coincidences but were too intricately planned to be just chance, because they recognized something deep within them—a God-shaped hole, a natural desire to know that eternal and unchanging being that nagged at the back of their mind all their lives. Above all, they knew and trusted that there was a God who loved them, and whose plan was much more important than theirs, and that the ultimate goal of life on earth was to glorify God, even if it meant while gritting one's teeth through one's afflictions and death. Isn't that called faith? They were sure of what they hoped in, and true to what they believed in, no matter what the circumstances.

And why should we do it? For all these reasons, and because Christ did it for us. Do you remember Jesus' response to Thomas' doubts?: "You believe because you have seen; blessed are those who have not seen and yet have believed." (John 20:29)

There's some incredible stuff to learn in that statement to Thomas. Jesus basically told Thomas what Paul wrote to the Roman Christians (Romans 1:18-20): people can see God in creation and hear his voices loud and clear; it is up to people to have faith and believe in God. That belief is a conscious effort to listen to the "right voices," or to "see the right things," that are markers of God, signs of his presence, his stamp upon creation, and proof of his interaction in our lives. Don't get me wrong: I'm not saying that God doesn't take on the responsibility of meeting us where we're at, or reaching out to us.

The problem is that there will always be room for human doubt. As the saying goes: you can lead a horse to water, but you can't make him drink. And, as Abraham told the rich man in hell (see Luke 16:19-31), even if they sent someone back from the dead to his brothers to tell them about the realities of God and eternity, they would not repent if they had not believed in the revelations God had given them on earth. The fact is that God can meet us or show himself to us a hundred million times and we could still walk away doubting that it was God. As a matter of fact, that is basically the theme of the Israelites in the Old Testament. Thankfully, another theme is that he never stops loving us, no matter how much we turn our backs on him.

Amazingly, and yet, often very tragically, God leaves the believing up to us. And that's really the crux of the whole issue. Either God is real or he isn't. Either he is who he is or he isn't. So there it is, choose you this day whom you will serve. It's entirely up to you. I can entertain and even doggedly believe that a charging and snarling rotweiler isn't really there, but that doesn't change the absolute of whether or not he exists or that he's ripping my throat out. In the same way, your beliefs in God, either way won't change the absolute truth of whether he is true or not; nor will mine.

There's an age old problem that philosophers and many other folks have delved into called the Problem of Evil. That term exists because it is very difficult for us humans to understand how a loving and all-powerful God could allow bad things and suffering to take place with his people. Many people have chosen not to believe in God because of this very observance of the world. Countless others have struggled deeply in their faith when they see someone they love suffer. The bottom line is that it takes an extra large step of faith to believe in God, his goodness, and his love for people when these things happen in our lives or to our loved ones.

In my lifelong struggle with the Problem of Evil and other such questions, I've recently been given a huge gift. Do you know what it is?: PAIN AND SUFFERING! That's right: I said it was a huge gift.

Before some of you think I'm off my spiritual rocker, or that the tumors have reached my brain and are affecting my thinking, allow me to make a brief commentary here. Suffering has a way of honing your faith, a way of whittling down what you believe and hope into the bare bones of your being. When suffering and faced with death, you suddenly realize that asking the nagging questions about God's existence, goodness, and love don't really get you anywhere. No matter which way you believe, the absolute is still true: He's either there or He isn't. Choose you this day whom you will serve, even though you can't "prove" it either way. You simply don't have time to waver any more; make your decision now! Pain and suffering force you to place your beliefs on the line, to hope against all hope that the decision you made was correct. So don't look back, just gather every scrap of faith, jump in deeper, and hold your nose till you can come up for air. You want a Biblical example? Look at Mark 9. A bunch of people are arguing because the disciples tried unsuccessfully to drive a demon out of a boy. Jesus is angered at their unbelief, and the father of the victimized child shyly asks Jesus for help, that is, IF Jesus can do anything. Jesus responds by saying that everything is possible for those who believe. The father's response (I imagine that he is crying, or that he screams this out of his agony for his son): "I do believe; help me overcome my unbelief!" That prayer is just enough; the father's molecule of faith suddenly bursts into a mustard seed and Jesus heals the son.

It is important to realize that God doesn't heal everyone, nor does he heal everyone who has faith in God that they will be healed. It is an extra step of human faith to believe that God can even be glorified through non-healing circumstances.

I was following until this point. But non-healing circumstances? How can they possibly glorify God?

Now that I have seen this with my Dad as he crosses the finish line into heaven, I truly believe that God CAN glorify himself through ANY circumstances. My Dad's dogged faith, the way he lives his life, and the way he leaves this world are a tribute to God. Did I pray for my Dad's healing? Yes. Did I believe it would come? Yes. Was I disappointed when it didn't? Yes. Yet is God glorified through my father's suffering and ultimately its end? Yes, indeed!

Yes, that's true, I guess. Daddy's devotion to God is nothing short of staggering.

> I'm still praying, religiously, for my own healing. I believe I will be healed. I believe that my work on earth is not finished yet. But I have had to recognize what that means: if God grants my prayer, it is for his glory, not my own. Jesus healed the man born blind because it brought glory to the Father (see John 9:3). I also have to recognize that God will not heal me because I deserve it more than others who ask for healing, or because I have more faith than others. That is just not true.
>
> Finally, I have to say by Jesus' example, "Your will be done, not mine." I admit, this is the hard part. I want to be healed for three reasons, and at different times, I will readily confess, certain reasons are more important than others. These three reasons are 1) my own desire to keep living, 2) the desire not to widow my future wife early in life, 3) and the desire to glorify God through my healing so that my friends and family who are struggling with God over the suffering will find it easier to believe in Him.

This includes me, even though Andy does not—cannot—know how deeply I'm struggling. But would I still believe in God, in His goodness, in His love, if He ultimately took Andy and *Daddy? I don't know if I could. How is that love? How is that good?*

> Lately, these three reasons have been very mixed up, and the second and third reasons are very related. The bottom line is that I am VERY concerned about the beliefs of my loved ones. I don't want anyone to fall away on account of my situation, or because of ANY suffering. I want God to heal me in such a way that it will be impossible for anyone to doubt Him ever again. I argue with him that because He wants relationships with those people, He MUST heal me to help them overcome their unbelief.
>
> But in saying, "Your will, not mine," I have to trust God that Mary, my family, and my friends will be okay. I trust that he will help them overcome their unbelief, no matter what the outcome of my physical health.
>
> My prayer now is that the empty God-shaped holes in peoples' lives, that itch to see him revealed, will be filled to over-

flowing, no matter what. Of course, I hope beyond all hope, and pray with all intensity that his will includes my healing. Because I believe that he will answer my prayer to fill what is empty, I can accept his will, live or die. Like my father, like Job, like my savior Jesus, I must live every breath of my life in the marvelous hope that I will one day see all my friends and family in heaven.

If by my life or my death I could will each and every one of you to join Job, my father, and my Father there, I would. But I can't. Each one of us must make up our own mind. Choose you this day whom you will serve.

We love you,
Andy Schrier

When I had poured over Andy's email ad nauseum, I could still not tear myself from my chair. The computer screen returned my stare. Andy's words rocked me. I was not believing like Job, or like Daddy, and definitely not like Jesus. I was selfishly and foolishly insisting that God be glorified on my terms. Healing on all counts was the only means by which I would accept God to be who He claimed.

But all people die, independent of the reality of God, I argued silently with myself, still sitting at the computer desk, my hands still resting on the keyboard. *So if God is real, and He is omnipotent, He must be able to bring glory to Himself through healing or through suffering and death, which are part of the human experience. Andy's suffering has already brought glory to God. His emails have been shared practically worldwide with thousands who find themselves struggling. We've gotten reports of his words encouraging so many in places farther than we'd imagined possible. Andy's right. I need to choose who I'm going to serve—a God who is limited to only being powerful when things are good, or a God who can turn even the most atrocious evil into something good.*

The choice seems pretty obvious, unless I take God completely out of the picture. But I simply can't believe that the world, the plants, the animals, humans, the beauty of nature, the complexity of even the tiniest living creature, all came to be by an accidental clashing of elements. Then what is the purpose in any of it? And where do those elements get their origin? No, that's too far-fetched for me. There must be a creative being who is not limited by time or space or matter. And if He exists, He must be all powerful. So I've been searching for the wrong thing. I've been expecting the obvious miracle—healing all around. Perhaps instead I should be looking for the little things; the hidden miracles.

The small internal voice on the train came back to me. God had given me Shaun. He was a hidden miracle—and a pretty huge one. Being able to come home was another. Motivated to hold tighter to my faith, I whispered, "Jesus, I believe. Help me overcome my unbelief."

WITH RENEWED FERVOR, I went back to my assignment helping Daddy. Once a day, Mom and I had to help him out of the bed so she could wash him down with a rag and change his pajamas. Other than that, Mom did most of the work caring for Daddy while I did the housework and took care of the dog, the grocery shopping, the cooking, and the laundry. When there was nothing that needed my immediate attention, I snuggled next to Daddy on the bed and just enjoyed his warmth. I prayed that he felt my presence and frequently whispered that I loved him. I could not bring myself to enter into a final monologue of farewell. It was crystal clear, however, that every night when I hugged him and kissed his cheek, it could be the last time. Each morning, when I woke, I expected to see Mom hunched beside his bed, shoulders shaking with sobs, mourning his passing. Instead, each day I found her faithfully sitting on the couch next to his bed, reading to him from the Psalms.

"YOUR FATHER cannot travel to Michigan for the wedding. And I can't leave him now. We'll have to figure something else out." Mom was on the phone with Andy. He didn't seem to be able to argue with her. Conversations like these were too much for me, and I had to leave the room. Maybe I called Shaun, checked my email, found a chore that needed my attention, or went to read a book—I don't remember. For whatever reason, I couldn't get Mom's words out of my head. *She and Daddy aren't going to their son's wedding?* And if they weren't going to Michigan, that meant they also wouldn't be a part of the family Christmas celebration we'd planned in the hotel for December 27, the day before the wedding. Something was fundamentally wrong with this concept and anger began to brew in a small corner of my consciousness towards the God I'd just determined to be good and loving. No matter how hard I tried, I couldn't reconcile my parents being separated from their family for two such important events. Troubled by my inability to hold to my belief, I reread Andy's email daily. With the strength it provided me, I determined to make my parents' Christmas Day here the best it could be. Perhaps Daddy wouldn't even wake up to see the work I put in, but Mom would know and so would I.

"Andy said they can wire a speaker to the phone so we can listen to the entire wedding!" Mom was excited to tell me this news.

"Oh, that's great," I lied. It was horrific that there was a need for such ridiculousness. I had to change the subject. "Mom, do you mind if I use the pewter dishes for dinner on Christmas Day? I think the pewter will look really pretty with all the glassware and the red linens."

"Sure, Sweetie. That will look nice with the arrangement our friends sent," she replied flatly. Clearly she was not excited about Christmas dinner at all. But I was. I had to be.

"I'd like to make us a special meal like we always have, even if it's not quite the same. But Grandma and Grandpa will be here and so will Tim and Leslie. We'll need something."

When Mom headed off to church the next morning, I began planning. Someone needed to stay with Daddy and I had offered, knowing Mom had been confined to home too much in recent weeks. I didn't really feel up to forcing myself through the motions of worship and prayer anyway.

I got out a place setting with all the glassware and pewter and laid it out in various ways, trying to determine how it would look best against the dark grain of the table. The red napkins and flowers offered the perfect pop of color. As I worked, I considered the menu I would serve. I'd ask Mom if I could get a ham and I'd make mashed potatoes, green beans, rolls, and a salad to go with it. Grandma was bringing some sugar cookies she'd decorated and we would have our traditional peppermint ice cream with hot fudge and whipped cream. As I arranged and rearranged dishes, I prayed through my anger. *God, I'm trying to believe. Help my unbelief. Show me how You are loving. Help me see the hidden miracles.*

"Look what the ladies from church gave me," Mom exclaimed, when she returned from church. She held a huge star-shaped basket, filled with small wrapped packages. "You can help me open everything up after lunch." She went into the sunroom to give Daddy a kiss, peeling her wool coat and leather gloves off as she went.

"What can I get you?" I asked, pulling out the makings of a salad and sandwiches and the Jell-O for Daddy. She joined me in the preparations after hanging her things in the closet and using the bathroom.

"Thank you for letting me go to church."

"Of course. My pleasure. I figured out stuff for Christmas dinner on Wednesday." Mom's demeanor quieted and she focused on toasting our sandwiches. After a sullen lunch, I cleaned up while Mom tried to feed Daddy. He didn't wake up long enough to eat much though.

"I can't believe they did all this!" I exclaimed, after we opened the contents of the basket. Mom sat on the floor in the living room, tears streaming down her cheeks. Candles, soaps, lotions, dried fruit and nuts, chocolates and popcorn, and cards with prayers, Bible verses and encouraging messages were all piled around her. The star-shaped basket had been emptied one item at a time as we lingered over each gift and note.

"They are such thoughtful, caring people." This was all Mom could say. She seemed overwhelmed by their generosity—humbled by their love. I stared in awe at the pile. *Another hidden miracle. You heard me, God! Thank you! How many others have I missed because I've been stuck in negativity for so long?*

Chapter 27

IT WAS ONLY four hours from our house in Ohio to Grand Rapids, Michigan. Tim drove Daddy's big blue Town Car. Grandpa sat in the front and Grandma and I occupied the spacious back seat. Despite the natural divider provided by the front seats, Grandpa and Tim took the opportunity to tease me relentlessly about Shaun.

"Has he given you a ring yet?" Tim asked. When I turned the color of a beet and sputtered a wimpy "no," he turned to Grandpa. "I think we need to have a talk with this boy! Don't you think so Gramp? He needs to get a move on it."

"Yup. Absolutely. We'll call him next week."

"He'll be at our house next week. And he'll be at the hotel tonight. Talk to him all you want," I responded, annoyed. But I really didn't mind. No one had ever approved of any of my boyfriends before, so Tim's and Grandpa's forwardness surprised me more than it irritated me. Besides, it was imperative that they approve of Shaun since I planned on him joining the family.

"Oh, he needs to wait until they are done with school," Grandma chimed in, ever the voice of reason. "He's a such a nice boy. He'll ask her when the time is right." I hoped this would be the end of it, but I should have known better. Tim had inherited Grandpa's teasing bone and the two of them would not let the matter go.

They had not dared to behave this way at yesterday's Christmas dinner. It was not out of respect for all the work I'd done to set a beautiful table and cook a delicious meal, either. It was because they knew how Daddy felt about the thought of his baby girl getting married, and they wouldn't speak of it in his presence, even if he was unconscious for the duration. By the time we finally arrived in Michigan, I had never been so relieved to get out of a car.

Andy was waiting for us at the hotel. I jumped out as quickly as I could and ran to hug him as he walked out of the lobby towards us. I noticed immediately that he looked shockingly healthy. His head was full of thick, curly hair once again, and his cheeks were rosy. I squeezed him tightly and could feel his heavily-muscled arms squeezing back with renewed strength. As I pulled away from him to let someone else greet him, his eyes twinkled with mischief I hadn't seen in quite a while.

"When's Shaun coming?" he asked.

"He'll be here sometime tonight."

"Can you wait that long?" He smiled deviously at me and I punched his arm. Grandma moved in to hug him and reached reverently up to touch his curls. Grandpa broke in to give the characteristic handshake/bearhug men do. I could not help but admire their appearance, the two of them. Both olive complected with rosy cheeks, both robust and energetic, both healthy. Only Grandpa's white stubble growing where his thick black hair had previously been belied his recent war on cancer.

"I'm in remission!" Grandpa declared loudly to Andy and everyone else.

"You're in remission and I'm taking a leap of faith and believing I am healed," Andy practically shouted. The small cluster of family let out a whoop in the lobby of the hotel, not giving a second thought to who might be turning to stare. Nothing could squash our joy that two of the three men who'd suffered horrific battles with cancer were now healthy.

After settling into our rooms, Grandma and Grandpa treated us all to a rather rowdy dinner. We returned to the hotel around 8:00 and as I rounded a corner to head toward the room I was sharing with Grandma and Grandpa, I almost ran into a man wearing a grey Old Navy fleece. Before I could think, his familiar arms scooped me up into a bearhug and swung me in a circle. No amount of teasing could have lessened my glee to be in Shaun's arms again.

The next day was a busy one. At nine o'clock in the morning, we all gathered in the hotel's conference room to celebrate our family Christmas. It was a plain room with beige carpet, off-white walls, and uninspired drapes. A folding table had been laid with scrambled eggs, bacon, fruit, coffee, and juice from the complimentary buffet. Mom hadn't had spare energy or time to make the traditional Dutch pastry we all loved, but Mary, also being Dutch, had brought some similar treats. No one complained, although the the exclusion of the annual delicacy was a harsh reminder of our missing patriarch and matriarch.

Otherwise, everyone was there in lively fashion. Dave had flown in from Hawaii. Katie and Jake had come from North Carolina with their three kids. Pete was there and Jen and Rod and their three children had driven from Maryland. And Shaun had driven a grueling twelve hours through a snowstorm to join us.

The first gifts opened were the matching button-down shirts Grandpa gave the men every year. I was happy to see that Shaun was included, even though we were not yet engaged. Next the children opened gifts. Then, as they played with their new treasures, oblivious to the somber atmosphere, the adults exchanged a few small items. After lunch (which must have been ordered from somewhere, but I really can't remember) and some more reserved celebration, we all departed to our own rooms to get ready for Andy's rehearsal dinner.

We reconvened at Andy's and Mary's church and awaited the instructions. We all had various roles to play. Grandma and Grandpa would sit in for Mom and Dad. Jen and Katie each had a singing role. Tim, Dave and Pete were ushers and I was a bridesmaid.

The rehearsal went quickly and before long, we were eating a spaghetti dinner in the fellowship hall and Andy was making his rounds through all of the guests, proclaiming his own healing and Grandpa's as well. I had to roll my eyes a little at his confidence in God's healing power without any evidence of such. *How can he be so sure,* I wondered, planting a fake smile on my face. *He doesn't know he's healed. As far as we know, the tumors are still there and could begin growing again at any time. He's a ticking time bomb. But isn't that the biblical definition of faith—being sure of what you hope for and certain of what you do not see? Maybe my annoyance is misplaced and I should be rolling my eyes at myself for being unable to believe. Lord, help my unbelief!*

I stood in silver heels and a black bridesmaid's dress, red roses in my hands, hair in an updo and makeup professionally administered, waiting with Mary and the other bridesmaids for the ceremony to start. Mary was beaming, as every bride should. She was perfect for Andy. Sensible and sweet, quiet and reserved, but every bit as passionate as Andy. *Is he going to die and leave her widowed?* I couldn't help but think it. *Will he give her children she'll have to take care of by herself? They will certainly be without a paternal grandfather.* My thoughts were cut short by a voice over the speaker.

"Okay, we should be connected. Are you still there, Shirley?"

"Yes, I'm here." I heard my mom's voice reply to the sound technician.

"Okay, Andy say something into the mic and we'll make sure she can hear that, too." From where I stood, I could see Andy step up to the microphone at one side of the platform, but Mary was safely out of his line of vision.

"Can you hear me, Mom?"

"Yes, I hear you. Dad is here and so is Leslie. We hear you." The familiar feeling of a wet face came to my attention. I was crying and I couldn't stop, even when the prelude music flowed into the processional. I followed protocol, walking to the front of the sanctuary with the music, turning one full turn to my left before stopping to face the front, standing quietly while the other bridesmaids did the same, turning to watch Mary and her father walk towards my blushing brother. The tears were persistent. So much for the professional makeup.

"Andy, I believe you have a song prepared for Mary?" the preacher asked after the giving of the bride. Andy nodded and walked to where his guitar waited by a microphone. He strummed a few chords and then his deep, folksy voice floated through the sanctuary serenading Mary with words he'd penned just for her:

> I've been through the fire and I've felt the pain;
> I was burned by the heat, but escaped the flame.
>
> I've been through the river, and I've swum in the deep;
> I came close to drowning and the banks were steep.
>
> But you walked beside me when my face hit the ground,
> And you stood beside me till I came around.
>
> Whoever walks with me along such a road
> Must truly be an angel to carry such a load.
>
> And how can I say thank you for seeing me through?
> I'll always be grateful, and I'll always love you.
>
> I've climbed over mountains, been cut by sharp stones;
> I lost sight of the path; that was my only way home.
>
> I've suffered the blows from and unwanted hand,
> But you stood beside me and helped me to stand.
>
> For only our God could create love so strong;
> It's a gift from Heaven to help us along.
>
> Whoever walks with me along such a road
> Must truly be an angel to carry such a load.
>
> And how can I say thank you for seeing me through?
> I'll always be grateful, and I'll always love you.

Oh God! She is an angel. What will happen to her? Is she simply sealing her fate today, binding herself to a man on death row? Jesus, protect her! Keep Andy alive so they can enjoy a happy life together, have children together, grow old together. Please God! When the ceremony was finally over, I proceeded back up the aisle feeling raw. I had to get myself together for the pictures and the reception later. I headed straight to the bathroom to wash my face and re-apply some makeup.

I made it through the pictures, despite the awkward absence of Daddy and Mom. There would be no pictures of them in Andy's wedding album. But we managed to get some beautiful shots of all of their children, promising to get them some prints. Then we headed off to the reception where I took my seat next to Shaun, Tim, Dave, Grandma and Grandpa. As dinner was being served, one of Andy's friends came to the microphone to make an announcement.

"As you know, Andy and Mary have a great sense of humor. So we'd like to honor that by doing something a little different. We want to hear your memories of Andy and Mary. It could be a funny story that happened when they were little, it could be something serious, or whatever you'd like. You could also use this time to share some marriage advice with them. So, the mic is open!" He stepped aside and almost immediately people began trickling forward to tell their stories—mostly of Andy doing or saying something funny. Some people shared tearfully about how Andy's emails had helped them through a time of trial. I knew exactly what I had to share and I made my way to the microphone.

"Hi, I'm Abby. I'm Andy's little sister, so naturally I have LOTS of stories about Andy. But there is one story which stands out as kind of capturing who Andy is." As I spoke, I looked around for Andy so I could watch his face as the story unfolded. He was watching me intently from the corner where he had been talking with a friend. A curious expression covered his face. Satisfied that I had his attention, I continued with my story.

"I'm the youngest of seven and I come after a line of three boys in a row, Andy being one of them. The older three children were much older than us and so the four of us younger kids played together all the time. But we always had to compromise so the boys would be happy and I would be happy. So, one of our favorite activities on rainy days was to build a big fort out of cushions and blankets and then have a tea party in the fort." Suddenly Andy turned bright red and ran into the nearby kitchen to hide. He knew exactly where I was going!

"So we were having one of these tea parties one day and Andy and Dave went to get some lemonade from Mom. They were gone a little longer than usual, but Tim and I, being the younger ones, didn't think much of it. They came back, Andy carrying full Dixie cups and Dave a plate of Mom's amazing chocolate chip cookies and we went about our tea party as usual." I scanned the room. Dave and Tim were grinning in our corner of the room. In the opposite corner, Andy's head was poking out of the kitchen door, bright red and buried in one hand.

"And then Tim took a sip of his lemonade." I made quotation marks with my fingers as I said the word "lemonade." "And he spit it right back out. Andy and Dave started laughing and I just sat there confused, until Tim started yelling, 'I hate you Andy! You peed in my cup! You peed in my cup!'" Andy's head had disappeared as peels of laughter filled the room. I reclaimed my seat and Tim and Dave clapped me on the back like one of the boys.

A little while later, I cautiously hugged Andy goodbye as he and Mary left for their honeymoon. I wondered if he'd be mad at me.

"I'm really proud of you, Sis," he said. I looked up at him in confusion. "You were great up there telling that story. I love you."

"I love you too, Andy. Have fun!" I winked at him and he blushed again.

Chapter 28

I RODE BACK TO OHIO with Shaun, who would be staying at our house for a few days before we visited his family in New York and then headed back to school together from there. That was the plan anyway, but when we got home, everything seemed up in the air. Daddy had gone into a coma. He was not waking to eat or get a sponge bath anymore. The Hospice Care nurse had told Mom it would only be a matter of days before he died now. With his body in such a deteriorated state, he could not survive without food for very long.

"He had a smile on his face during the ceremony," Mom said. "He even woke up enough to high five me and then Leslie when Andy and Mary were pronounced husband and wife."

"That's neat," I replied. I didn't know what else to say. *He must have been waiting for the wedding. Now he can let go.* I spent my time alternatively snuggling with Daddy or with Shaun. There was nothing left to say—nothing left to do, but I didn't want to miss a moment of it. When Thursday came and Daddy was still hanging on, Shaun and I had to make a decision.

"You know if we go today, we're going to have to come right back tomorrow, right?" I asked, not willing to utter the reason we'd have to return.

"Yeah, I know, but there's nothing for you to do here except wait and we've been waiting all week. My family would really like to meet you. I know you want to be with your dad. You make the decision."

"I want to go." So we packed our things and drove nine hours to Long Island. We quickly filled Friday with meeting as much of Shaun's family as we possibly could, spending the morning with his mom and brothers and then heading to his paternal grandparents' house for the afternoon to meet his dad's family. When I finally went to bed on Friday night, I was exhausted. I fell into a deep, dreamless sleep, but was awakened by Shaun's mother at seven the next morning. The cordless phone was in her hand.

"I'm sorry. It's your mom," she whispered. I knew immediately that Daddy was gone. I took the phone with a trembling hand.

"Daddy's with Jesus, Abby. He saw Andy and Mary when they came home last night and then he started to slip away. He died around two o'clock this morning."

I lay in the unfamiliar bed and sobbed. *How can it hurt so much when I knew it was coming? God take the pain away! It's too much!*

I don't remember the rest of the day. My brain felt like an arm whose circulation had been cut off for so long you had to pick it up just to move it. I know Shaun made some phone calls to cancel our plans for the rest of the weekend and then we hopped in his car to head back to Ohio. I remember that everyone he spoke to offered their condolences and his mother was full of hugs and apologies. *It must be awkward to have to be the one to tell your son's girlfriend her father died when you've just met her. She must feel at such a loss to know what to say. Poor woman.*

We arrived back at my parents' house and my siblings were starting to show up as well. Andy and Mary had returned from their honeymoon the night before to prepare for a reception for those who couldn't make it to their wedding. I dove into the planning of the memorial service with my family. Children played, oblivious to the dismal task the adults were taking on and the absence of their grandfather. I remember thinking, *I should be really upset. I should be crying right now.* But it was as if all my tears, all my emotions had been spent. At church the next morning, I nodded and looked sad as countless people said, "Your father is in a better place now," or, "We loved and respected your dad so much. What a wonderful man he was," or, "You are in our prayers." I knew these words were attempts to show love and concern, but they were empty to me. They wouldn't bring Daddy back. The worst was, "Oh, you must be heart-broken, you poor thing!" Well, no. In fact, I felt very little except annoyed by people's ignorance.

The same happened at the memorial service on Monday. I shuffled through it all, holding on to Shaun like a shield from unwanted sympathy. The next day, it was finally time to go back to school. I was unspeakably grateful to be away from meaningless clichés and the expectations of how I should be grieving.

Free from the unknown, I was now able to pour my energy into catching up on what I'd missed the previous semester. Shaun and I were both in the musical for J-term, which thankfully rehearsed all day every day, keeping my body and mind occupied. Between that and all the make-up work I had to do from last semester, I barely had time to think. There was little news from Andy and Mary, but I didn't expect them to be calling frequently while they were enjoying newly married life.

In February, classes started back on a regular schedule again. I still had a long list of assignments to check off of my make-up list. Concert Choir and Singers' rehearsals started back up, along with a new set of classes. Rehearsals for the musical were moved to the evenings. It seemed to me I had uncovered yet another hidden miracle in the busyness of this season. There was no time for mourning.

But once the play was finished and my make-up assignment list was dwindling, I began to grow restless. Too much time on my hands meant too much reflecting on the past and the future—both dangerous territory.

I checked the last assignment off my list just before Mom's ominous phone call. In my numbness, I couldn't comprehend what was being said, I just heard distinct words seemingly independent of one another. *Andy. Emergency room. Tumors. Lungs. Breathing too slow.* The world spun around me as though I was peering into a kaleidoscope. All I could do was focus on the tiny point in the center that seemed to be still. For a couple of days this worked. Breathe, eat, sleep, go to class, sing, do homework, repeat. Don't look at the periphery. Always look ahead at the next task, never look at the dizzying world all around.

Then this blow came from Andy's own hand:

2-26-03

Dear friends,

I'm writing today to bring you all up to speed on my life. I am sorry that I have been so quiet since the wedding. As you can imagine, I've been very caught up with details of family, job, marriage, finances, and other related subjects, that I've neglected the important task of updating the prayer armies. Until the last few weeks, we have not been concerned very much about my health issues. God has given us a good month or more to just adjust to marriage. Mary is a wonderful woman of God, and our love grows stronger with each passing day. Our honeymoon was great: a week in the Smokey Mountains of Gatlinburg Tennessee. Lots of hiking and a new hobby of mine: antique shopping.

We came back to Ohio for a reception and immediately found that my Dad had passed away. It was both very sad and very joyful, as everyone came home for a few days and a beautiful celebration of Dad's life and love for the Lord. We are pleased with how well Mom seems to be settling in to the life-changing adjustment. In many ways, she feels the loss, but she can also celebrate the wonderful legacy he left to her and the children and grandchildren.

Some of you may not have heard this yet, but my grandfather was granted remission from his leukemia just before the wedding. Understandably, he was embarrassed that it was not Dad or I who was healed. But the family did what I hope was an adequate job of convincing him that we don't get to choose our gifts from God, just accept them. After all, we have been praying for all three healings, not just one.

And, as for my father, I know he is a cancer survivor. That's right; my Dad became a cancer survivor the moment his cancer took his body, his strength, and his wonderful mind. He survived the struggle for the one thing that the devil wanted to take most from him: his faith in God. My Dad survived cancer without letting it take his faith and belief that no matter what happens in life, God is still in charge. My Dad is a cancer survivor.

As for [me], my last few weeks have been an amazing battle with pain control. As I had been on vicodin for my gas pains since before the wedding, I had been taking it for quite sometime. Unfortunately, it wasn't doing the trick; it wasn't cutting the mustard. My gas pains seemed to get worse, and as I upped the doses, my gas pains got worse.

I found out last week, after a long overdue consult to my original (and wonderful) Gastroenterologist, Dr. A. (not to mention his wonderfully dedicated office staff), that any painkillers related to codine were probably shutting down my bowels and causing more gas pains than they alleviated. On top of that, the nausea was making it difficult to keep my food down, a crucial battle when preparing for my next chemo treatments. Until we heard that news from Dr. A, we had intended to start chemo by the end of that week, if possible. But Mary and I really wanted to get a chance try to get the pain under control, so we switched to a pain control narcotic called Duragesic.

The pain control was effective, but unfortunately, too high. I was dizzy, nauseous, sleepy, and mentally not coherent. After standing (somehow) through a wedding on Saturday, Mary noticed that my breathing had become frightfully slow. She took me to the emergency room on Saturday night. After consulting with some physicians, and a chest ex-ray, they informed us that tumors had spread to the lungs.

All I wanted to do was sleep, so they sent Mary home and kept me for tests. I was quickly awakened at 3 am as they shocked my system with a drug called narcan that was to reverse the effects of the Duragesic. It was the scariest experience of my life. I won't talk about it here.

In any case, by morning I was perked up and free from the effects of the duragesic. Drs. L. and A. decided to keep me in and monitor my effects on Sunday, Monday and Tuesday morning. Monday, my breathing came back to normal, but I was encountering severe pain from bloating in my abdominal region and in my legs due to the fluid they had pumped in my to rehydrate me.

Dr. A. was convinced that most of my bowel pain and bloating was due to the confusion to the colon over the last week with the switches of drugs and the bowel shutdowns.

At this point, we have resumed use of the Duragesic patch at half the original strength. This amount seems to agree much better with my body. I have, however, spent two very painful nights wrestling with bowel pain, bloating, laxative, and the toilet to get my swelling down and more under control.

I am home now. Thanks to those who knew what was going on who were able to visit us or call us. We will now focus on getting this pain managed, and once it is, I think we will start a chemotherapy drug called gemcytabine. I'm not sure if that is the spelling, but it seems to be the recommended form of treatment and should be easy enough on my body to allow me to continue with my part-time job as Fund Developer for a local organization. and our church's outreaches to poverty, including the Hattie Beverly Center tutoring program that I used to direct.

Like I said, God has been good. He has been truly amazing to us.

Due to my energy level, length of the email as is, and my creative powers being all used for a sermon/testimony that I will be giving at my Church on the evening of March 9th (Lord willing!) I will not expound on spiritual themes at the moment. I will leave you with this poem that I wrote many years ago. It expresses how I have learned that fear is only itself—fear.

Thank you all for your prayers.

Love,
Andy Schrier

VACANT FEARS
Where is my God right NOW?

I thought I'd find Him in plateaus of peace
only to find a torrent of anxiety
throwing me back into a gulf so deep
I cannot think or cry or sleep.
Instead, I'm helpless;
I quake with fear
and hope the storm will pass me by
and leave me somehow stronger here.

I don't always find God in the pleasant eye,
nor in the gale of the raging storm,
But when He takes me safe beyond
to yonder solid rock for just a while.
And as I catch—my breath—I smile:
and laugh at myself for vacant fears.

Someone had spun the kaleidoscope as fast as possible and then let it go, the colors and shapes swirling before me, confusing, indistinguishable and nauseating in their metamorphosis. He had said it—or written it. The words I could not ignore. *Daddy passed away. Andy has cancer in his lungs.* And he said it so matter-of-factly, as if the very words didn't sting him at all. They reduced me to a sobbing puddle on my bedroom floor. Daddy's words nearly a year ago suddenly overwhelmed me. "He's not dead yet." *No*, I whispered to my empty room, angry with Daddy, angry with God, angry with Andy. *But you are. And he will be soon, too!*

Chapter 29

MUD AND COW MANURE sucked me in like quicksand. I struggled unsuccessfully to break free from their grasp. Cows, ignorant of my plight, grazed just feet from where I sat in a ditch of some sort. I was at Laughter Farm, in the pasture adjacent to the house. There was Daddy, coming to feed the cows. I called to him, but my voice stuck in my throat. The mud's grip tightened and dragged me a bit farther in. Desperate, I used every ounce of my strength to call out again. "DADDY!" It emerged as little more than a whisper. But he turned. He saw me! I would be free momentarily. And then, he turned and walked out of my field of vision, where my voice could no longer reach him. He had abandoned me! But wait, there was Andy, not much more than a boy. But he was strong enough to get me out. I was just a small girl. "ANDY, HELP!" He looked up from the bundle of wood he was carrying. His eyes did not register the danger I was in. "Help me," I sobbed. He too began to turn away from me as I sat there, drowning in mud cow dung.

Shaking, I emerged from sleep. Dread and anger filled me all at once. Glancing at the clock, I forced my eyes closed again. The sun would not be rising for a couple of hours. But I didn't really get back to sleep. The images of the dream were etched into my mind and closing my eyes made them more real somehow.

IT WAS A MONDAY, or maybe a Wednesday. A day full of classes, either way. Who knows which ones they were. I went, I took notes, I held my eyelids open. Lunchtime meant I could see Shaun briefly. He was nearly bursting with excitement about his favorite class and professor. His chatter kept me awake and my mind off of the horrors of last night. After we parted, I stopped at my mailbox, which was in the same building. Leafing through the flyers and junk mail, I discovered a plain white index card with neat writing which I did not recognize penciled on it. Curiously, I read the words someone had anonymously written for me.

"Isaiah 41:10—So do not fear for I am with you; do not be dismayed, for I am your God. I will strengthen you and help you. I will uphold you with my righteous right hand."

Beneath the verse was a personalized note: "You are in my thoughts and prayers."

Suddenly I was wide awake. My mind was occupied for the remainder of the day with who'd written that note. Analyzing the handwriting was fruitless. There was no one whose printing I had access to that matched the notecard. It was loopy and neat, which implied a female, and clearly excluded Shaun. *But who knows that's my favorite verse?* There were only a handful of people, and unless they were experts at disguising their penmanship, it was not any of them. The dilemma was maddening. But the verse was successful at keeping me going for another couple of days.

Then, just as I began to have nightmares again, just as I began to despair of Andy's life, another notecard came with another verse. I don't remember what it was, but it became my sustenance. Then there was another, again at the most opportune moment. *Whoever this anonymous person is, they certainly know what I need.* Each of the verses was pertinent to the fear, anger, or hurt I found myself facing that particular day.

SPRING BREAK WAS APPROACHING. Concert Choir was going on tour somewhere in New England, but our director had agreed to allow me to go home so Mom and I could visit Andy and Mary in Michigan. We would sleep at Mary's parents' house about half an hour away from their tiny apartment. After saying goodbye to Shaun, I bummed a ride home with someone. I took a day to rest, do laundry, and see some friends, and then Mom and I headed west in Daddy's car. It seemed wrong to drive it without him. He'd always insisted on being the sole driver, no matter the distance, but now he wasn't there. Instead, Mom and I split the drive in half, both of our small frames swallowed in the giant vehicle. The image made Daddy's absence all the more poignant.

Our time with Andy and Mary was short, but sweet in many ways. We only stayed two or three days so as not to impose on the precious time these newlyweds had left. When Andy was awake, he practically glowed with his love for Mary. She blushed and giggled in his presence. After dinner, Andy would go to bed or fall asleep on the couch while we chatted. Mom and Mary and I would talk and laugh until we could no longer keep our eyes open. On the second evening, we had stayed a little later than we wanted, so we hurriedly hugged Mary goodbye and hopped in Daddy's car to head to Mary's parents' home. Mom was too tired to drive, so she handed me the keys.

"You know how to get there?"

"I think so." I pulled out of the driveway and into the dark, unfamiliar streets, feeling anxious about guiding such a large car. Before long, I noticed a vehicle behind me. It drew dangerously close to us and I slowed my speed a little in an attempt to send the driver a message. He didn't get it. Ahead of me, a traffic signal turned yellow, then red and the car in front of me stopped. Anxious that the vehicle behind me wouldn't stop, I left several car lengths between us and the car in front of us and eased to a very gradual stop. Anticipating the crash did not make it any less of a shock. The car behind plowed into us hard enough that my head jerked forward and then back again in the snap of a finger. My right arm instinctively reached in front of my mother to brace her.

"Are you alright, Mom?" I asked in a panic when I could finally think.

"Yes, I think so. Are you?"

"Yeah, just shakey. I saw it coming."

"You did an excellent job not hitting the car in front of us."

"I knew he was going to hit me, so I left plenty of room." Neither of us could think clearly enough to get out of the car and assess the damage or exchange insurance information. We just sat there for a moment, squeezing each other's hands. In the meantime, the light had turned green and the car ahead of us had left. I glanced out my window to see a man just a few years older than me walking towards us. The driver. My instinct was to start yelling at him, but instead, I rolled down my window.

"Are you guys alright?" he asked.

"Yes, I think so. Just a little shaken," I replied, surprised by his kindness.

"I'm sorry. I didn't see you there." *Yeah, 'cause you were too close*, I wanted to scream.

"We'll need your insurance information," Mom piped up, her emotions calming enough to gather her wits about her.

"Oh yeah." The man turned to walk back to his own car. Mom opened up the glove box while I began to search for a pen. As we rummaged through Daddy's things, the light from the car behind us shifted and then faded away. I turned to look behind us, and, sure enough, the man was gone.

"Mom, he left."

"What do you mean, 'he left?'"

"He's gone. He just drove away. We have to call the police I guess." Mom closed the glove box compartment and reached into her purse to find Daddy's cell phone which she'd grabbed for just such an emergency. An officer arrived surprisingly quickly and took our report. After looking over the car and determining that it was basically untouched, he informed us that there was very little he could do since we had no information on the man responsible for the hit and run. We hadn't even thought to get the make and model of his car. *Daddy, why aren't you here! You'd have made sure we got everything we needed. That guy wouldn't have dared to leave if you'd been in this car!*

The next day was our last with Andy and Mary. The warm spring sunshine allowed for a long walk through the historic neighborhoods of Grand Rapids. I listened to Mom and Mary discussing the local Historical Society's regulations regarding refurbishing a home within the historic district, but my thoughts were really on Andy. For so long I'd fluctuated between clinging to God for my sanity and doubting God's ability or desire to heal. Sometimes I even doubted His existence. But now I was just angry. I had established the necessity of His existence and even of His love and goodness. But He must not love me.

What did I do to You? In my mind I was shouting. *Andy used to have limitless energy. He used to play sports tirelessly all day, every day. Now he can barely catch his breath while we walk a mile. A very slow mile. He's a good man—smart, funny, loving. He loves kids, especially poor ones. He is dedicated to You. He's got so much more he could give You. Why are You punishing him for whatever it is I did to piss You off? What about Mary? Are You just going to leave her alone, husbandless and childless? How could You!*

Chapter 30

EVEN WHEN I WAS BACK at school, I struggled to suppress my anger. I knew it was incongruent with what I'd always been taught about God—that He doesn't punish us that way, but the sicker Andy got, the harder it was to argue it away. I tried to lose myself in schoolwork and in spending time with Shaun. I had the fortitude to stop wasting my efforts on burying my sorrows in alcohol. Busyness had always worked before, and for a while it did again. But updates kept coming via Mom or Mary that Andy's health was slowly deteriorating. His faith remained strong, although I couldn't fathom how. I couldn't help but think that I was the obstacle in the path of Andy's healing.

About a month after my brief visit, I was sitting at my computer and discovered an email from Andy's email address, although reading it revealed that he was not the author.

> 4-25-03
> Dear Friends of our Friend Andy:
> The past few months have seen some ups-and-downs in Andy's health, beginning with some changes in pain management in mid-February as he and Mary sought to change medication to find something more effective. Lately, Andy spent the past weekend of Friday, April 18 through Monday, April 21 in the hospital for what was believed to be pneumonia after having some trouble breathing. Upon returning home, hospice care was established on Tuesday, and Mary has been informed Andy's need for added oxygen more than likely isn't from pneumonia, but actually symptoms caused by the cancer spreading to Andy's lungs. He remains on an antibiotic just in case.
> Andy continues to sleep for the majority of the day and has an abdominal catheter to relieve him of the fluids that build up in his

abdomen. Mary has been taught how to use the catheter in order to relieve Andy's pressure when suitable, instead of 3 times a week, often draining many liters at a time. At this very moment today, though, he is up for a shower with the assistance of Mary and the hospice care provider, and has maintained a truly healthy appetite... little surprise to those of you who know his eating capabilities!

God continues to hold Andy in His hands. That is exactly where he needs to stay, as we continue to pray for Andy's healing and well-being. Andy is often not alert enough for visitation or phone calls, let alone email correspondence, so the "effects of the prayers of fervent, righteous men and women" are the only thing that will "avail much" at this time. Though frustrating to all of us, Andy is under the care of the Great Physician, so there really is no better hands in which to put him.

God also is holding Mary tightly as well... her face still lights up in His joy, though her days are much more draining and sobering. She continues to "stand by her man" throughout and has been blessed with being able to take time off of work for few weeks. One tough item for her has been familiarizing her self with the process of hospice care and projected health concerns based on the symptoms Andy exhibits. Please pray for true rest in sleeping and continued peace for Mary.

As you can see, the theme for this update is continued prayer. Andy and Mary wish to continue to encourage all of you, and those with whom you share this email, to lift them up before God that His will be done and He is glorified. We are reminded also that there has never been a request or petition to God that would tax his abilities or max-out his grace and love... wrap your minds around that concept!

We'll continue keep you all posted.

Andy and Mary Schrier

Mom had told me about the hospital visit, but it was easy to pretend I had misheard her through the crackle of the phone. Seeing the words on my computer screen made pretending impossible. I stared at the words, until each letter became a meaningless squiggle. *Meaningless, meaningless, everything is meaningless.* Forcing myself to look away, my eyes found the clock and suddenly I was jarred into alertness. It was time to meet Shaun for dinner. That would help.

Later, we sat on Shaun's couch, his arms enveloping me, shaking with my sobs. *He's not dead yet.* Daddy's words from a year ago screamed at me. *Meaningless!* I mentally screamed back. At the moment, I felt more in tune with the author of the book of Ecclesiastes than anyone else, past or present.

"I'm so sorry," Shaun crooned, clearly unable to access any helpful words. "I wish I could do something."

"Well you can't!" Filled with misplaced rage, I bolted out his front door, not caring where I was going. I jogged for a half mile or so, certain he wouldn't be able to keep up. But the tears overtook me until I could no longer see where I was going, so I slowed to a brisk walk. An all too familiar feeling engulfed me. *Shaun's right. He can't do anything. But I can. I'll give God my life, if it will appease Him enough to save Andy's. Oh God! Why are You doing this? Why Andy?*

Suddenly aware of my surroundings, I glimpsed my own house over the hill. *I can't go there! I need to go somewhere where I can think.* So I continued past it and spotted the empty bleachers of the soccer stadium. I climbed to the top row and thumped heavily onto the aluminum bench. No more tears came. I was raw. No, I was angry. I shook a trembling fist heavenward.

"Okay, what do You want me to do?" I was whispering through gritted teeth. "Throw myself down these bleachers? Go home and find a knife? I could drive it straight into my heart and be gone in minutes. Would that make You happy?" But even as I visualized all the options, I knew I didn't have the courage to follow through with any of them. *I'm too weak. It would hurt too much. I'm such a coward. I can't even save my brother.* "Why are You doing this to me?" I had never addressed God so boldly, but somehow it felt liberating to speak the words, even in a guarded whisper. "What did I do to You? Do You want me to swallow a bunch of pills? I could actually do that."

I jumped as Shaun appeared next to me and then I knew I couldn't even make myself overdose on medication. It would ruin him and his faith. It would ruin Mom. Even if it saved Andy, would losing one child over another be any better for her? And if it didn't work, she'd have two children to bury, right after her husband. I was completely trapped.

Shaun must have been too afraid to speak. He just sat next to me, one arm around me, my head on his shoulder, his head folded over mine.

"I'm sorry I snapped at you," I was finally able to squeak. "It's not you I'm mad at." I paused, afraid to confess the truth, as if saying it to another human would be worse than the things I'd just said straight to God himself. Apparently I didn't need to clarify.

"It's only natural to be angry with God, Babe. I was definitely mad at God when my friend Tommy died a couple of years ago. I thought He couldn't be good—couldn't be loving. But He is. You know how I know?" I looked at him questioningly. "Because He gave me you."

I lay awake later that night and stared at my ceiling. I knew one thing for certain—I didn't deserve Shaun. But he wasn't about to leave me for all of this and I owed it to him not to leave him either.

"Okay God. If You love me, heal Andy by tomorrow morning. Otherwise, I'm done with You."

I slept surprisingly well that night, certain something would change the very next day. But when I awoke, there was no phone call, no email stating a miraculous recovery. And that was my confirmation. God was no longer relevant to me. I went to my first class feeling confident I'd made the right decision. He didn't love me, so I would no longer love Him.

At first it was easy. I met Shaun at Tuesday morning Chapel and successfully ignored every word. It did not apply to me. I went to another class, then went to check my mailbox before lunch. There, at the worst possible moment, was another notecard. Romans 8:38-39 was written on it in that same flowing print:

> "For I am convinced that neither death nor life, neither angels nor demons, neither the present nor the future, nor any powers, neither height nor depth, nor anything else in all creation, will be able to separate us from the love of God that is in Christ Jesus our Lord."

I tore up the card and threw it in the nearest trash can. But the thought of God loving me was unshakable somehow. It began to eat at me from the inside. By the time my afternoon class was done, I could barely think. My head was spinning. *God says He loves me. But Andy's still dying. But it was there, on the notecard, straight from the Bible. But Andy's still DYING. It's not possible.*

Shaun and I both had a break between class and Concert Choir rehearsal, so he picked me up and we drove to his apartment.

"I can't go to Concert Choir," I told him, finally reduced to tears, yet again. "I just can't do it. I don't want to see anyone, I don't want anyone asking how Andy's doing. I can't handle it." He called our director and convinced her to let me skip rehearsal. But he still had to go. So I sat there in the empty apartment and wept.

"God, do You hate me?"

"No, My Child. I do not hate you. I love you."

"Are You mad at me?"

"No, I'm not mad at you, My Child."

"Show me! Please, show me how You love me if Andy's still going to die." Suddenly it was as though the room was black. I could see nothing of my true physical surroundings, only images of past events. I saw my professor sitting across from me at her desk, encouraging me to see a counselor. I saw. Mrs. N. assuring me that she would arrange with my professors for me to leave early. I saw Gail at the train station, coming to take me home. I saw the basket filled with Christmas gifts for Mom. I saw my friends in Concert Choir and Singers gathered around me in a football huddle praying for me. I saw notecard after notecard, perfectly timed and worded waiting in my mailbox to uplift me. And I saw Shaun over and over, never leaving me, always loving me.

Then my sight was normal again. The dingy tan carpet and hand-me-down furniture were firm beneath me. The windows, blackened from the dust of the road just feet away, filtered the bright afternoon sunlight. The built-in bookshelves crowded with textbooks, movies, and video games reflected the life of the man I loved. I stared in awe at everything around me, evidence of a bachelor in need of a woman's touch. Suddenly I didn't feel guilty that I would be that undeserving woman, I felt overwhelmingly blessed.

I thought of my friends, most of whom were gathered in a room singing praise to God—a God of whom I had a clear picture for the first time ever. They would have prayed for me before rehearsal officially began and several of them would have difficulty focusing on rehearsal out of concern for me. My heart joined them in offering praise to God as I imagined them rehearsing the harder passages of Tchesnokoff's *Salvation Is Created*, my favorite choral piece. *Thank You Lord for music and for friends.*

I thought of those in authority over me—my professors, my advisor and voice teacher, and of Mrs. N., all of whom had offered me grace and allowed me to grieve. Some of them had understood my situation better than others, but they'd all allowed me to go home. *Thank You, God, for the gift of that time to care for Daddy.*

And then I considered all those at home—all my family and friends there—the love, the prayers, the gifts, the care for Mom. All I knew to do was fall on my knees before God, right there on the dingy carpet.

Father, forgive me for not seeing! Forgive me for doubting You! Let me never doubt Your love for me or Your goodness again. I believe that You can work all things together for the good of those who love You, and I choose to love You again, because You loved me all this time. Help me to love You more and more. Whatever hardships come my way in this life, keep me close and never let me doubt You again. I'm so sorry!

Tears of repentance flowed as I knelt on the floor of my boyfriend's empty apartment. The torrent cleansed me from within. A heaviness I'd grown quite accustomed to was gradually lifted from my core and my body felt tangible relief. Joy spread warm in the wake of that heaviness, spilling from my heart into every part of me.

When Shaun entered his apartment a little while later, I was sitting on the couch waiting. He seemed shocked by the genuine smile that greeted him.

Chapter 31

MOM WAS GOING TO SELL the house in Ohio and move back to Laughter Farm in Maryland. So the plan was that I would go back to Ohio for a week or two after Shaun's graduation and then head to Maryland to spend the summer with Jennifer and her family. I was excited about the possibility of getting to know my oldest sister better and about spending time with her kids. After all, our age difference had meant she'd left for college when I was a mere toddler. But mostly I was thrilled because Shaun would be staying in his apartment and it would only be an hour drive to see him—that is, once he returned from his month abroad in Nepal, his final undergraduate course.

The first days back home I spent catching up on sleep and enjoying the new car Grandpa had gotten me as an early graduation present—a slightly used, silver Honda Civic. He'd gotten a car for every grandchild who had graduated from college, and even though I still had a year left, he'd agreed to get me mine early since I would need it at Jen's and to drive back and forth for my practicum experience in the fall. It was a beautiful little machine, even if the gigantic Oldsmobile I'd driven since high school did have a special place in my heart.

I was planning to sleep in again that Saturday morning, but Mom woke me around 7:00. She sat down on the edge of my bed, the cordless phone still in her hand, tears welling in her eyes. I knew the news before she was able to form the words.

"Andy's gone," she finally managed. "He passed away peacefully early this morning. Mary doesn't think he suffered much. He was able to talk to her up until just before the end." We held each other for a moment and then she left as quietly as she had come.

I lay there in my bed crying, mourning, rejoicing. His pain was done. He was with Daddy and the God he loved and served so faithfully. *Poor Mom, she will miss him. I can't imagine what it must be like to lose a child. God, let her feel You near to her. Help me help her through this.* Then I thought of Mary. *How does one call a woman to tell her her son is dead? God, comfort her. Give her peace. Wrap Your arms around her,* I prayed, through my own intense pain. As I prayed for the others who loved my brother, I felt a tangible calm come over me. The pain was intense, but this peace I couldn't mentally grasp was miraculous in its effect on my outlook.

The proclamation that "he's in a better place" began almost immediately as the news of Andy's death spread. Somehow it didn't bother me as it had when Daddy had died. Rather than trite, I found that I believed it and took comfort in it. I missed him desperately, but envisioning him playing ultimate frisbee or soccer on grass greener than emeralds in company including Daddy, Jesus, and angels, somehow made it impossible for me to question the goodness of it.

His memorial service a few days later was a celebration of this very fact. Shaun had been unable to make it home from Nepal in time, but I was far from alone. Surrounded by family and friends, there was no space for loneliness. Even Andy's friends I'd never met, but who had followed his emails, felt like family.

The words of the pastor and the songs played spoke of the beauty and joy of heaven. *What are Andy and Daddy doing up there? Dancing? Discussing the finer points of theology with a sudden full knowledge of all things? Singing and playing the guitar together before the throne of God? Or are they so in awe, that all they can do is lay prostrate before Him in all His glory?* The images made me long to join them, and I wept, knowing that the many wonderful memories I had of these two men were all I had left until it was my turn to meet Jesus. But they were both finally whole again and I had no choice but to rejoice in that.

Chapter 32

I SETTLED IN QUICKLY to the basement guest room at Jennifer's house. Not only did I have a private bedroom, I had my own bathroom across the hall and, with my new little car, I had everything I needed. I could come and go as I pleased. My sister's neighborhood was full of young, well-to-do families in need of a babysitter or pet sitter, and she'd made sure I had plenty of work for the summer.

The first task on my to-do list was to pick up Shaun at the Baltimore Airport.

"I wasn't sure they were going to let me on the plane," Shaun had told me over the phone, once his flight from Delhi had landed in London. "In Kathmandu, the guy at the desk literally just wrote the flight number and my name on a piece of paper and told me that was my ticket. I was worried, but he assured me it would be enough. Of course, the guy at the Delhi airport wasn't so thrilled with it. He was like, 'What's this? Where's your ticket?' I told him that *was* my ticket and he looked at me like I had ten heads. At that point, I'd already been stuck in the airport for eighteen hours, so it was all I could do to stay calm. Eventually, he let me through, thank God! I think I might have lost it if I couldn't get home to you!"

I felt like I might have lost it, too. And then there he was at the baggage claim. I had always rolled my eyes whenever couples at an airport embraced, unencumbered by the crowds around them. This time it was Shaun and me who exhibited affection without a hint of shame. Sprinting into his arms, I felt as though I were flying, and when he lifted me and swung me in a circle, the sensation was even more acute. *Let the whole world know how much I love this man,* I thought as we kissed, right there in the midst of hundreds of other travelers.

"I'm so sorry about Andy. And sorry I missed the memorial," Shaun said, as he finally set me back on my feet. His arm encircled me as we walked to the parking garage.

"It's okay," I replied, and meant it. He seemed as surprised as I was. "There were so many people there who loved Andy, it was kind of like one gigantic family." It was a lame explanation, but Shaun accepted it, gathering from my tone and body language that it was an accurate summary of how I felt.

"I have a surprise for you." Not wanting to linger on the subject of my brother, I brought Shaun's focus elsewhere. I hadn't told him about my car and he must have assumed I was still driving the Oldsmobile.

"Ta-da!" I exclaimed, motioning to the adorable little Civic waiting for us in the parking garage.

"Wait, this is yours?"

"Yup! Grandpa got it for me early so I'd have a reliable car for all the driving I'll need to do this year." I was nearly exploding with pride.

"It's really nice!" He climbed in the passenger seat after putting his luggage in the back and we headed towards—well, I didn't really know where home was right now. But it didn't matter because Shaun was there in the seat next to me.

We settled into a routine that summer. We took turns driving the seventy minutes to visit one another one evening during the week, depending on his work schedule at the clothing store and mine babysitting. We were often able to spend more time together on the weekend. Once, we even had a picnic at Laughter Farm, which was eerily vacant and overgrown waiting for Mom's return.

One Friday in July, Shaun and I were planning our visits for the weekend and the next week.

"I have to go to an all-day training at another store on Sunday, so I won't get to see you," Shaun informed me. "How about you ask your sister for a recommendation for a nice restaurant near you and on Monday, we'll get dressed up and go out for a fancy meal."

"Okay," I agreed enthusiastically. *Is this it? Is he going to propose on Monday?* My heart fluttered and words failed me.

That same day, I visited the local DMV. It was taking a little while to get my car registration transferred from Ohio. I don't remember if it was because I was a college student and didn't have a permanent residence or what, but it became a huge headache. Each time I went to the DMV, there was some glitch preventing me from making the necessary switch. This time was no different.

"Why don't you let me see what I can do?" Jennifer offered when I returned to her house exasperated.

"Good luck," I replied but consented to letting her try. Sure enough, when we both returned from work Monday afternoon, she had figured the mess out and had been able to get everything in order.

"Here are your temporary plates." She handed me two pieces of printed cardstock. "These are technically only legal in Maryland. Now, they said it will be a couple of days before the actual license plates arrive in the mail, but once they come, you're good to go."

"Oh my goodness, thank you so much! I hope you didn't have to wait too long." Jennifer's expression indicated otherwise, but she didn't complain. It was just like her to bend over backwards for those she cared about.

I glanced at the clock. 5 p.m. *Oh no! Shaun will be here in an hour and I probably still smell like spit up and Play-doh from the kids I was babysitting all day!*

"I'm gonna go get ready for our date tonight." Lingering barely long enough to see my sister's knowing smile, I nearly leapt down the basement stairs and into the bathroom. Panic began to set in. I had to look perfect. *No time to shower. My hair takes hours to dry properly. I'll have to straighten it. And I have to get dressed and do my makeup. What am I going to wear? Okay, what do I do first? Yikes! Diamond earrings. I should definitely wear those. Oh, my straightening iron—I have to get that heated up. Good grief, Abby, get a grip!* I glared at myself through the mirror.

"It's Shaun. He loves me no matter what. It's fine!" I managed to calm myself enough to think straight. Plugging in the straightening iron to warm up, I strode to my closet to pick something appropriate. *Hmmm, I don't want Shaun to think I think anything is up, especially if it's not. But he did say we were going to a fancy restaurant, so I certainly can't just wear jeans.* I tried on several outfits and finally settled on a jean skirt and nice top before moving back to the bathroom to attend to my hair and makeup. Straightening curly hair takes a good half hour, and by the time I was finished, I feared I would make us late. The bedroom clock said 6:05. Surely Shaun was upstairs talking to Jennifer or waiting in the driveway for me. He was always punctual, if not early. But he was nowhere to be found and his car was not in the driveway. I sat anxiously on the steps to the side door of the house, waiting.

He said 6:00! I gave him several recommendations and he said he'd take care of the reservation. What's going on? At 6:10 his car finally pulled in. I stood, ready to hop in the passenger seat, but he turned off the engine and stepped out of the car. *Is he wearing swim trunks? And an undershirt?* His facial expression looked as if nothing was amiss.

"Hey Babe! You look great! I passed an Applebee's on the way here. Sound good?"

Applebees?

"Um, sure. But I thought we were going to one of the restaurants Jen had recommended—somewhere fancy?" He smiled mischievously at me.

"Oh, I found a great place in Harrisburg I want to take you tomorrow. Let's get some food. I'm starving!" *Harrisburg? Tomorrow? That means driving to Pennsylvania. With illegal plates! What do I do?* I forced myself to enjoy Shaun's company, though I haven't the foggiest notion what we talked about. Internally, I was weighing my options. *Should I tell him I couldn't drive to Pennsylvania, or should I just let it go and risk it?* I decided to casually mention it before he dropped me off.

"So, I'm not legally supposed to cross state lines until I get my permanent license plates, which will take a few days. Should we wait until the end of the week?" Shaun was completely unphased by this information.

"No, I already made our reservation. Maybe I have a special plan . . ." He winked at me.

"I thought you had a special plan for tonight," I muttered.

"That's what I wanted you to think. I just like to keep you on your toes! You look gorgeous, by the way." Well, how could a girl stay mad? We said goodnight and I went to bed, but I couldn't sleep. I was at war with myself. Shaun was clearly planning to propose tomorrow night, but that's what he'd wanted me to think tonight, too. I couldn't get all worked up just to be disappointed again. And if he wasn't planning anything, would he ask me to drive illegally? Was it worth the risk? What would be the consequences of getting pulled over with a temporary, out-of-state license plate?

I POSED THE DRIVING CONUNDRUM to my sister the next morning without mentioning my suspicions of Shaun's covert activites.

"What should I do?"

"I think you should drive the speed limit and stay alert for cops." Jennifer had a knowing smile on her face and I did not dare argue. *It really is going to be tonight. And she knows.* Her confirmation granted me permission to obsess over what I imagined might be in store for me later in the day. *Where is he taking me? What will he say? He's so eloquent when he plans out just what he wants to say. Will he get down on one knee? When did he get a ring? Did he ask Mom or Grandpa? When did he call them? No one said anything to me. But Jen clearly knows, so Mom must know.*

It was a white-knuckle drive that night. Passing at least two vigilant cops, I prayed it would be worth it. Finally, pulling into Shaun's driveway, I was pleased to see that he was wearing dress pants and a tie. I begged him to drive his car, even though mine was much nicer (and typically cleaner as well). But he'd washed and detailed his at some point during the day, anticipating my concern. It even smelled clean when I climbed in.

It was another half hour drive to the restaurant, but I was not disappointed when we arrived. It was a victorian home which had been tastefully converted into an upscale eatery. There were items on the menu I'd never heard of before. Both Shaun and I were very pleased with all we'd ordered.

It was obvious that we were both nervous, as we floundered to keep the conversation going.

"Oh, so I was wondering," Shaun began during a lull, "what size ring should I get?" I was completely caught off guard. *What are we doing here?* But I calmly answered his question, thinking perhaps he was trying to throw me off. When our meals were finished and Shaun had paid the bill, he led me back to his car without incident and we drove back toward his apartment. I kept up with the conversation somehow, but if confusion was his goal, he'd succeeded. Then, just when I'd convinced myself that I was heading home with my relationship status unchanged, he drove right past his apartment.

"Where are we going?"

"I was wondering if you'd like to go over to campus and sit on our bench by the stream for a little while." A lump caught in my throat. *This is really going to happen.* I squeaked out an "mm hmmm" and silence took over. Shaun parked the car and we silently walked hand in hand across the covered bridge and into the grass. The pine needles and moss created a soft bed under our feet and my heals began to stick.

"Hold on a second, Babe. I need to take off my shoes." Just as I hooked my fingers through the straps of my shoes, Shaun's strong arms swept me up and carried me across the soft ground. He set me gently on the bench where we'd sat so many times before. It was where he'd met me when I first heard Andy's diagnosis, and again when I'd received that anonymous note. It seemed sacred.

For a long moment we sat silently watching the sun disappear before my thoughts snapped back to the present. *What is he going to say? Is he going to get down on one knee? Not in this dirt, I'm sure. What should I say? I should have thought of something clever and romantic. I certainly don't want to throw myself at him all dramatic and clingy! Eeew!*

"I love us," he eventually began. "Abby, I can't imagine ever being without you. I want nothing more than to grow old with you." Then he stood in front of me, blocking the moonlight until he lowered his knee to the ground—dress pants and all.

"Abigail Schrier, I want you to be my wife. Will you marry me?" In his hand lay an open ring box. It was too much. I couldn't take it in. I froze. Here, where he'd taken on so much of my pain, he was offering to share in whatever came our way for the rest of our lives. *I don't deserve such dedication.* An internal voice nudged me—*I gave him to you because I love you.* It was all the reminder I needed.

"Of course I will." The words must have been nearly inaudible, I had to force them out. Shaun breathed a sigh of relief and sat back on the seat next to me. He took my left hand and slipped the ring easily onto my finger.

"Whew! It fits!" He pulled me in for a passionate kiss until I pulled away and punched the meaty part of his shoulder.

"That's for pretending you didn't have it!" I'd found my voice again! He chuckled gleefully.

"Sorry. I was trying to throw you off! But do you like it?"

"Um, it's kind of dark. I can't actually see it," I told him honestly. The moonlight was so dim behind the trees. "But if it's from you, I love it!" This was also true. Shaun could have put a piece of crumbly sandstone on my finger and I'd have found a way to wear it with pride. I threw my arms around his neck and kissed him again. *Thank You for Shaun,* I prayed.

"I have a confession to make," Shaun said with a smile, as we headed back to his apartment to make phone calls.

"Yeah?"

"You know how I said I had to go to a different store for training on Sunday?" Suddenly, I knew exactly where he was going with this.

"You didn't? You drove all the way to Ohio and back? In one day? Just to talk to my mom?"

"Uh huh."

"Oh Shaun! I thought you'd just call her!" His face indicated that he was horrified by my suggestion.

"Oh no, I took her out for dinner and asked her for your hand properly." I leaned across the console to plant a grateful kiss on his cheek.

Chapter 33

RED, YELLOW, ORANGE and brown leaves floated outside the window of the campus apartment some friends and I occupied for our final year of college. The leaves and the crisp air reminded me that Thanksgiving was just around the corner. It had been nearly six months since Andy had died and ten and a half since Daddy's passing.

I stretched and sat down at my computer before hopping in the shower. It was Friday and I had managed to arrange my schedule so I only had one class on Fridays. It afforded me time to relax, work on my practicum with my church's music ministry, practice for my senior recital next semester, or do any number of other things more appealing than going to class. I scanned through my emails and noticed one from the professor of my lone class. It was cancelled. *Well now what am I going to do with my day? I really like that class and the professor. God, is there something You want me to do today?* My thoughts turned to Grandpa who was now resting in a bed at the Hospice Care Center in Ohio. Just days ago, Mom, now fully reestablished at Laughter Farm in Maryland, had gone to be with Grandma and Grandpa until he was gone. In the past week he had finished teaching her how to manage all of his finances, gotten all of the final details of his will in place and made sure Grandma was well situated. I suddenly felt an urgency. *Grandpa needs me. I've got to go to Ohio.*

I immediately called Shaun who was working at a car rental company nearby.

"I'm going to drive out to Ohio to see Grandpa. I just feel like it's going to be very soon and I want to be there for him." I had to make him understand why I couldn't wait until Thanksgiving break in less than a week. Shaun was hesitant, but not for the reason I'd anticipated.

"Well, if you need to go today, I understand, but I can't get out of work today. If you can wait until tomorrow, I'd like to go with you."

"Okay, let me talk to Mom and see how he's doing today. Call me on your lunch break."

"I will. I love you, Babe."

"I love you, too." I hung up just long enough to dial the number on my calling card and then Mom's number.

"Hi Mom. I don't have any classes today so I was thinking of coming to see Grandpa. But if I wait until tomorrow, Shaun can come with me. What do you think, can he hang on until tomorrow?" I wasted no time on pleasantries.

"Of course I can't promise," Mom replied matter-of-factly, "he's not really responsive today, but he's stable and breathing well. I think you'll be fine if you wait until tomorrow. I'd prefer that you have Shaun with you."

So I packed an overnight bag and a dress for church on Sunday, then busied myself getting extra homework and rehearsing done so I wouldn't need to worry about it for the rest of the weekend. Shaun and I left in his car around six o'clock the next morning, hoping to get to Grandpa around noon. I had no desire to waste time.

Finally, after some confusion and a stop at a AAA office to get a map, we entered Grandpa's room at the Hospice Care Center. Mom and Grandma hovered over his bed. Their anxious expressions, hushed voices, and vigilant postures told me the end was very near. I slipped between the window and the bed to greet him. He did not respond to my kiss or to my hand reaching for his.

"It's me, Grandpa. It's Abby. Shaun's here with me, too." There was no indication that he heard me. I backed out to allow Mom to take the spot next to him. She immediately reached for his hand. Grandma sat on the other side of him, holding his other hand. There was nothing for me to hold onto except Shaun, and so we stood at the foot of his bed, my left hand on Shaun's chest, diamonds from my new engagement ring sparkling in the sunlight from the window. *Reminding him that I'm taken care of will give him peace,* I thought. But I did not feel at peace as I took in the scene before me. *He's so pale! Oh, God, he's so pale! Oh . . . oh, his breathing—it's awful! It must hurt him so much! Oh, God I hate this! I hate cancer! God don't let him suffer like this.*

"The Lord is my shepherd," Mom began to quote Psalm 23. We all joined her, not caring that we were quoting different versions. "I shall not want. He makes me lie down in green pastures: he leads me beside still waters. He restores my soul: he leads me in the paths of righteousness for his name's sake."

I watched Grandma's lost expression as she quoted mindlessly. *She looks so fragile. What will she do without him? Lord Jesus, help her!*

Our volume increased as Grandpa's breathing grew heavy and ragged. "Yea, though I walk through the valley of the shadow of death, I will fear no evil: for you are with me; your rod and your staff they comfort me. You prepare a table before me in the presence of my enemies: you anoint my head with oil; my cup overflows. Surely goodness and mercy shall follow me all the days of my life." The sound of struggled breathing filled the room until we could no longer speak over it. Then, his great, gulping breaths began to slow until, at last, they stopped altogether. *Is that it, God? Is he gone, now? Is he at peace, finally?*

"And I will dwell in the house of the LORD for ever." Mom ended the Psalm in a choked whisper. All eyes turned to Grandma who continued to sit faithfully at Grandpa's side, gazing lovingly at his face. After a few moments, she looked from Mom to me and back again, as though just realizing what had happened.

"He's gone, isn't he?" she asked. Mom and I nodded, afraid that if we spoke the words, she'd melt into a heap. But Grandma seemed to glow.

"Did you see him?" she asked. Confused, I looked to Mom, but no answer was on her face. "I saw Jesus!" Grandma continued. "He came through the door. He was all dressed in white and He stood next to us. And then He was gone." Perhaps she was just a tired old lady experiencing hallucinations, but my history with God made it hard for me not to believe Jesus really had come to usher my grandfather into heaven. Or at least an angel. That He'd allowed Grandma to see it was her own, private, hidden miracle.

Chapter 34

MONTHS HAD PASSED. Holidays had been celebrated dutifully, empty reminders of the men we'd lost. Grandma had settled into an apartment at a beautiful retirement home, alone. Mary remained in the apartment she and Andy had shared for so brief a time, alone. And worst of all, Mom occupied that giant farmhouse at Laughter Farm, once echoing with the voices of her children, all alone. Many weekends, I'd driven home from school to be with her and spent the evenings holding her while her sobs shook both our bodies and her wails pierced my heart. Oh, we'd had plenty of joyful times, too, particularly planning my wedding. Mom and I had shopped for my dress, picked out flowers, food, and a photographer, and chosen the music and decorations together. Now, it was finally all coming to its glorious culmination. Tomorrow, Shaun and I would be married!

Throughout the sleepless night, I heard the rain's relentless pummelling of the earth. *It has been raining for days, why should this day be any different?* As soon as the black sky began to turn a bleak grey, I finally gave up on sleep and snuck outside. There was no pink sunrise as I'd imagined there would be. I stood sheltered under the roof of the massive front porch at Laughter Farm and squinted to watch the sky pour forth upon the circle of grass in front of the house. The area was supposed to seat my wedding guests in twelve or thirteen hours. Water cascaded off the edge of the roof in front of me, making it nearly impossible to see more than a few feet ahead. The white pillars Shaun and I had meticulously painted a week ago were drenched. I knew I should be disappointed. I had dreamed of a sunset wedding on this front porch since I was a little girl and now I would have to let a crowded white plastic tent suffice. But I knew the man who'd be waiting at the altar was the most tangible gift by which God had shown His love for me.

I headed inside for coffee and my mother's company. A grin spread across my face when I found her in the kitchen grinding up the beans. She hugged me tightly.

"I'm sorry it's not a very sunny day for a wedding." Her eyes were sympathetic for what she assumed I must be feeling.

"Maybe it will stop. Either way, what matters is that Shaun and I get married."

Literally skipping through the day, admiring the buzz all around me, I gave input on which kind of flowers should be at the center of the dais and where strands of white lights should be hung. Grandma and Katie helped me pick earrings to go with the Celtic pearl necklace Shaun's mom had loaned me. There was chaos and stress over the saturated ground, the outdoor pictures, seating in the tent for the ceremony, the transition to the reception, and so much more. I let everyone else handle it. I didn't want anything to threaten my joy. None of it mattered except becoming Shaun's wife.

Finally, my brother Dave, clad dashingly in his dress blues, led me down the back steps and over a carpeted path to the tent where Shaun was waiting. My friends and family had done just fine managing the challenges the weather presented.

"Who gives this woman to this man?" our friend Jason asked.

"Our mother and I do," Dave responded, choking ever so slightly over the words we'd deliberated over. Surprised, I ventured a quizzical look at him. Sure enough, he seemed to be struggling to control his emotions—this brother of mine who was quite possibly even more stoic than our father had been. I brushed it off as a moment of grief and turned towards Shaun. As Jason continued leading the ceremony, and I stared into Shaun's eyes, I noticed tears there as well. Inches away from us under the crowded tent sat Mom and Grandma, also crying. Soon, Shaun's mother joined them. Then both of his grandmothers. By the time the ceremony ended, there were very few dry eyes in that tent. Mine were somehow among them.

Years before, I'd told Daddy I wanted to dance with him to *Butterfly Kisses* at my wedding. I couldn't bring myself to drop that wish, and so I'd asked Dave to dance it with me. As the music began to play and I found myself in my brother's arms instead of my father's, sorrow hit me without warning. My face joined the others that were dripping. Dave held me tightly and I thought I felt a tear fall to the top of my head. We clung to each other as we danced, each word of the song seeming like a dagger.

As the song ended and I saw the faces of the onlookers—people I loved—all streaked with tears, I took inventory of each precious person.

Glancing from face to face, I silently thanked God. Every face represented the miracle of burdens shared among those who love each other.

Wasn't that what it was all about anyway? When one person feels another's pain so deeply it hurts them as well and they share the burden through acts of kindness and love, isn't this a reflection of the miracle of God's great love for us? There is no greater gift than the gift of love.

God help me to always love others the way it's described in the Bible. Give me opportunities to be the hidden miracle that others need in their time of suffering and need. Help me to seize those moments wholeheartedly, pouring Your love over them as it overflows in me. Help me to always love Shaun in this way. And help me never to miss those hidden miracles in my life again.

POSTSCRIPT

MOST PEOPLE DON'T RECEIVE a vision from God these days. Many of you may not even believe what I described truly happened. But it did. I can't explain why. I'm no more special than any other person on this earth. But perhaps it happened because God wanted me to write about it—not hoard the memory as my own supernatural phenomenon, but share it with everyone willing to read about it. Because we all need to know how desperately God loves us, how vigilantly He pursues a relationship with us. And even when we don't need that reminder, perhaps we need to be reminded how God can use us for those who do, even in ways which may seem small in our eyes. A note, a prayer, a Bible verse, a song, a small gift, or just silent presence can communicate so much in the wake of suffering.

I wish I could say my faith was permanently rock-solid after my vision—that I never again doubted His love and goodness. I wish I could say depression never again immobilized me or caused me to think irrationally. But that was not my reality.

What I can say is, from that moment on, when tempted to question all I'd placed my hope in—poured my very life into—I had tangible evidence to reflect on. It was His hidden miracles which, once I opened my eyes to look for them, reminded me of His love and pursuit of me. Those little miracles are still all around me, and I believe they are all around you, too, if you'll ask God to show them to you.

I don't know what would have happened if God had not intervened in such a miraculous way for me. I don't think it would have been pretty though. I had become so despondent because I put God in a box. I had thought the only way He could make good come from my circumstances was by changing them miraculously. But I learned that God's love is at its most powerful when it is most needed. If He'd chosen to miraculously heal my family members, I may never have seen how He'd loved me through the darkest time of my life. This seems obvious or simplistic, but I had lived so long under the assumption that the only way God could love me was to heal them that the revelation was cathartic.

The truth of the matter is, sometimes life just sucks. Forgive me for being crass, but I don't think there's a more eloquent way to put it. Life sucks. That's just the reality of a world in which evil exists. But God's love is a promise—a miracle—that doesn't change no matter my circumstances. When Daddy died, God didn't love me any less. When I turned my heart from God, He didn't turn away from me. When Andy and Grandpa also died, God's love did not change in its intensity and passion for me. God doesn't promise us freedom from suffering, but He does promise to be with us in it. Psalm 56:8 says, "You've kept track of my every toss and turn through the sleepless nights, each tear entered in your ledger, each ache written in your book." (MSG) I don't think it means that He merely sits back taking notes.

I hope that in sharing my story with you, I can bring some small measure of encouragement to you, whatever your situation may be.

APPENDIX A
Andy's Emails, Poems, and Song for Mary

Early May, 2002
Dear Friends,

I woke up at 3am a few nights ago and looked out my window. Shrouded by trees and mist, I saw a lamppost, burning brightly through the night air. It so struck me that I stared at it for a few moments.

It reminded me of C.S. Lewis' "The Lion, the Witch, and the Wardrobe," where the kids enter the hidden world Narnia through a wardrobe. After entering, the hanging fur coats in the wardrobe turn to fir trees, and eventually they see a lamppost ahead. The lamppost becomes the symbol of their entrance into the new world, and the wardrobe the symbol for the old. Well, I feel kind of like Lucy entering the wardrobe and an unknown world for the very first time. Only I didn't want or ask to go in; I was sort of hurled in and the door locked behind me. What is in this world? I don't know; it's all foreign to me. And somehow, I have to find another way out. But as I walk on, I see the lamppost ahead, burning brightly. I have a feeling the lamp will be walking ahead of me for some time now, until I get out of this dark forest, maybe even longer. If I turn to the side or the back, I stare at the trees and the darkness and I grow scared: these trees are so big, and what could be behind them?! Why am I here?

But if I turn again to the light, I see the lamppost out in front again, almost waiting for me; if I look closely, the lamppost is shedding tears for me, relieved that I have turned back. Whatever questions I had that were so pressing only seconds ago are gone with the mist, and my hope is restored again, for this, indeed, is God in front of me.

And, I do feel a thousand voices cheering me on and lifting me up in prayer.

My family and my girlfriend, Mary, are right there, holding my hand. I cannot thank you all enough. I will do my best to keep up with all of your individual correspondence, as well as putting out an update with prayer requests at least once a week. Thank you to everyone who was able to make the party, services, or reception last weekend in Grand Rapids, and to everyone who has expressed their love through mail, email, and phone messages. I cannot tell you how much each heartfelt word does for my spirits and for those around me.

UPDATE:

Okay, enough of this banter, here is an update: I have moved in to my parents' house in ohio. They have taken it off the market. We met with a liver surgeon this Monday. He is unable to operate right now, and a liver transplant is a very bleak option because the recurrence rate for liver cancer in transplants is near 100%. But, he is a wonderful doctor and a great man, and he is going to help us get into the system and fight the insurance battles. Our first task, however, is to find the source of the tumors, or primary, as the docs call it. Where did this thing come from? Whatever the answer, it is going to be extremely rare. This just doesn't happen in people my age. Anyhow, I woke up yesterday and was told I could only eat green jello. Then I had to choke down this laxative for 6 hours until my system cleaned out, all in preparation for a colonoscopy and some other tests today. So we are about to leave for the hospital, where it looks like we will be focusing our treatment. It is one of the best hospitals in the country, and my broth Dave spent lots of time there in Med School. Needless to say, I can't wait to eat tonight, and Mary is coming down for the evening.

Otherwise, we just don't know a whole lot. Chemo and radiation are probable, but we do have to make an appointment with an oncologist yet. We are still very thankful that the doctors in Grand Rapids moved so fast to uncover it.

To those struggling with Why:

I know a lot of folks are struggling with the Why, God? question in all of this. Is it God's will?

Well, I'm not a seminarian or a pastor, but I've had to work out my thoughts on this in a hurry. One of my good friends gave me the image that God is crying and pounding his fist on the table because of this cancer. I love that image, and I think it is right. Somehow, to me, that image seems inconsistent with it being God's will, or at least that he wanted it to happen this way. I may be toying with semantics, but that's how I feel. God did not want this anymore than he wanted Satan to inflict Job. However, God did ALLOW my cancer to happen. I also believe firmly that he will, as Romans 8:28 proclaims, use it for good. Though he may be crying at our pain, he may also be joyfully crying in anticipation of how this may affect his kingdom. I think my little brother Tim stated it best, "I consider it an honor that our family can suffer for God," first in my father's cancer a year ago, and now in this time.

Finally, I don't feel like asking why of God will get us anywhere, for two main reasons. First, for me task the question, "God, why me?" is basically to ask the question, "God, why not someone else?" With God as the only judge of human value, how could I ever dare to assert that my life is of more earthly value than anyone else;s? Secondly, I look at Job who kind of asked God why in the last several chapters of the book. Did he get anywhere? No. Except maybe smarter because he got a lecture from God on who was in charge.

There may be moments where I break down and start to ask God why, but where will it get me? Nowhere but back to leaning on God. For my family, Mary and I, that is our challenge: that through this suffering, we will be able to stand up and say that God is still in charge. I know there will be moments where we will be tested, but, as one of my high school friends pointed out to me this week, there will never be more temptations than we can bear (I Corinthians 10:13)

God bless you all.

Love,
Andy Schrier

May 10, 2002
Dear Friends,
David Wilcox, a songwriter, performs a song called "Farthest Shore." In it, he writes these words:

> Let me dive into the water,
> Leave behind all that I've worked for
> Except what I remember and believe
> And when I stand on the farthest shore
> I will have all I need. (Wilcox)

I've tried to live the last few years of my life by a Christian creed of that nature. i've always known that you can't take it with you when you go. But I always thought this meant material possessions. Especially in the last two years of my life, I've tried to not worry at all about material possessions and throw my all into the Hatty Beverly Center, that tutoring program in Grand Rapids that I worked so hard for. I've tried to invest my very fibers in something worthwhile, not seeking to get anything back. In doing so, to use a cliché, I've found myself.

I'm not trying to boast but to be real. But even this, this thing that i've labored long over, the young people and tutors I love so much, the countless hours, the success, the pride-I can't take any of that with me either. It all has to stay behind-even what I've worked for in this life.

Now I stand on the farthest shore, and I truly have all that I need. I dove into the water and left behind so much and so many that I love. I can still see all of it on the other shore. But now that I've left everything, I stand here alone, naked, not ashamed, yet vulnerable. I truly have nothing that I came here with. I turn my back on the other shore, wide-eyed into the wilderness, ready to face...well, I don't know what.

But I do have something: what I remember and believe, what I've learned in my life's journey so far.

It's funny how God uses places to teach you things. For example, he has always let me struggle here in Ohio. I've fought several battles here. When I first moved here, I struggled with shyness, popularity, not being good at sports, fitting in, and owning a faith that was really my parents' and not mine. Then, during college, I came back here for the summers. One summer, I wrestled my toughest battle ever against depression and anxiety brought on by my RA year at college and a breakup. And now, I'm here again to fight this battle.

And through it all, God used Grand Rapids to teach me the stuffing in the middle of the oreo, what I needed to know in between. In Grand Rapids, I learned the life lessons I needed to know to not care about popularity, to take ownership of MY faith, to conquer anxiety and depression, and to find the passions in life that make me tick.

It's a tale of two cities, if you will, the best of times and the worst of times. But I will always have those experiences as I go through this.

Finally, I realize that I have my family and friends. I'm not sure how the analogy fits, but this great cloud of witnesses is cheering me on, praying for me, encouraging me, crying for me, telling me wonderful things about myself, showering me with gifts and mail, and above all, time. If I ever struggled with popularity in my life, my diagnosis with cancer sure has cleared that right up. And I'm not really sure why. I don't feel like I deserve all this attention. I'm really just a messed up sinner like everyone else.

Someone told me that I don't deserve to go through this. I agree. No one does. We all deserve a lot worse. Only because of what Jesus did on the cross are we able to even limp through one day of life on this earth. He's given me 25 beautiful years, and often, in the words of another favorite artist, "this blessedness of life sometimes brings me to my knees."

Because of this, if I have to leave everything on that shore and say goodbye forever, I'm okay with that. Yeah, I've got dreams that I haven't realized, but that will probably be true even when I'm 80. If it comes down to that, I hope to see you all in heaven. (By the way, this is not a stance that I developed in the last few weeks in reaction to my situation. It is, however, a stance that I have kept strongly since the developments in the last few weeks. Maybe that matters to someone.)

As I see it, this is not a time for weak-kneed or pew-padded Christianity. Not that there is really any time or tolerance on God's part for such things, but for me, this is more urgent of a time for sincere belief than ever. You see, I'm about to look death in the face and say, "Do what YOU will, but unless GOD will, YOU will NOT." I can't say that with a shaky voice or with any wavering in my belief. I truly pray and believe that if we, as a prayer army, can challenge ourselves to be true Jesus followers, the we will be more than conquerors through Jesus Christ, in any trial, not just this one.

MEDICAL UPDATE

I received an endoscopy/ultrasound on my pancreas on Monday. The initial procedure was supposed to be for an hour, but they decided to take a needle biopsy and knocked me out for another two hours. In my delirium afterwards, they also gave me a chest X-ray to see if the lungs could be the primary. I have spent all week recovering from this procedure, basically sleeping off the drugs and getting the gas out of my system.

We received the results on Thursday of this week. The pancreas does indeed seem to be the source, or primary tumor. There is a small tumor behind or in the pancreas. In general, pancreatic cancer is a nasty thing, relative to other cancers of course. However, there is a bit of good news: the cancer has been diagnosed as a germ cell cancer. Typically, these types of cancers are very treatable with chemotherapy, and very responsive (in the way we want it to be).

Our first appointment with our oncologist, Dr. I., is this Tuesday at 10:45 am. She would like to start chemotherapy soon, which is good. Now that we know what we are dealing with, we can hopefully begin to deal with it.

Our service last Sunday was wonderful. Thank you for your prayers. I think the Lord used it to speak to many, including my father and I who led the service. It was a very positive experience for both of us.

Thank you all for everything! As always, we feel surrounded and uplifted by your prayers and support.

Love,
Andy Schrier

May 16, 2002
Dear Friends,

Before Daniel went into the Lions' den, he must have been a wreck. Oh, I'm sure he prayed like crazy beforehand, trusting that the Lord would protect him. But I don't think there is a human alive who could have enough faith in God to walk into that den without a serious degree of fear and trembling.

I guarantee you that Daniel had nervous diarrhea that day. Of course, he trusted that God would save him, but look at those fangs, those teeth, those huge, majestic, and hungry beasts. Look at the piles of bones strewn around the den. Everyone in the kingdom probably knew criminals that had been ripped apart by those animals.

After a while, when I imagine that those things started purring like kitties, Daniel probably relaxed and became amazed at something that he had known all along: that God would take care of him. In my imagination, there are countless people of faith who, though they believed in God's provision to the best of their human faculties, probably trembled with anxiety and questions at the moment of truth. Well this is my moment of truth, and I'm scared. I have faith, but I also have fear and trembling.

We were planning to start chemotherapy on Monday, May 20, but a phone call from my oncologist changed that just a few hours ago. The tumors appear to be growing fast and she wants to start tomorrow. Friday, May 17th, a month and a day after I was originally diagnosed in Grand Rapids, will be the first day of chemotherapy. I will be in the hospital for five days, receiving the first drug in doses as much as my system can handle.

I will be miserable at times, nauseated, puking, and without energy. Eventually I will lose my hair, and my 150 pound frame will probably do some shrinking.

I'm scared. It is indeed a terrible thing not to be able to have control of one's body. If you think about it, which I have, cancer and chemotherapy are really very interesting, and perhaps ironic enigmas. Germ cell cancer is really my own cells, from my own body, growing without supervision and organization in a way that threatens to take over the very mass that allowed their existence. They're like the prodigal son in a way.

Chemotherapy, on the other, hand, is a technology that God has revealed to man about how to combat this phenomenon of cancer. It is a series of chemical treatments that poison the cancer. But the chemicals are so strong, and often poisonous to certain parts of the human body, that they must be delivered with caution, anti-nausea drugs, and a lot of fluids to flush them out of certain organs. Some folks, after enduring chemotherapy for so long, prefer to die of cancer before the drugs kill them. While a miracle, and often successful, chemotherapy often weakens the spirits of those who receive it, sometimes more than they reduce the cancer.

My chemotherapy is not one of the worst, nor one of the easiest. At times it will be very miserable and difficult. I will be on four three-week cycles that last from now until the beginning of August. This process, standard for germ cell cancers of my sort, is 48% successful in blasting the cancer into remission, which is a far cry from liver and pancreatic cancers that are virtually incurable.

So, while I am scared, I also still have my faith, and I hope and pray that I will never seriously question it as I go through this process. So please forgive me if this email is a little longer than the last. Tis is the last day of my normal life that I will have for a while. In the meantime, i don't know if I will feel well enough to continue my lengthy updates; they may have to become shorter for a while. i'm just not sure. When I come out of this in August, I will be done. I will have turned 25 during the process. As I said at Madison Square Church the day I left Grand Rapids, there aren't many 25-year old cancer survivors walking around, but I intend to be one.

PRAYER LIST
1) Please pray for my strength and my faith.
2) Pray for my thought life to stay positive and joyful.
3) Pray for Mary and my family, as well as any friends who may see me; it may be more difficult to watch someone go through this than to actually be the person who goes through it.
4) Pray for my relationships with Doctors, nurses, and other patients; I want to have a good attitude and represent Christ in this process.

5) Pray for the medical community at the hospital to have keen attention to detail and wisdom to see things that they need to.

Finally, I am by no means the greatest poet on earth. But my poetry means a lot to how I express myself. I would like to share this poem with everyone, and it follows after my postscript. To me, it captures my struggle, my relationship to God (Daddy), and the standards I'm setting for my own outlook on this whole ordeal. If it makes sense to you: great. If not: sorry.
Thank you for everything.

Love,
Andy Schrier

P.S.: I will have constant email access while in the hospital, with my laptop by my side, so please continue writing. I will respond to as many as possible.

TO DADDY

Daddy, daddy,
This I pray,
Which mountain shall we
Climb today?

My burden's heavy
And my faith -so small -
Next to those mountains
That you built so tall.

Daddy, daddy,
This I cry:
How could you lead me,
So young, to die?

I've followed you as close
As anyone, I guess;
So how could my journey
Be so much less?

Daddy, daddy,
This I know,
I've got more questions
When I'm feeling low.

Now Daddy listen here:
It's hard for me to be brave,
On my knees in a hole
That may soon be my grave.

Daddy, daddy,
A joyful life I've known;
Did I use up my quota of joy
With fifty years to go?

Just give me another fifty
And I'll spread your joy like seeds,
It'll grow faster than cancer,
with deeper roots than weeds.

Daddy, daddy,
One more thing to say:
Don't leave me all alone
And then go on your way.

This pain is a burden
And my fear is at its height
I can only bear it daddy,
If you stay tonight.

Daddy, daddy,
This I pray,
Which mountain shall we
Move today?

A mustard seed,
Is that faith enough?
You rewrote the book
On how men are to be "tough."

Daddy, daddy,
I ask you one more thing:
You healed so many people,
You stole from death its sting.

I know you can heal me
And how will you choose?
My feet are way too small
To wear any of your shoes.

Daddy, daddy,
This I choose:
Enough of my silly questions-
We don't have time to lose.

As long as I live this moment-
Perhaps more down the way-
I'm gonna live each minute
With such joy to burst a day.

But Daddy, daddy,
May your will be done.
I'm happy to walk with you,
Until another day is done.

And knowing that you treasure
Each minute you walk with me
Is enough to boggle my mind;
I have to believe it before I see.

6-6-02
Dear Friends,

  The name Israel means to strive or struggle with God. Jacob, a patriarch of the nation of Israel, won the name after wrestling all night with a man that turned out to be either God or an angel. The story seems oddly placed in Genesis 32: one moment Jacob is very concerned with avoiding Esau's wrath and getting his family home and across a river quickly, the next moment he is wrestling with some random guy in the desert. Now I'm a wrestler, but I prefer not to stay up all night fighting folks that I just happen to meet in the desert at midnight.

Whatever details are clouded here, it is clear that this man was not able to defeat Jacob, so he touched his hip and dislocated it, and gave him the name Israel. In fact, Jacob would not let the mysterious stranger go until he had blessed him. So the man blessed Jacob; after the man left, Jacob realized that he had wrestled with God himself. Jacob, however, walked away with a limp.

Honestly, this story shocks me sometimes: how is it that God can get away with blatant physical damage of one of his children? Doesn't this pose a serious problem to those of us who believe in God as a compassionate and benevolent lover of his people? How can I trust a God who blesses and physically harms within the same breath of his almighty power?

I think I understand this passage a lot better after this week. If I can make an analogy that a hip is something we stand or rely on for emotional stability, then God has dislocated one of my hips this week.

In his own unique way, God made me aware that in the last week I have placed too much hope and trust for my healing in the medical process. After all, my prognosis is favorable compared to most other cancers. Also, my chemotherapy isn't one of the toughest treatments being used. From a medical perspective, this is a favorable cancer to have.

And, in God's equally unique way, he has dislocated my hip; he has violently severed me from the hope that medicine will cure this cancer. Why? So that I can be totally reliant on Him for the cure.

Now some may say that I shouldn't even proceed with chemotherapy in that case. However, there is an important distinction to make between such stance and one that places all hope in God for healing, acknowledging that God can use chemotherapy and medicine as weapons in his vast arsenal. Indeed, he allowed "science" to "discover" this knowledge in the first place, in order that his people be less afflicted.

To some, this may seem like a total contradiction, or a paradox. "What is the difference," you might ask, "you're still receiving chemotherapy?"

The difference is in my attitude and my allegiance. God has made it mentally impossible for me to continue trusting in anyone or anything but Him for healing. As far as I'm concerned, I have cancer in my body that will kill me unless God intervenes on my behalf.

Back to Jacob, I believe that something similar happened to him. Perhaps God desired Jacob's trust. So, at a moment when Jacob needed speed and physical ability most for survival, God interrupted his hope, blessed him, and made it impossible for Jacob to trust in his own physical ability. Why? So that Jacob would be totally dependent on God for survival in a tough situation. Instead of running, Jacob had to trust that God would protect him and fight for him.

We serve a jealous God who deserves and desires our affection, trust, and total reliance. As one of my pastors remarked in a sermon a few weeks ago, those of us in middle and upper class America live in the wealthiest, most plentiful society ever. It is extremely difficult to rely on God when we live in green pastures as we rely on God when we journey through the deserts of life. We place a lot of trust, hope and faith in our own abilities, diligence and finances, rather than in God who allowed us to acquire them.

I would like to challenge that maybe we need to boldly pray for God to dislocate our "hips," or the things that we stand on aside from God. I will warn you, weak-kneed or pew-padded Christians should not pray this prayer, because it will mean a total paradigm shift in your hopes and trusts. For those who are bold enough, I think we will change radically from a pat-myself-on-the-back, sometimes self-worshipping brand of Christianity to one where we are totally dependent on God for survival, and totally in awe of the fact that he provides for our needs.

And isn't that exactly where we ought to be?

UPDATE AND PRAYERS

Mary has moved in safely. She is getting along well with her roommate, my sister Abby, who is also home from college from the summer. Mary's addition to the family during this time is priceless. God has blessed our relationship, along with her relationship with the rest of the family. It is also extremely good to have Abby back.

My hair started to fall out on Monday morning, so I shaved it off along with the facial hair. Being bald is both an adjustment, as well as a poignant physical reminder of the battle itself. It was a difficult wake-up call at first, but we are able to laugh about it now. I wear a lot of different hats (when you usually hear people say that it means something else!).

I am finished with the first cycle of chemotherapy. The tumor markers, as well as the drastically decreased level of tumor-associated pain in my abdomen, shows that there was a definite and favorable reaction by the tumors to the chemotherapy. This is very encouraging news, as well as that my body has held up very well under the chemicals. My blood counts appear to have dropped dramatically over the weekend, such that I can get sick very easily until the bone marrow replenishes itself. In all likelihood, this happened because the different chemo drugs continue to work for weeks after infusion. This weekend is my brother Tim's wedding and I will be around a lot of people, so hopefully I can enjoy their company and not their diseases.

Finally, on Sunday June 9th I begin the second cycle of chemo. That means hospital from Sunday to Thursday. I am NOT looking forward to this. I will then be down for several days when I come home, recovering from the Cysplatin. This is, by far, the hardest and nastiest part of the treatment. Each day in the hospital gets worse.

I will need to hear from people during this time through email and snail mail, which my family can bring to the hospital. Please do not be afraid of flooding the boxes. From June 9th to about the 18th is when I need the most support and love to help me remember that the hospital treatments are worth it, and that life is worth fighting for. And of course, all of your wonderful, childlike prayers are desired as well.

Please pray for good communication between Mary and I, even while I'm drugged and tired. Pray for the wedding, that we will enjoy the wonderful occasion and family, and that I will not pick up any diseases. Pray for this hospital stay, that our attitudes will stay positive, that I will not get too bored, and that I avoid diarrhea. Also pray for all of our interactions with the nurses and doctors. Please pray that the chemotherapy will continue to do more damage to the tumors than to me. Please pray for a swift recovery.

I will write again as soon as I get home from the hospital. Thank you for all your prayers and support.

Love,
Andy Schrier

6-20-02
Dear Friends,

Mary and I have a favorite spot here in Ohio. We call it the town's best kept secret. It is a huge reserve of flowers and trees, elegantly landscaped by a local division of Ohio State University. While azaleas were in bloom, we would visit our favorite spot known as "Azalea Allee." Right now, however, the crowning piece of the whole secret arboretum is in full bloom: the Rose Garden. We love the combination of amazing colors and smells as you walk through garden after garden, rosebush after rosebush.

I'm not a rose gardener, but I love watching how they grow. Roses grow like vines, and some of them are quite covered with thorns, with as much as 20 thorns in an inch of vine. Just like any other plant, roses have to compete with other plants for all of the natural elements they need for survival, their thorny bases curling sometimes for several yards before producing the beautiful and fragrant blossoms for which they are so beloved. They stand dormant most of the year, fighting for sun and for life, choking out all of the other plants in their competition for survival, then for a short time, they produce these beautiful, heart-wrenching, color-filled, aroma-laden flowers.

Roses are parallel to human life; those nasty thorns are as much a natural protection as a reminder to us of how tough life really is. Sometimes survival is downright difficult, while the twisting and turning of the vines remind us that life isn't always going where we expect it to be. In fact, we spend most of our lives twisting and turning, surviving, growing, competing for resources, and very little time in full bloom. Yet for a brief time every year, we are showing our best colors, we can smell and taste the fruit of our own labors, we glory in the goodness of life. To take the analogy further, the amount of beauty that comes out of a rose is totally dependent on the Gardener. Wild roses grow, but without a caretaker are limited to the vicissitudes and whims of their own environment. For those that are watched, however, sometimes the Gardener has to do things that may truncate the beauty, like prune the blossoms, so that the flowers will be better in the future. Sometimes the Gardener has to change the direction of the plant, or spread poison that may kill nasty bugs.

I would think that the roses rarely understand the actions of the Gardener. It never feels good when we are pruned, changed in direction, or poisoned, but somehow, when the roses come out, the Gardener's way seemed to make sense in the end. Since I'm speaking about roses, let me share a timely example that has to do with love. First we look at it from a human viewpoint: the pruning. I was removed from my job, my girlfriend, and my church in Grand Rapids to fight a disease. I moved five hours away to be with my family while I tackle this illness. My girlfriend Mary could not stand to see me fight the battle from afar, so she obtained a leave of absence from her work to move in with my family for the summer. Now both of our lives are interrupted, and we can't spend any time working on productive things, like the ministries that our lives once were.

But now that the roses have bloomed, we have started to see things a little differently. First of all, Mary is able to go through the tough times with me. Secondly, during the good times, we have a lot of time to spend with each other. This is not the pressured, time-confined seeing each other, either. God has allowed us a lot of long hours for talking, walking, going places, joyful long hours of just being together, laughing or silent, not having to worry about normal-life pressures, locked in accompanying each other through one great struggle. What a gift! No worries about jobs, very few schedule constraints, and each day to spend together discovering God's mercies in our lives.

It is amazing to look back and see how the Gardener allowed our rose vines to twist together at just the perfect moment. Neither of us wanted me to get cancer and move away; we didn't like the painful twists and turns that were made without our control. But now the only question we have is, "Why did we even question the Gardener in the first place?"

I struggled to find a good Biblical example of a spiritual couple, but I think Ruth and Boaz paint an amazing picture of another two roses that the Gardener intertwined through lots of pruning and change of direction.

First of all, Ruth was a Moabite widowed daughter-in-law of the Israelite Naomi who had taken refuge in Moab due to a famine in her hometown of Bethlehem. When Naomi, also a widow, decided to return impoverished, struggling and bitter to her homeland, Ruth declared her allegiance to her mother-in-law, including to her God. This is significant because Ruth was a foreigner to Israel, and because Naomi herself was bitter towards her own God. So Ruth declares her allegiance to Naomi and they return to Bethlehem in Israel.

From God's command in Leviticus 23, Israelites were required to leave the corners of their fields ungleaned by harvesters so that poor folks and foreigners could get what they needed to eat. It was humiliating work for those who chose it, but Ruth had few alternatives for making ends meet, so she began working in the fields of an Israelite named Boaz.

The situation looked bleak for Naomi and Ruth, and then suddenly, the roses bloomed and the Gardener's work started to show its beauty. Boaz, who was related to Naomi, took notice of Ruth because her commitment to Naomi impressed him greatly. He overlooked the fact that she was a foreigner, respected her integrity, and made sure she had enough to eat from his fields.

Then, through the wonderful and intricate kinsman redeemer process, Boaz married Ruth, making the quality of life for Ruth and Naomi suddenly a lot better. Ruth even had the honor of becoming the great grandmother of David, the great king of Israel.

Through Ruth's faithfulness to a Gardener she didn't know, her, Naomi and Boaz were brought to see the faithful work of the Gardener.

I feel like Mary and I are in a similar situation to Ruth and Boaz because God has pruned and twisted us, and even poisoned me. But through it all, just like Ruth and Boaz, we see the hands of the Gardener. Romans 8:28 says that God works through everything for the good of those who love him, and right now we can testify that in this situation, he certainly has kept his promise.

MEDICAL UPDATE

The Bleomycin treatment on Monday was better than usual, perhaps because they gave me some different countering drugs, and the side effects were less than usual. We have a catscan of the tumor region on Friday morning to determine the effectiveness of the chemotherapy. Needless to say, this is a pretty big thing. On Monday we will discuss the results and other tumor markers (indications of what and how the tumor is doing, such as chemicals in my blood that are produced by or in reaction to the tumor) with my doctor, and we will receive the final Bleomycin treatment in this cycle.

I have recovered from the hospital treatments. I feel pretty good and strong right now. I will be enjoying a crew of visitors this weekend. My appetite is very good. I am enjoying being somewhat productive with my days, and of course, spending lots of time with Mary.

This is a good time to pray for the wisdom of the doctors as they determine what all that these signs are saying. Please pray for a good, accurate catscan on Friday morning. Please pray that I will drink the barium solution for it with relatively no problems (I hate that stuff). Please pray for our Doctor's appointment on Monday. I will probably give a brief medical update that night, just to let people know how it went. Pray that we will see the tumor well, or even that we will not see it at all (meaning it has been completely destroyed.) This is brave, but we can pray for it anyways. Pray for the last bleomycin treatment on Monday after the appointment, that it will be effective and the side effects minimal. Please pray for Mary and I, that our love continues to blossom.

Thank you all for your prayers, emails, snail mail, and thoughts. We are convinced, thoroughly, that prayer made a huge difference in how I held up under the chemotherapy of this cycle. There is just no other good explanation, except that God's people are praying effectively and frequently and for the right things. Again, I'm sorry if I can't keep up with all the correspondence, but every word of it means a lot to me.

Love,
Andy Schrier

6-25-02
Dear Friends,

I'm sorry I didn't write last night; my treatment had me feeling quite sick, so I went to bed early. We did have our meeting with our Doctor yesterday, with the results of the catscan. I have to say that at first we were rather disappointed with the news. It appears that the tumors are smaller, with some of the smallest ones even disappearing. However, there is also a 6cm mass in the liver that decreased only by a half centimeter. Overall, we were not impressed by the rate of tumor destruction. At that rate, we could be here a long time.

However, if we choose to look at the bright side of things, the tumors are stopped in their growth, and there is decrease in size. They are in check for the time being. I also gained 4 pounds during this cycle, which is no small task. I have been eating like a horse, and I feel great. My tumor pain has been gone since we first started chemotherapy. So things are mixed. It is taking some time for us to process this last bit of information.

Mary and I have to remind ourselves that God is still in control, and that only he can conduct the healing. We are trusting him for it still. We have dedicated ourselves to more earnest prayer for complete healing.

I will send out my normal update at the end of this week. Please pray that God will strengthen our faith throughout this week to deal with this news.

Thanks for your prayers and thoughts.

Love,
Andy Schrier

6-29-02
Dear Friends,

It has been a difficult week for my family, one where our faith has been tested very strongly. At the risk of sounding too dramatic about our own problems, I want to let you know what we are going through this week.

As some of you may know, or I may have mentioned, cancer has hit our family on three generations. My maternal grandfather has chronic leukemia, my father is in remission from cancer in his bladder wall, and then there is me. This week we had a slim range of disappointing to disturbing news on all three of us. First, my father is suffering from hydronephrosis, or failure of the kidneys to drain properly, probably due to his surgery over a year ago to combat the cancer. He is currently recovering from surgery that he underwent on Thursday to correct this problem. Secondly, as I reported on Tuesday, we were disappointed about the lack of destruction of my tumors as reported in my latest catscan. Finally, my grandfather's leukemia, it was discovered on Tuesday, has taken a more aggressive form and is now throughout his body. He will receive a more aggressive chemotherapy to combat this beginning on Monday. Needless to say, my mother and the rest of us have felt very assaulted this week. Our faith has been called into question almost openly. How we respond to such a week, such dire circumstances when the situation wasn't exactly favorable to begin with, is as crucial as it is challenging.

I can tell you how I felt like responding on Monday and Tuesday. Better yet, I can illustrate it with a Bible story. My favorite Bible passage is I Kings 19. It involves Elijah the prophet after his encounter with Ahab on Mt. Carmel and the destruction of the prophets of Baal. After such a victorious experience, Elijah feels overwhelmed by the pressure from Jezebel, flees into the desert, lies down under a tiny shade tree and prays to die. He then falls asleep, is attended by an angel, and continues into the desert for forty days to the mountain of God. When God speaks to Elijah, it is in the voice of whisper, not in earthquake or fire, and Elijah tells God basically that he is tired and overwhelmed. God then tells him to go back where he came and get back to work.

For me that is always the punch line of the story. How often that you tell a near-suicidal person to go back to whatever it was that caused them to be near suicidal? Elijah didn't get some miracle sympathy from God in completing his task. He didn't talk God into ending Jezebel and Ahab with a wave of his hand and restoring the nation to fearing him. He didn't erase all of the danger for Elijah so that he could return to Israel without fear of harm.

Instead: Go back the way you came. God simply said get back to the task at hand, restoring God's kingdom and standing up to those that opposed him. He gave Elijah instructions and a new helper in Elisha and sent him back to work. God must have known that Elijah wasn't yet at the end of his faith rope, and so he sent him back to it to climb some more.

After the news on Monday I wanted to quit the chemo. I wanted to switch to something more aggressive. After all the news about my other family members, I'm sure we all felt like we didn't want to keep fighting. We felt like running into the desert. The mess was too overwhelming for us and too tough for us to face alone. All humans, no matter how tough their faith, and no matter how strong their resolve, will be at least tempted in such moments to question their faith. Some will give in to that temptation, some will give it up, and others will resist. But the temptation is very real in such moments.

And to me, God very gently said, "Go back the way you came." In other words, get back to work, get back to your chemotherapy, maintain a positive attitude about your family members, and believe MORE in my healing power for all three of you.

I've always struggled with regularity in my prayer life, but I felt very strongly this week as though God wants Mary and me to spend more time in prayer. We have committed ourselves to that goal.

So, through the fire, we have gained in strength and faith. We have learned that we aren't even close to near the end of our faith ropes, but that we have a lot more mileage left. And it's a good thing, because all three situations, plus other things going on, require a lot of earnest, true faith-wrought, child-like, standing firm kind of prayer.

MEDICAL UPDATE

It is already the end of the second cycle. We go into the hospital for five days on Sunday around noon for the big treatment. We will be home on Thursday afternoon, if all goes well.

Please continue to pray for rapid and total tumor destruction, especially during this cycle. If we can pray for this as a united effort, I am convinced that God will act. Please pray for Mary and me to have good attitudes throughout the hospital stay. Pray for side effects of the drugs to be nonexistent, specifically nausea and diarrhea. Please pray that we will fill our time with useful things and not get too bored. Please pray that we will continue to pray together every day while in the hospital, even when tired and when we don't feel like it. Please pray for a quick recovery time after this treatment is over.

I have given up trying to do email in the hospital. The systems are too unreliable. Basically, I will be email silent until I emerge on Thursday, but your messages will still be appreciated.

One last thing: in my last update from last week, I said that God poisoned me. Someone thought that I meant He gave me cancer. Not at all what I was trying to say. I simply was making a small reference to chemotherapy, as I think of it as poison. I can understand the confusion, but I want to make it clear that I don't think God "gave" me the cancer.

Thanks for everything,

Love,
Andy Schrier

7-6-02
Dear friends,

as of friday afternoon, it is very good to be home, once again! as usual after the hospital stay, i am pretty tired and out of it. so i just try to sleep it off and get back to normal over the next few days. we spent an extra day in the hospital this week because my counts were too low to start me on sunday. so we didn't start till monday and didn't get home until a day later on friday. it made for a long week. but it is nice to be home in my own bed. i see that there are a ton of email messages to read, so i will do my best to catch up with them as i feel better in the days ahead. thanks for all your prayers and thoughts. i will write an update that has some coherence to it when i feel a little more coherence.

i miss everyone very much and i hope everyone is doing well. as for now, please just pray for strength and rest. all else will come back in time.

Thanks,
Andy Schrier

7-9-02
Dear Friends,

Sometimes my will power has to be put in serious check. Every problem that I've ever needed to solve before, with some notable exceptions of course, I've been able to just stir up the creative juices, the resources, the physical power, or just the sheer willpower to overcome. I'm not trying to brag, but it's just how we do things, isn't it? We muster up the willpower and we get things done.

Yet this battle to me is like no other problem I've ever had. No matter how much willpower, diligence, resources, physical, or mental strength I have, it matters not at all to this cancer. In short, I can't do any more than I am already doing. No matter how much of my natural resources I command, I can't will the cancer to go away any more effectively. Nothing I do, aside from praying and keeping a strong positive mental attitude, will make any difference in the amount of tumor destruction that occurs.

This is perhaps the hardest thing for me to face. I've always been able to do something more to take care of the problem. Now, I cannot. And it is very frustrating.

One thing that does comfort me is a passage in Luke 18 that tells me I can pray a lot more. It must be a little known passage (I've never heard it preached on) about a widow and a judge. The judge in this particular town does not fear God or have any respect for other humans. Yet a widow in this town comes to bother the judge every day for justice against her adversary. The judge admits that he neither fears God nor has respect for other humans, but decides to rule justly in regard to the widow simply so that she will leave him alone. Otherwise, he says, she might drive him nuts with her pestering. So even in the case of this judge, the widow is granted justice. Jesus goes on to comment on the illustration that we can bring our requests to God the same way. The difference is apparent that because he cares about us, justice will be granted even quicker on our behalf. Luke even mentions that the reason Jesus told the story in the first place was to encourage the disciples not to give up and to keep praying.

It does seem kind of weird at first, to pray to God about something so much that he is pestered by our prayers. This passage enlightens us a great deal about prayer. I find it more revealing than a lot of scripture.

Of all the passages on prayer, we don't know how God really receives it. Does it come in bags to his office like letters, or has he switched over to a more efficient email-like system lately? Does he have to spend three days a week answering reading mail, and four days on a really busy week? Does he tally up requests for certain things? Do certain prayers "weigh" more because of who sent them on into heaven or because they may have been more heartfelt and less selfish than most? And how long does it take him to make decisions on really tough matters that have accumulated thousands of prayers?

Scripture doesn't answer a lot of these questions for us, and it probably doesn't need to. We probably don't need to know all those things. But in Luke 18 we learn a couple really basic things about prayer that I find very reassuring. First of all, aside from the fact that we don't have an understandable metaphor for how, God does receive our prayers. Secondly, the passage strongly indicates, at least by analogy to the judge, that God is interrupted or distracted by our prayers.

I think that is significant. That means a bit more to me than that he hears our prayers. I like the image that whatever God is doing, I can distract or interrupt him by sending up a prayer about something. I also like the idea that I can distract him for long periods of time. And not because I like to distract God, but because just like anyone else, I dislike bad listeners. I hate it when I say something and wonder if it got heard. I like knowing that God heard what I said. I like knowing that if I ask for healing 30 times a day, every time I asked for it God turned around stopped what he was doing to listen and mark the request for justice to be restored to my body.

And not just anybody, but God himself. Jesus told this analogy at the risk of being associated with a judge that didn't care about people or God, but made it clear that he was not that kind of ruler. In fact, he is so much more benevolent and caring about us than any earthly judge could be, and that is what makes the analogy so powerful. We ARE in good hands, and are requests DO matter, no matter how many times we log them in his book.

This passage gives me a great deal of hope. One of the points behind my email updates is to focus our prayers so that we pray for the same things, and I think that helps out when it comes to asking God about things in unison.

Sadly, one of the things we forget to do most is pray. We hear about situations, talk about them to our companions, think about them a bit, and then forget to pray. At least I fall guilty of this way too much. This passage makes me want to capture every thought when I think about healing and turn it into a prayer.

I like the idea that I can "pester" God. I like the idea that each one of us matters to him enough that he cares about our needs that much. Especially in a world of cold injustice that doesn't care about how things turn out. We have someone to fight for us. I'm sure you can imagine how comforting that is to me when I want so badly to be healed and to return to normal life.

MEDICAL/PERSONAL UPDATE

I am back to normal after the hospital treatments of last week. My Bleomycin treatment on Monday seemed worse than normal. It gave me a bad headache and cold/hot flu-like symptoms for the evening. I usually have this to a small degree, but it was worse this week. I look forward to another week and a half of "normality" before going back to the hospital to start the fourth cycle near the end of July. I am enduring a bit of a cold.

I have had problems with boredom since coming home from the hospital. The issue for me is that I like to feel useful and I have very few productive things to do while I am here. It is very hard for me to be completely stopped and away from normal work, but I am praying that God will teach me something through being still, as well as giving me things to keep my mind occupied as I have this downtime.

My father and grandfather are both doing well this week. My grandfather's chemotherapy is underway, with little news as to the results yet. My father continues to heal up from his surgery and has started going back to work.

Please pray for complete healing for all three of us, my grandfather, father, and I. Please pray that my chemotherapy will continue to blast my tumors and cause total cancer destruction with minimal side effects to my body. Please pray that I will only have to endure the four cycles of chemotherapy. Please pray for my cold to heal and my blood counts to stay high, or for me to stay healthy when they don't. Please pray for Mary and I, that our relationship will continue to progress under the stress. Please pray for the caretakers in our family, namely my Mother, my grandmother, Mary, and my sister Abby as they continue to be strong day in and day out.

Thank you to everyone for keeping up with me this long. I know this is a tedious, enduring, patience-demanding struggle without immediate results, but I am thankful for every single person who stays updated on my condition, thinks and prays for my family and me. I eagerly anticipate the day when I can victoriously thank you all for participating in this prayer struggle. I praise God for your faithfulness.

Love,
Andy Schrier

7-22-02

Dear Friends,

I've gotten a lot of feedback on the emails I've written so far, mostly the spiritual nature of them. I guess I just want to say that the inspiration for these writings has come only from God. How do I know this? Well, if it were just me writing them, I could produce them any time I wanted, and I can't. I've learned over time that I have to wait on God to give me the inspiration for a writing. Thus I truly believe that God deserves all the credit for anything that was of value in my emails.

I feel it is important to acknowledge this for two reasons. First of all, it is always important to give God the credit for anything he does. He doesn't like people stealing his glory. Secondly, I hope it can be an encouragement to you as friends and prayer warriors. I hope it shows that his hand has been in this situation from the beginning, working in my faith to ready me for this battle. I hope this proves his presence, confirms his intentions to do something positive out of this mess, and gives you all the more reason to continue in this prayer marathon.

If there is anything I have learned so far in this process, it is that trusting in God for the long term during a battle is very difficult. I've learned that it is one thing to stand up in front of others and declare your faith as you start the battle, even going on the strength of that for a while, and another thing to keep trusting in the Lord as the battle drags on through its everyday twists, turns, ups and downs. Because we are humans and we have free will, our inner enemies of doubt, discouragement, depression, and worry take their toll as time goes on and the music and encouragement others fades. Eventually, you find yourself alone and the questions in your head start to ask whether you can live up to the claim that you staked yourself to from the beginning. To use a cliché, this is where the rubber meets the road.

There is a biblical example for this phenomenon in the life of Asa, King of Judah, in II Chronicles 14-16. In Chapter 14, when Judah is attacked by a large army, Asa goes to God first for protection, relying on him for strength to defeat the attackers. God fights for Judah, destroying the army. In Chapter 15, Asa loudly and publicly renewed a covenant with the Lord, declaring his intentions to seek God with all their hearts. That was in the 15th year of Asa's reign.

But something happened in Asa's heart by the 36th year when the King of Israel attacked Judah. Asa turned to the military strength of another nation to save Judah from this peril. So hard was his heart by this time that he even put in prison Hanani the prophet who delivered the message that Asa had done wrong. Three years later, Asa was struck with a minor foot disease. He refused to turn to the Lord for relief, but relied on physicians to cure his condition. He died two years later.

I think God used the life of Asa in this passage to prove a major point: that relying on God for deliverance through tough times is usually a marathon and not a sprint. It is easy to verbalize strong declarations about one's faith in God, but a lot tougher to live it out in the long run. Asa started out well, but for one reason or another, he couldn't finish strong. As a result, he seems to have lost what started out as a very neat faith.

It is difficult to march through the everyday parts of the battle and still really, truly trust in the Lord for victory. Some days are more difficult than others. I think Asa is a warning to us to keep this in mind through our battles. Doubt, depression, discouragement, and worry are powerful and devastating, but perhaps not so much as apathy. I have a hunch, though no biblical proof, that this is what killed Asa's faith over the years.

It is difficult to stay focused on God throughout the endurance of our trials. I guess that is why James wrote about perseverance.

MEDICAL UPDATE

We begin the fourth cycle tomorrow (Tuesday, July 23rd). We will be in the hospital from Tuesday through Saturday. As usual, it will take me several days after the treatments to recover my mind and strength. Hopefully this will be the last cycle. At the end of it (two or three weeks from now) we will have a catscan that will determine how the destruction of the tumors is progressing. After that, I will either go home, continue more cycles of the same treatments, or begin some different treatment options.

We are having some trouble with the insurance company. Since they have transferred us to Ohio, they have been very unclear about what they're paying and not paying and we have to appeal some of the decisions. We hope this doesn't get into a frustrating mess.

Mary and I got engaged on Friday! We are pretty excited about this and we have set the date in December.

As usual, I will be out of it for a little over a week, with no access to email.

My grandfather is not feeling well at all right now. He has very little energy. My father is still in pain dating back to his surgery. Hopefully some new antibiotics will clear this up.

Please pray for healing for grandpa and Dad. Please pray that this cycle will result in lots of tumor destruction. Please pray that the hospital stay will be tolerable and go quickly. Please pray that my blood counts will be high enough to start chemotherapy on Tuesday. Please pray that Mary and I will continue to pray and keep a positive attitude everyday during the hospital. Please pray for our relationships with doctors, nurses, and other hospital folk. Please pray for Mary as she attempts to figure out the insurance mess.

Thank you all for your prayers and support.

Love,
Andy Schrier

8-2-02

Dear Friends,

My eyes are closed. It is dark anyways. I stumble around with palms outstretched feeling for sensation and feedback. There is a sense of danger here, as though I may be walking into a trap. But, alas, it is just more trees, leading nowhere. I wonder how many times I have touched that tree, looking for my way out, and passed it by, hoping that by touching it, I gained some ground.

When your eyes are closed on a moonlit night, you can still have a general sense of where the moon is. You can't tell how close or how far away it is, or where it is in relationship to anything significant, but you can tell that it is there, beating down on you from the general direction in which it comes. And so, in blind hope, a person in such a predicament will continue to feel around in the general direction of the moon because it is the only reference point they have.

Well I still feel like I'm wandering around in the wardrobe, following a lamppost that faintly glimmers in the eyes-closed perception of my mind, always representing a faint hope that my mad journey will one day end.

As the characters in Narnia also did, I have lost all sense of time in this new world. My perception of the other world that I came from comes only in faint memories, sometimes distorted and very far away. I've been hobbling around in here for so long that I fear what it will be like when I actually return. How will I act, what will I do, what will I say, how will I be different? I'm afraid of returning to my other world, yet I still seek it. Indeed, my only hope is bent on reaching it as soon as possible.

How will I ever describe this world to anybody? Will they believe I was here? Will they care? Yet I want out of this wardrobe more than anything I can imagine. There is also a sense of shock and amazement. I still can't believe I'm here. Every once in a while I pinch myself. Is it really true? There are some days that are very frustrating. What possible good does it do to have me walking around aimlessly in this thing anyways? And I sure can't step out whenever I want to. Nope, I'm trapped here, until the lamppost leads me out. This could be days, weeks, months.

So everyday I wake up, not knowing how many more days it will be until I can leave the wardrobe and this world behind, returning to "normal" life. Somedays I wonder how much more I can take, or if I can take any more at all. But that thought isn't relevant, because I can't control the results of that anyways. I don't have any choice. I can't be anywhere but where I am.

There are two comforts that get me through every day. The first is that I actually have that day to live. The second is that the lamppost really is in charge and could miraculously end this whole journey at any point.

It is both amazing and exhausting to believe in a miracle for one's everyday hope and sense of direction. I don't know that I can say much more about it than that.

My greatest fear is that I will somehow get stuck in this wardrobe, that I will never be able to come out.

Since the results of the last catscan, I have been unable to place my faith for healing in chemotherapy or medicine. At the beginning of the last hospital stay, our doctor informed us that she had consulted with a germ cell tumor expert at the University of Indiana regarding my case. Together they determined that they don't believe that I have germ cell cancer. They now think I have some sort of hepatocellular, or gland-based tumor. This seems like an abnormality, mainly because the tumors have reacted to the germ cell treatment and are under control. So for now, the conclusion they have reached is that I have some sort of hepatocellular cancer and they aren't exactly sure of how we should treat it yet. The next catscan will reveal what tumor damage has been caused during these last two cycles, and based on these results, they will determine whether to continue with my current form of germ cell treatment, or whether to switch to a treatment that is more geared against a hepatocellular tumor.

The next catscan will take place on August 12th, with a conference with the doctor to take place the following day. On August 13th, in that conference, we will review the catscan and decide our next medical moves.

Needless to say, this is disappointing news to us. It is very hard not to know what we are dealing with exactly. It is much harder to be placed under a mystery category than under a category where the doctors know exactly what to do and follow a prescribed regimen for your health.

It is also very hard to wait for news on the catscan. Do we hope and trust that all is simply healed, or should we be more realistic and prepare ourselves for the option that we have more cycles to go? That option seems unbearable. Is it weak faith on our part not to expect a miracle?

Finally, it is difficult to anticipate a possible change of chemotherapy. Although we don't love the treatments I am receiving now, we are used to them. There is a comfort in that which could change when my body is introduced to new drugs and new treatment schedules.

Last, but not least, the doctor is letting me go on vacation with my family this week. Every year we take a trip to the beach in North Carolina. This year I had ruled out the possibility of being able to go, due to the cancer, but they have canceled the Bleomycin treatments for the rest of this cycle due to the switch of diagnosis. Therefore, I don't have any treatments until the week of the 13th. They gave me a growth factor shot that will keep my immune system in good shape while I am gone. This is encouraging. It will give me a whole week to feel normal and fun with my family.

I know the tone of this writing has been considerably more dismal than my others, but I'm trying to be realistic about my feelings. I'm not trying to win sympathy points as much as trying to understand myself and convey my feelings to others. I do this because I know most of you care, and maybe it will help you pray for me. I am well aware that this has become the hardest fight of my life, harder than anything I've endured before. The constant mental battle is ever there, never leaving and sometimes better than others, sometimes worse.

Please pray for the final destruction of tumors during these last few days of the fourth cycle. Please pray for a good and accurate catscan and conference with the oncologist. Please pray for a good vacation. Please pray for our spirits to be rejuvenated. Please pray for my father's pain and my grandfather's chemotherapy.

Thanks to all of you,
Andy Schrier

8-12-02
Dear Friends,

A friend of mine once sent me a quote by C.S. Lewis. I don't know the origin of the quote, but it has since intrigued me and I've never forgotten it. The quote reads: "I believe in God as I believe in the sun; not because I can see it, but because by it I can see all things."

I think this quote intrigues me because I've questioned the existence of God before. I've struggled with doubts about the tangible whereabouts of a being that I can't physically see, yet in which so many people place their faith. I've struggled with the uncertainty that this stirs in my soul, and I've wrestled my way back to a faith in that being, a faith that is totally mine and not reliant on anyone else's.

Throughout this process I've learned the truth of this quote by C.S. Lewis. For some of us it takes believing in the Lord to see his work in our lives. That's not to say that he doesn't work in our lives if we don't believe in him, but that some of us don't have a perspective that will allow our belief system to accept that it is in fact God working within us. In other words, if someone doesn't know the work of a particular artist, one will never recognize the artist's touch that distinguishes that person's art from other paintings. Or, if one doesn't believe in the wind, one can't believe that the wind was responsible for blowing down a tree.

This last week, Mary and I both witnessed tangible evidence of the Lord working in our lives in a powerful way. To us, it was a miracle that we will never forget. The power of the moment was not in being able to physically see God, but to see the things he showed us and to witness his work in our lives in an amazing way.

Last Friday, we journeyed with my family down to the outer banks of North Carolina and sat on a beach for a week. When we left, I was at a pretty bad point. I was sick of being a cancer patient and battling a situational depression that was growing stronger and nastier. It was getting hard for me to be joyful about anything, and I really didn't think I could handle any more cycles of chemotherapy. I felt trapped.

We took two days to travel to the beach. When we arrived at our cottage on Saturday night, Mary and I went for a walk on the beach. We both felt "at the end of our ropes," and that the depression on top of everything else was just too much to deal with. We cried about it for a while and then we prayed. I told God that we needed to hear from him and that we felt as though we couldn't go on. It was a bold prayer, but one that we were compelled to pray. There are few times in my life where a prayer was uttered with such desperation and sincerity of need. And I've never wanted to have God give a booming response so badly in my life.

And it didn't take long to feel, not hear, God's response. On Sunday, the effects of the depression began to melt with the sun and wash away with the waves. I felt much better, and the laughter and conversation of my family helped to pull me out of the slide I had been in. As my mental health improved, and Mary saw positive changes, we both increased in our joy.

As if that wasn't enough, God wanted to make sure we got the message. On Sunday evening, I received an unexpected phone call from my good friend and prayer partner in Grand Rapids. He had felt God's presence urgently directing him to cry and pray for Mary and me as he drove to church that evening. When he got to church he gathered others and led them in prayer for us, and also brought us up as a concern during the service.

After the service, he felt that he had to let us know. So he tracked down our phone number and called to let us know that he didn't know exactly what our needs were or why he had been struck by the notion to pray for us, but that we had been prayed for. I listened as chills ran down my spine. In my entire life, I had never experienced such a profound answer to prayer in such a desperate time of need.

Mary and I experienced a deep wave of awe. God cared enough about us to let us know he had heard our prayer.

But he wasn't done yet. He continued to work on us as the week went on.

The source of my depression was an overwhelming sense of uselessness and boredom. I had been ripped away from my job and many other things I loved, and there was no telling how long it would be until I could resume normal life. My sense of purpose and joy had been eroded by the long months of chemotherapy.

Throughout the week, God spoke to us through a series of messages, including conversations between us and my parents, our own conversations, and our daily devotional time. He reminded us we had been set aside for this time in our lives for a purpose. That purpose, he revealed, was to take lots of time to spend with him everyday, to get to know him in a completely different way. As we brainstormed about it, we realized that this was, in fact, a gift. How often in my busy, "normal" life have I wished for an extended period of quiet time for reading and reflection? How often in my life have I craved to really take meaningful time for such things as prayer and scripture memorization, but been too busy to actually follow through? How often have I desired to bury myself in good books, not worrying about the busyness of life to keep me from finishing them? By the time Friday of the vacation arrived, Mary and I were actually excited about how we would spend our time with God when we returned. We are still excited to see what he will teach us as we spend time everyday in prayer, scripture memorization, singing praises, and thinking about his goodness. My joy has returned. Only God can wipe away depression in a week. Only God can rejuvenate me and give us strength in the midst of a great battle. And only God will see us through. I rejoice and thank him for all of these things.

MEDICAL UPDATE

Tomorrow (Tuesday, August 13) is a huge day. Today I had a catscan which we will find out the results of tomorrow in a meeting with our oncologist. Based on the results of that scan, we will determine which chemotherapy to pursue. I will then be admitted to the hospital later in the afternoon for five days. So, I will be in the hospital until Saturday, and out of communication on email until then. I will probably have my sister write a quick email tomorrow containing any medical information that we learn.

Please pray for my father's continued healing; he is still in a lot of pain. Please pray for my grandfather's strength as he receives his treatments. Please pray for Mary and I, that our spirits will stay strong during the hardest part of the cycle, the hospital stay. Please pray that we will view every day as an opportunity to know God, and that we will be disciplined in our efforts to seek him. Please pray for wisdom for the doctor as she decides which chemotherapy will work the best. Please pray that God will use the chemotherapy to destroy all of the tumor cells. Please pray that my depression will continue to stay away as I focus on God. Please pray for Mary's strength as she walks through this with me.

I thank you all for your prayers, especially in response to my last email. I hope that you can take encouragement from the miracle that God has worked in our lives this last week. I think God intentionally used praying people as part of this miracle to encourage us that prayer is important and that it works. So please don't give up.

Love,
Andy Schrier

9-7-02
Dear Friends,

When in the course of human life, Christians endure suffering, they often turn to the Biblical example of Job for comfort and direction. Job's refusal to turn his back on God, despite the remarkably depressing circumstances of his life, are a shining paradigm to us all. In fact, even most folks who don't profess faith in Jesus Christ know of Job and his trials, and many take comfort and strength from his ordeal. Suffering is a human phenomenon, and misery loves company, so to associate ourselves with others who go through suffering is a natural human response and coping mechanism.

While I love and respect the story of Job, I've come to appreciate another Biblical example of suffering much more. Genesis chapters 37 and 39 through 50 tell us about Joseph, a promising and extremely talented young man, the youngest and favorite son of the patriarch Israel. Joseph's hardships began at the young age of 17 when his brothers sold him into slavery; they despised him because their father favored him, and because he had dreams that indicated that one day he would rule over him. Joseph ended up in Egypt, far from his homeland, while his brothers convinced their father that his youngest son had been killed by a wild animal.

Alone, as a slave in a foreign country, Joseph surely was tempted to give up on life, slip into a depression, blame God, be angry at his brothers, or waste his life away as in servitude, living in a shell of bitterness and hatred. Instead, there is no indication that Joseph gave into any of these temptations; in fact, he made up his mind to make the best of the situation and let God use him. It must have taken a great deal of positive mental energy and a great faith in God to believe that God could indeed have a purpose for Joseph in such a tragic circumstance, especially for a teenager (I guess we don't know for sure that Joseph was still a teenager when he arrived in Egypt, but, for me at least, the strong possibility that he was somehow adds to the story). It is exactly this spirit of Joseph's that I find inspiring.

Like a flower that refuses to wilt, Joseph maintained a positive attitude and worked diligently, allowing all of his talents to be used, and God blessed him. His owner, Potiphar, rewarded Joseph's trustworthiness and abilities by placing Joseph, even as a foreigner, in charge of his entire household.

Tragedy struck again for Joseph, however, when Potiphar's wife falsely accused him of making advances towards her. Potiphar banished his Hebrew slave to prison.

Even after this tragedy, and even in prison, Joseph refused to bow to the lure of discouragement. In a prison that was full of former leaders from Pharaoh's court, Joseph's talents and leadership abilities caught the prison warden's eye. The warden placed Joseph in a position of immense responsibility and authority in the prison. So great was his trust in Joseph that the warden did not pay attention to the decisions and responsibilities that were under Joseph's authority.

It was in prison that God provided deliverance for Joseph. Joseph correctly interpreted the prophetic dreams of two inmates, the former royal cupbearer and chief baker. According to Joseph's interpretation, the cupbearer was restored his position at Pharaoh's side, while the baker was hanged. After two years, Pharaoh had two dreams which none of his advisors could unravel. The cupbearer remembered Joseph and recommended him to Pharaoh. When called before the monarch, Joseph reported that the dreams predicted seven years of prosperity followed by seven years of famine. He then advised that Pharaoh place someone in charge of storing up food during the years of plenty so that there would be food during the years of scarcity. Pharaoh, immediately impressed by Joseph's wisdom, placed Joseph in the very position he had recommended; he became second in command to Pharaoh himself.

In the years that followed, to make the long story short, Joseph stored up enough food during the plentiful years that other nations came to Egypt to buy food during the years of famine. During that time, Joseph's own brothers came to Egypt looking for food, and through that process, the family was reconciled and moved to Egypt, restoring Joseph to his beloved father. Thus, through the tragedy of Joseph being sold into slavery, God provided salvation for all of the Hebrew people from the severe famine.

So why do I prefer the story of Joseph to that of Job? Because I'm amazed by Joseph's courage and strength in the face of his suffering and tragic circumstances. I'm sure Joseph went through moments of doubt, worry, fear, and discouragement, but his perseverance through times of trial enabled him to make the most of his life, and allowed God to work through his life.

Throughout my struggle with cancer, I have found it hard not to give in to feelings of despair, doubting God's faithfulness, fear and discouragement. At times, it has proved difficult to engage in the very things that give me joy and hope, and to cherish the very things that make life worth living. God has challenged me through the story of Joseph to not just persevere through suffering, but also to maintain a positive attitude, take joy in life, and above all, to trust in him for deliverance.

MEDICAL UPDATE

Tomorrow, Saturday September 7th, I will go into the hospital for my sixth round of chemotherapy. We are continuing Cisplatin and Etoposide treatments. As reported by my sister Abby, my last catscan showed very little tumor destruction. However, my tumor marker was down significantly again. The tumor marker is a protein in my bloodstream that is produced by the tumors. Compared to what it was when we started the first cycle, it is approaching zero. This is a very good sign because it means that there is significantly less tumor activity.

One theory that might explain this is that the tumor cells are in fact being destroyed, but are leaving behind masses of scar tissue that are showing up on the catscan. After this cycle, we will do another catscan, and we may perform another test to see if the scar tissue theory is true or partially true. If not, we will probably continue Cisplatin and Etoposide treatments indefinitely.

The depression is very much at bay. I have enjoyed myself during the last three weeks of reading, spending time with Mary and my family, and a wonderful weekend trip to visit friends and church in Grand Rapids. God has been very faithful in helping me keep my thoughts positive. I have finally arrived at the point where I appreciate the loads of extra time I have on my hands. I also have a good bit of energy, and my weight has increased so much that I weigh more now than I did when I was healthy. Time to start exercising.

Mary and I have decided to move back to Grand Rapids in mid-October whether I am in remission or not, mainly because we don't want her employer to hold her job open indefinitely. Also, since I have energy most of the time, I would like to find a job. Obviously, I would need my employer to be somewhat flexible as to my chemotherapy treatments. There may be about one week out of every three or four weeks that I will be unable to work due to the chemo. Ideally, I would like some sort of writing job that would allow me to work a bit more to my own schedule.

So I ask my friends and church family in Grand Rapids who read this to keep their eyes open and please write me if there are any job openings available that would be compatible with my circumstances. Needless to say, we are very excited about this move. It places us near Mary's family, a wonderful church home, a job that Mary loves, and a huge and wonderful support group of loving friends that we were forced to leave. Above all, it will allow us to get on with our lives in as normal a fashion as possible. This is important because we didn't expect that this would take this long, and there is no telling how long the disease and treatments will drag on.

As usual, I will be out of email contact for five days until Wednesday. Thank you all for your prayers, contacts and thoughts.

Love,
Andy Schrier

10-6-02

Dear Friends,

I know it has been a long time since I have written an update, and I'm sorry. I've been struggling a lot lately, mentally and emotionally, and I haven't written or talked to many people.

During the last few weeks, I have encountered a huge flare up of anxiety and depression due to the mental stress of my situation and my family's struggles. But God has been faithful in leading me through this situation through the love of Mary, my family and friends, and through professional and medical help. I am now seeing the light at the end of the tunnel and I am starting to feel like myself again.

Mary and I are happy to be moving back to Grand Rapids this coming weekend (Oct. 11th). We are not completely satisfied with leaving my father and grandfather during their struggles, but we are glad to try to get on with our lives again. We are excited to rejoin our church family, wonderful friends, and Mary's parents. Mary will return to her job, while I will hopefully find a job soon.

Medically, my tumors are under control, but not gone. Catscans have shown very little tumor deterioration, but no progression either. After seeking a second opinion from a national expert on germ cell tumors in Indianapolis, we have learned that my cancer is almost certainly not germ cell, but either pancreatic or liver cancer. Knowing this makes me feel lucky to be alive, as this diagnosis is much less favorable than a germ cell diagnosis.

We have also decided that my body needs a rest after six cycles of chemotherapy. I may resume a different regimen of chemo if and when the disease flares up again, but for now, I am trying to get enrolled in a clinical trial at Wayne State University in Detroit. The trial involves a new drug taken orally every day with very few side effects. It would allow me to rest my body, grow my hair back, live pretty close to normal life, and yet still be doing something about the disease. I hope to secure an appointment at Wayne State this week to see if I qualify for the trial. I have also nailed down an appointment with a new oncologist in Grand Rapids.

While my Grandfather is doing relatively well under new chemo treatments, my Father is really struggling with back pain, kidney function, nausea, and other complications. It is very difficult to watch him suffer through this time, waiting for doctors to find out what is wrong with him.

Please pray for my Father, for a decrease in pain and an elimination of these complicating health factors. Please pray for my Grandfather, that his chemotherapy will be effective and minimal in side effects. Please pray for my anxiety and depression to completely disappear. Please pray for Mary and I as we move to Grand Rapids. Please pray for me to qualify for the clinical trial at Wayne State. Please pray for me to find a decent job.

A special thanks to all of you for your continued support, cards, emails, gifts, visits, prayers, thoughts and phone calls throughout this long battle. Thanks especially to those who we leave behind in Ohio, and we look forward to seeing those of you in Grand Rapids.

Love,
Andy Schrier

10-21-02
Dear Friends,
    Almost everyone of a Christian background has memorized Psalm 23, verse 4, which says, "Yea, though I walk through the valley of the shadow

of death, I will fear no evil." As a young, imaginative kid, I often wondered what King David meant by "the valley of the shadow of death." Was it some nasty place in the writer's homeland where hungry predators roamed, waiting to kill and eat humans?

As I've grown up, I've studied a bit about the land of Israel, including an intense month-long visit four years ago. I've also listened extensively to a series of lectures by Ray Vander Laan, an expert on Jewish background to the Bible. I've even had the privilege to visit the "valley" where David fought with Goliath. In Israel, I learned, a valley is almost always a dry riverbed, called a wadi, that flows out of the central mountain ridge of the country, channeling water either west towards the Mediterranean Sea or East to the Jordan rift valley. These wadis remain dry, harmless and quiet throughout most of the year. But the rainy season or an isolated storm in the mountains can cause a flash flood that cascades without warning down the wadi, destroying everything in its path, and likely killing any animals or humans unlucky enough to be caught unawares at the bottom of the wadi.

When sheep roam through the desert land of Israel, searching for water, they may be inclined to drink from pools of water left at the bottoms of the wadis. What the sheep doesn't know is that drinking from those pools could get them swept away by a flash flood. Therefore, shepherds guide their flocks away from the bottom of the wadi, searching for living water, or still water: water that won't get them killed.

A skilled shepherd may even take his flock of sheep into the wadi if the shepherd knows it is safe, and that no flash floods are coming. As long as the skilled shepherd is with the flocks, keeping an eye out for signs of flooding, the sheep will be safe in the wadi.

In the 23rd Psalm, David clearly compares himself to a sheep and the Lord to his shepherd. In my opinion, "the valley of the shadow of death" is David's reference to the walking along the bottom of the wadi. At any moment his life could be snuffed out by a flash flood, but because he knows that the shepherd is watching, he has no fear.

As sheep in His flock, God sometimes has us walking on the high, safe banks of the wadi, looking for water that is still, quiet, or living. Other times, he will lead us directly into the bottom of the wadi, into the valley of the shadow of death, where, if He were not in charge, we would be washed away.

I've certainly lived most of my life on what I perceive are the comfortable, relatively safe banks of the riverbed. What I have come to realize is that there is a considerable risk in always walking on the banks where death is not imminent. The danger is that of losing perspective, of not realizing one's need for the shepherd.

I've also realized that when you walk in the valley of the shadow of death, at the very bottom of the wadi, you depend on the shepherd for the peace and safety of every moment. Only with the shepherd's guidance can you live without fear and anxiety of turmoil and death.

Right now, God is leading me through a valley where the shadow of death is long, dark, and menacing. Several tumors sit dormant in my liver, threatening at any time to attack again. No one knows when or how. And no one can tell whether or not further treatments will be effective in containing these killers. The prognosis for liver cancer is not good. In fact, I'm glad I don't know what the doctors say the percentages for living should be. The fact is, I don't depend on the limitations that medicine or its percentages might place on my life.

Because I know the shepherd, because I know he leads me through this valley, because I know he controls the real percentages of whether and when I live or die, I have peace. My cup overflows. And most certainly, goodness and love will pursue me with reckless abandon for every day of my life that I have left, be it two months or two hundred years, and I anticipate the rich feast of living with Him in His dwelling for the rest of eternity.

MEDICAL UPDATE

Mary and I have moved back to Grand Rapids. It is wonderful to be back in our church and near our large group of friends and Mary's parents. Right now, I have a lot of energy, and I even played ultimate frisbee yesterday. It is nice to have this break from chemotherapy, and I am eagerly searching for a job. My hair has even started to grow back in the last week.

As I mentioned, I am taking no treatments at all right now. The tumors appear to be dormant, not shrinking, but not growing either. We have met with our new oncologist here in Grand Rapids, Dr. E., and he will keep an eye on the tumors. Dr. E. also thinks that this trial at Wayne State University would be a great thing for me to be enrolled in. I am speaking with a receptionist from that clinical trial today who wants to set me up with an appointment.

Please pray for Mary and I to just enjoy and appreciate the time we have right now without treatment, attempting to live "normal" lives. Please pray for me to get into the clinical trial at Wayne State. Please pray for God to be destroying the tumors even without me receiving treatment. Please pray for me to find a good job, and that I won't be discriminated against because of my illness. Above all, please continue to pray for my Dad. He is still in a lot of pain. Also, please pray for my Grandfather to continue to do well.

Thank you all for your prayers, thoughts, and support.

Love,
Andy Schrier

11-25-02
Dear Friends,

The man named Shimei hurled rocks and insults at King David and his exiled party. He did no real physical harm to David and his men, but his diatribes were aimed a bit more accurately. "You are a man of blood!" he shouted at the King, amongst of tirade of other harmful words. If none of his other ill-intended remarks struck David, certainly this one caught him like a knife in the back.

Some time earlier in his reign, David had aspired to build a Temple in which God would reside. With great intentions in his heart, he probably began to form great ideas and visions about this wonderful temple and how all the world would…and then God told him, "no."

God told David—the shepherd-boy-become King, the man after God's own heart, mighty warrior against Israel's nemesis, the Philistines—God told David that he didn't want him to build a temple. Why? Because he had blood on his hands; he was a man of battle, a warrior, a man of blood.

Imagine saving up for and envisioning the perfect gift for your favorite person, a gift so well-intended that it would last forever. Then imagine that person telling you, "No. You are not to give me this gift because…" Whatever the reason given, you would be devastated.

In spite of God's rejection of David's gift, he delivered the message with a great deal of sensitivity. The Temple would be built, God promised him, by David's son Solomon, who would succeed him on the throne of Israel.

This was no small promise on God's part, and subsequently no small response on David's. If David's ego was hurt by God's statement about him as a "man of blood," he quickly let that hurt go in response to God's generosity. The promise to David insured that his son Solomon would reign, and that a temple would be built, keeping Israel focused on God for yet another generation. This pleased David immensely, and he humbled himself in gratitude to God.

Now we know—from a comfortable distance, when we aren't going through tough times—that God always keeps his promises, even though we may have to take a few significant detours to get there. But it is a little more difficult to trust God to fulfill his promise when the detours start going down treacherous cliffs, up steep mountains, across icy and frigid land, through deserts—anywhere but in the direction of the fulfillment of God's promise. The detours cause some of us to question if God really gave us that promise, or maybe that the terms aren't quite as we remember them. Some of us doubt that God ever spoke at all, or if He's real, or if He isn't just playing some kind of game, with humans as the pieces on the board.

Although there doesn't seem to be record of it in the Bible, I would be willing to bet a sizable amount of change that David went through some of the mental anguish that I described in that last paragraph.

You see, God didn't just fulfill that promise right away for David; He took David—and Israel—on some significant detours before the details of the promise came true. And in those moments, David had to have wondered—any mortal would have to wonder—whether or not God was off His Throne-rocker, or if David was for listening to Him.

The trouble started with Absalom, one of David's many—and most beloved—sons. Before David's death, Absalom declared himself King of Israel, converted enough of David's old faithful followers, and acquired such a significant army that David and those loyal to him had to flee from Jerusalem rather than face death at the hands of the renegade King Absalom. They fled east, into the Judean wilderness where David had run from King Saul. During this flight, David and his men encountered the wrath of Shimei, a relative of the house of Saul.

If I were in David's shoes at the time, I would have seriously questioned God's promise about putting Solomon on the throne. I would have been angry, shaking my fist at God and crying out, "Why, God, won't you do what you promised? How can you fulfill your promise to have Solomon rule and build you a temple when Absalom has seized the throne and seeks the death of his own father?"

Enter Shimei: hurling stones and insults at David, kicking a man while he's down. That one line spoken by Shimei, "You are a man of blood," must have haunted David at the time. Not only was it a reminder of why God didn't want David to build the temple, it was a direct reminder of the promise to have Solomon on the throne and providing the Lord's residence—a promise that, at the time, seemed to crumble before David's very eyes. It's possible that Shimei's comment cut David even deeper; it could have said to David, "You're the king, but God doesn't want you building his house because you've fought too many wars; you're not even worthy of building God a house!" When we are down or depressed, statements like this resonate and echo within us, haunting us and reminding us of our failures and shortcomings. We forget the promises of God, and our inadequacies seem larger than His mighty power.

I don't know how David's attitude held up during this trying time: did he question God's promise? Did he doubt his abilities and blame himself? Did he feel weak, hopeless, and depressed?

It is likely that he did, because when Absalom's troops were defeated, and Absalom himself killed, David could think of nothing but the loss of his son. Joab, the commander of his army, delivered a sharp warning that David needed to shape up and take control of his kingdom before he lost it again.

So King David regrouped himself, and on his march back to Jerusalem to restore his kingdom, he even forgave Shimei. The kingdom was restored to David, and God's promise fulfilled as Solomon eventually succeeded his father and built the Temple.

Six months ago, my Dad received a message from God that we took as a promise for my healing. The promise came from 2 Chronicles 20, when several armies set out to attack Jerusalem. In humility and desperation, King Jehoshaphat gathered his people at the temple and cried out to God for deliverance. He then set out to fight the much larger invasion force, making the tactically suicidal blunder (if God isn't fighting for you, that is!) of placing a group of singing Levites at the front of the army. By the time the Israelites reached the enemy camp, they found that the invading armies had killed each other off, to a man.

My Dad, Mary and I took this as a promise for God's healing, that the invading armies of cancer cells would kill each other off, to a cell. I must admit that I have had trouble trusting God for the fulfillment of this promise through the detours, road blocks, man-eating potholes, and washed-out bridges of the road I've been on. Like King David, I've encountered some resistance, I've faced mountains that looked hopeless, and, like King David, I've need people along the way to challenge me to get back on the right track.

And there's still a bit of the story that isn't quite finished: the fulfillment of the promise. God is always faithful, and he always speaks the truth. Just because the road is tough, just because it may travel through a mine field, just because the road may appear to be going the wrong way—these things don't mean that the road isn't going where God intends.

It is hard to focus on God for the fulfillment of this promise. It is sometimes difficult to muster up the mustard seed of faith needed to believe in His healing power and to wait on Him.

Yet, for the first time in my life, I find myself believing that promise more than ever, and wanting its fulfillment more than ever. As our wedding day "creeps" closer and closer, Mary and I thank God for the energy and strength we have had to focus on our wonderful relationship. But more than anything, we want to be able to stand before God, family, and friends on December 28th and proclaim without a doubt that God has healed me of cancer. It would be an amazing testimony to the Lord's power for Him to heal me while my body is free of anti-cancer drugs and treatments, to declare that though humans are still limited in knowledge, God's power never wanes.

Another Old Testament king, Hezekiah, knew the power of God's healing. When he learned he would die, he cried out to God. God healed him and granted him another 15 years of life.

Well I'm pleading to God for another 50 years of life. I want another 50 years to love my wife, my family and friends, and, above all, to praise God for healing me through whatever means of communication I can. I would like for everyone to join with me in this prayer, not for the glory of Mary and I, but for the glory of the Lord and his mighty power.

How many of us are empty and waiting for the Lord to show himself to us? How many of us are broken and need to see a miracle? How many of us wonder if God even works miracles anymore? I know that sometimes I wonder all of these things.

But now Mary and I approach the Throne of Grace with confidence, boldly asking God for healing before our wedding and before any more medicine is put into my body.

Anyone can pray this prayer; not just Christians and church-goers, not just pastors and elders. God wants to reveal himself to everyone: broken people, hurting people, people who wonder if he exists, people who don't think they're worth anything, people who have no faith in anything, people who wrestle to understand God, people who have told God that he isn't worthy of their worship, people who are afraid to believe in something so amazing. The list could go on.

So no matter who you are or what your faith is, will you join Mary and I in our bold prayer? Will you pour your heart out for God to show His mighty power? Will you ask Him to reveal Himself in this situation? If you have any care for us, will you please ask him for another 50 years for me? Please join us, even if this is the only prayer you have ever dared pray in your life, and then see what the result is.

My medical update is short, thankfully. I'm still holding up well, looking well, and getting my hair back. We are enjoying ourselves very much and checking on the tumors every four weeks. We are still waiting to find out about the Wayne State trial.

Thank you all for your steadfast prayers, thoughts and support.

Love,
Andy Schrier

12-14-02
Dear Friends,

I'm not going to apologize for the length of this email, but it is a lengthy one. You may not want to open it work because it may take you awhile to read I don't want your boss to get mad at you. But I would appreciate it if you would take the time to read it. I think I've been waiting to write this my whole life; it has been an entire lifetime of stuff that God has been teaching me. In short, I feel that I've poured my very soul into this writing. I truly hope and pray that it will point to God and not to me.

Two years ago, God blessed me by sending me on a trip to New York City. I was there for a conference, but I remember more of the city than I do of the conference.

One night, I was trailing my group down Broadway Avenue, seeing the sites and letting the best Chicken Parmesan dinner I had ever tasted settle in my stomach. As I moseyed past the B.B. King Blues Club, a tall man in a long trench coat walked directly out of the club, and straight towards me. I immediately recognized the face, but I was off in dreamland; with a big grin and a nod, the man spoke a friendly "hey" to me as I passed.

"Hey," I said as I continued walking past, but staring back at his highly recognizable face. I was already a crucial 5 feet past him, and he was immediately mobbed by a throng of other admirers and picture-takers as he stepped towards his car. He graciously said a few words and smiled for a few shots before being driven away. Only then did it hit me who had just said "hey" to me: it was none other than Bill Cosby!

I laughed at myself for being a daydreamer. If I had been more alert, all I would have had to do was stop when I first recognized him, put out my hand, and said hello to have met Bill Cosby, one of the coolest and funniest celebrities I could ever hope to run into.

Although the event was quite exciting, I mentally kicked myself a hundred times during the next several days. I had the chance to meet Bill Cosby, but because I had my head in the clouds, I missed my opportunity. It passed me by. The only thought I could console myself with was, "well, at least I know he's real."

That's kind of the attraction with seeing a celebrity; it's that exciting feeling of, "hey, I've seen them on TV," or, "I've listened to his music. That person really is real, in person, not just something the TV producers want me to believe in." To actually get to know that celebrity would be more of a rush, even if it is simply a "hey" or a handshake, or a question about Jello pudding commercials.

As a result of that incident, the rest of the weekend became a hunt for celebrities. We checked every face in hope that we might find a movie star or a musician and be the first annoying tourist to ask for their autograph. Then we would share our stories with other tourists at the conference who would say, "Oh yeah, well we saw Master P!" And then we'd reply, "Yeah, but BILL COSBY! Top that!" And they would sullenly realize that we were right, because everybody knows that nothing tops a Bill Cosby sighting. Except God himself.

Sometimes, in my spiritual life, I've felt like that New York weekend. I run around everywhere looking under rocks and behind every tree, talking to every person, listening to every sermon, looking for a chance sighting of God. Sometimes, after a long period of searching I get frustrated. I think of the U2 song, "I Still Haven't Found What I'm Looking For." I'll cry out to God, frustrated that I can't see him: "God can't you hear me? Where are you and why can't I see you? If you are so powerful, why can't you reveal yourself to me? Don't you want me to believe in you, after all? Don't you want to have a relationship? How can I believe in you if I can't see you or hear you?"

Often what I really want is just a glimpse of God: like Thomas, to see the nail piercings in his hands and feet, or like Moses, who saw a very small glimpse of God's glory as he passed by. Sometimes, ironically, I want to be struck blind, like Paul, and hear God's booming voice in such a way that my life is totally changed and I will never doubt God's presence again. I would bet that 98% of Christians would admit to feeling this way at some point in their lives, if not often, and the other 2% are probably liars or in denial. Yes, there are Christian liars, just as there are many non-Christian truth-tellers.

I'll admit, it is much harder to believe in God than it is to believe in Bill Cosby. But just as I missed my chance at getting to know Bill, some of us miss our chance at getting to know God. We are so busy hunting for God in the places where we expect him to show up that we miss where he has already shown himself. Can I get an Amen? Does anyone else feel that way? I know I sure do.

For example, I could have spent the last six months of my life praying for my Dad's healing from cancer, saying, "God show yourself by healing my Dad; if you really are who you say you are, then you will heal him. And if you don't, its going to be very tough for me to believe in you."

As I dodge the proverbial bolt of lightning for my irreverence, I realize that if I pray that prayer too doggedly, expecting God to only act one way (MY way), I will miss the other messages, the other sightings of God that may be going on. But once I quiet myself, I listen to my Dad's prayers, and I heard God through Dad's pain and suffering and his weak voice: "God, thank you for being Sovereign and in charge. Help us to honor you with this day. May your will be done in our lives."

"Your will be done," where have I heard that before? Oh, yeah, Jesus prayed that in the Garden of Gathsemane (Mark 14:36), when he was "overcome with sorrow to the point of death," (Mark 14:34) and when he sweat blood through his pores in agony (Luke 22:34). Did God have the power to heal him? Certainly; Jesus was God and probably could have healed himself of the anguish. Did God have the ability to stop the course of the Cross? Sure. But did God have a purpose for his son's suffering and death that no one who loved Jesus one earth would have understood at the time? Without a doubt! That is the very hope that our faith is based in.

Jesus . . . my Dad . . . Job . . . "Your will be done, not mine" . . . "Though he slay me, yet I will hope in Him (Job 13:15)" When your body is racked with pain; when your mind falters; when everything you love in this world is right in front of your eyes but your sight is failing; when you might have to leave all of it behind; when your loved ones cry out for healing for you but don't get it; when you can't sleep at night because you wonder when you're going to die; when you watch the one you've committed your earthly life to dry up in your arms with your tears fresh on their face; when you watch bad things happen to good people; when six million of your people are slaughtered by a ruthless dictator; when you have to endure a death that will take on the sins of the world and separate you from the Father—How do you continue to believe in God? More so, How do you continue to love him and trust him? My father did it, Job did it, everybody in Hebrews 11 did it, Jesus Christ did it. How? Why?

Because they saw God in the rocks and trees and landscapes, in the human body, in the stars, in history, in the Bible, in the deep yearning within the deepest parts of their soul, in all the little things in their lives that seemed like coincidences but were too intricately planned to be just chance, because they recognized something deep within them—a God-shaped hole, a natural desire to know that eternal and unchanging being that nagged at the back of their mind all their lives. Above all, they knew and trusted that there was a God who loved them, and whose plan was much more important than theirs, and that the ultimate goal of life on earth was to glorify God, even if it meant while gritting one's teeth through one's afflictions and death. Isn't that called faith? They were sure of what they hoped in, and true to what they believed in, no matter what the circumstances.

And why should we do it? For all these reasons, and because Christ did it for us. Do you remember Jesus' response to Thomas' doubts?: "You believe because you have seen; blessed are those who have not seen and yet have believed." (John 20:29) There's some incredible stuff to learn in that statement to Thomas. Jesus basically told Thomas what Paul wrote to the Roman Christians (Romans 1:18-20): people can see God in creation and hear his voices loud and clear; it is up to people to have faith and believe in God. That belief is a conscious effort to listen to the "right voices," or to "see the right things," that are markers of God, signs of his presence, his stamp upon creation, and proof of his interaction in our lives.

Don't get me wrong: I'm not saying that God doesn't take on the responsibility of meeting us where we're at, or reaching out to us. The problem is that there will always be room for human doubt. As the saying goes: you can lead a horse to water, but you can't make him drink. And, as Abraham told the rich man in hell (see Luke 16:19-31), even if they sent someone back from the dead to his brothers to tell them about the realities of God and eternity, they would not repent if they had not believed in the revelations God had given them on earth. The fact is that God can meet us or show himself to us a hundred million times and we could still walk away doubting that it was God. As a matter of fact, that is basically the theme of the Israelites in the Old Testament. Thankfully, another theme is that he never stops loving us, no matter how much we turn our backs on him.

Amazingly, and yet often, very tragically, God leaves the believing up to us. And that's really the crux of the whole issue. Either God is real or he isn't. Either he is who he is or he isn't. So there it is, choose you this day whom you will serve. It's entirely up to you. I can entertain and even doggedly believe that a charging and snarling rotweiler isn't really there, but that doesn't change the absolute of whether or not he exists or that he's ripping my throat out. In the same way, your beliefs in God, either way won't change the absolute truth of whether he is true or not; nor will mine.

There's an age old problem that philosophers and many other folks have delved into called the Problem of Evil. That term exists because it is very difficult for us humans to understand how a loving and all-powerful God could allow bad things and suffering to take place with his people. Many people have chosen not to believe in God because of this very observance of the world. Countless others have struggled deeply in their faith when they see someone they love suffer. The bottom line is that it takes an extra large step of faith to believe in God, his goodness, and his love for people when these things happen in our lives or to our loved ones.

In my lifelong struggle with the Problem of Evil and other such questions, I've recently been given a huge gift. Do you know what it is?: PAIN AND SUFFERING! That's right: I said it was a huge gift.

Before some of you think I'm off my spiritual rocker, or that the tumors have reached my brain and are affecting my thinking, allow me to make a brief commentary here. Suffering has a way of honing your faith, a way of whittling down what you believe and hope into the bare bones of your being. When suffering and faced with death, you suddenly realize that asking the nagging questions about God's existence, goodness, and love don't really get you anywhere. No matter which way you believe, the absolute is still true: He's either there or He isn't. Choose you this day whom you will serve, even though you can't "prove" it either way. You simply don't have time to waver any more; make your decision now!

Pain and suffering force you to place your beliefs on the line, to hope against all hope that the decision you made was correct. So don't look back, just gather every scrap of faith, jump in deeper, and hold your nose till you can come up for air.

You want a Biblical example? Look at Mark 9. A bunch of people are arguing because the disciples tried unsuccessfully to drive a demon out of a boy. Jesus is angered at their unbelief, and the father of the victimized child shyly asks Jesus for help, that is, IF Jesus can do anything. Jesus responds by saying that everything is possible for those who believe. The father's response (I imagine that he is crying, or that he screams this out of his agony for his son): "I do believe; help me overcome my unbelief!" That prayer is just enough; the father's molecule of faith suddenly bursts into a mustard seed and Jesus heals the son.

It is important to realize that God doesn't heal everyone, nor does he heal everyone who has faith in God that they will be healed. It is an extra step of human faith to believe that God can even be glorified through non-healing circumstances.

Now that I have seen this with my Dad as he crosses the finish line into heaven, I truly believe that God CAN glorify himself through ANY circumstances. My Dad's dogged faith, the way he lives his life, and the way he leaves this world are a tribute to God. Did I pray for my Dad's healing? Yes. Did I believe it would come? Yes. Was I disappointed when it didn't? Yes. Yet is God glorified through my father's suffering and ultimately its end? Yes, indeed!

I'm still praying, religiously, for my own healing. I believe I will be healed. I believe that my work on earth is not finished yet. But I have had to recognize what that means: if God grants my prayer, it is for his glory, not my own. Jesus healed the man born blind because it brought glory to the Father (see John 9:3—keep reading that passage; this is also a great example of people who SAW God's power, but didn't SEE it). I also have to recognize that God will not heal me because I deserve it more than others who ask for healing, or because I have more faith than others. That is just not true.

Finally, I have to say by Jesus' example, "Your will be done, not mine." I admit, this is the hard part. I want to be healed for three reasons, and at different times, I will readily confess, certain reasons are more important than others. These three reasons are 1) my own desire to keep living, 2) the desire not to widow my future wife early in life, 3) and the desire to glorify God through my healing so that my friends and family who are struggling with God over the suffering will find it easier to believe in Him.

Lately, these three reasons have been very mixed up, and the second and third reasons are very related. The bottom line is that I am VERY concerned about the beliefs of my loved ones. I don't want anyone to fall away on account of my situation, or because of ANY suffering. I want God to heal me in such a way that it will be impossible for anyone to doubt Him ever again. I argue with him that because He wants relationships with those people, He MUST heal me to help them overcome their unbelief. But in saying, "Your will, not mine," I have to trust God that Mary, my family, and my friends will be okay. I trust that he will help them overcome their unbelief, no matter what the outcome of my physical health.

My prayer now is that the empty God-shaped holes in peoples' lives, that itch to see him revealed, will be filled to overflowing, no matter what. Of course, I hope beyond all hope, and pray with all intensity that his will includes my healing. Because I believe that he will answer my prayer to fill what is empty, I can accept his will, live or die. Like my father, like Job, like my savior Jesus, I must live every breath of my life in the marvelous hope that I will one day see all my friends and family in heaven.

If by my life or my death I could will each and every one of you to join Job, my father, and my Father there, I would. But I can't. Each one of us must make up our own mind. Choose you this day whom you will serve.

Two weeks from today, Mary and I get married! Hallelujah! We are very excited. I am still feeling well, looking well, and loving life right now. Our move back to GR was one of the best decisions we ever made, though we miss Mom, Dad, and Grandpa very much. I've been working a bit as a free lance writer and editor for Zondervan Publishing, on a wonderful Bible project. I am currently investigating some other opportunities for work to augment that income. We hope to have that all nailed down by the wedding, but God continues to be good to us. We continue to pray for healing before any more medication is put into my body. Merry Christmas to everyone.

We love you,
Andy Schrier

YOU MUST BE AN ANGEL

I've been through the fire and I've felt the pain;
I was burned by the heat, but escaped the flame.
I've been through the river, and I've swum in the deep;
I came close to drowning and the banks were steep.

But you walked beside me when my face hit the ground,
And you stood beside me till I came around.

Whoever walks with me along such a road
Must truly be an angel to carry such a load.

And how can I say thank you for seeing me through?

I'll always be grateful, and I'll always love you.

I've climbed over mountains, been cut by sharp stones;
I lost sight of the path; that was my only way home.

I've suffered the blows from and unwanted hand,
But you stood beside me and helped me to stand.

For only our God could create love so strong;
It's a gift from Heaven to help us along.

Whoever walks with me along such a road
Must truly be an angel to carry such a load.

And how can I say thank you for seeing me through?
I'll always be grateful, and I'll always love you.

2-26-03
Dear friends,

 I'm writing today to bring you all up to speed on my life. I am sorry that I have been so quiet since the wedding. As you can imagine, I've been very caught up with details of family, job, marriage, finances, and other related subjects, that I've neglected the important task of updating the prayer armies. Until the last few weeks, we have not been concerned very much about my health issues.

 To sum it all up, life has never been better. I'm finding that all my fears from obsessive compulsive disorder and depression are just, well, vacant fears. Meanwhile, God has given us a good month or more to just adjust to marriage. Mary is a wonderful woman of God, and our love grows stronger with each passing day.

 Our honeymoon was great: a week in the Smokey Mountains of Gatlinburg Tennessee. Lots of hiking and a new hobby of mine: antique shopping. We found some really cool things for our apartment and just relaxed and rested for a whole week. I recommend the area highly; even though it is touristy, you can find a variety of ways around the tourist traps to some neat hiking, shopping, and antiquing spots.

 We came back to Ohio for a reception in Ohio and immediately found that my Dad had passed away. It was both very sad and very joyful, as everyone came home to Ohio for a few days and a beautiful celebration of Dad's life and love for the Lord. We are pleased with how well Mom seems to be settling in to the life-changing adjustment. In many ways, she feels the loss, but she can also celebrate the wonderful legacy he left to her and the children and grandchildren.

Some of you may not have heard this yet, but my grandfather was granted remission from his leukemia just before the wedding. Understandably, he was embarrassed that it was not Dad or I who was healed. But the family did what I hope was an adequate job of convincing him that we don't get to choose our gifts from God, just accept them. After all, we have been praying for all three healings, not just one.

And, as for my father, I know he is a cancer survivor. That's right; my Dad became a cancer survivor the moment his cancer took his body, his strength, and his wonderful mind. He survived the struggle for the one thing that the devil wanted to take most from him: his faith in God. My Dad survived cancer without letting it take his faith and belief that no matter what happens in life, God is still in charge. My Dad is a cancer survivor.

As for, my last few weeks have been an amazing battle with pain control. As I had been on vicodin for my gas pains since before the wedding, I had been taking it for quite sometime. Unfortunately, it wasn't doing the trick; it wasn't cutting the mustard. My gas pains seemed to get worse, and as I upped the doses, my gas pains got worse.

I found out last week, after a long overdue consult to my original (and wonderful) Gastroenterologist, Dr. A. (not to mention his wonderfully dedicated office staff), that any painkillers related to codine were probably shutting down my bowels and causing more gas pains than they alleviated. On top of that, the nausea was making it difficult to keep my food down, a crucial battle when preparing for my next chemo treatments. Until we heard that news from Dr. A., we had intended to start chemo by the end of that week, if possible. But Mary and I really wanted to get a chance try to get the pain under control, so we switched to a pain control narcotic called Duragesic.

The pain control was effective, but unfortunately, too high. I was dizzy, nauseous, sleepy, and mentally not coherent. After standing (somehow) through a wedding on Saturday, Mary noticed that my breathing had become frightfully slow. She took me to the emergency room on Saturday night. After consulting with some physicians, and a chest ex-ray, they informed us that tumors had spread to the lungs.

All I wanted to do was sleep, so they sent Mary home and kept me for tests. I was quickly awakened at 3 am as they shocked my system with a drug called narcan that was to reverse the effects of the Duragesic. It was the scariest experience of my life. I won't talk about it here.

In any case, by morning I was perked up and free from the effects of the duragesic. Drs. L. and A. decided to keep me in and monitor my effects on Sunday, Monday and Tuesday morning. Monday, my breathing came back to normal, but I was encountering severe pain from bloating in my abdominal region and in my legs due to the fluid they had pumped in my to rehydrate me.

Dr. A. was convinced that most of my bowel pain and bloating was due to the confusion to the colon over the last week with the switches of drugs and the bowel shutdowns.

At this point, we have resumed use of the Duragesic patch at half the original strength. This amount seems to agree much better with my body. I have, however, spent two very painful nights wrestling with bowel pain, bloating, laxative, and the toilet to get my swelling down and more under control.

I am home now. Thanks to those who knew what was going on who were able to visit us or call us. We will now focus on getting this pain managed, and once it is, I think we will start a chemotherapy drug called gemcytabine. I'm not sure if that is the spelling, but it seems to be the recommended form of treatment and should be easy enough on my body to allow me to continue with my part-time job as Fund Developer for Restorer's Inc. and Madison Square Church's outreaches to poverty, including the Hattie Beverly Center tutoring program that I used to direct. Like I said, God has been good. He has been truly amazing to us.

Due to my energy level, length of the email as is, and my creative powers being all used for a sermon/testimony that I will be giving at my Church on the evening of March 9th (Lord willing!) I will not expound on spiritual themes at the moment. I will probably send that word out after it is written and delivered. I will leave you with this poem that I wrote many years ago. It expresses how I have learned that fear is only itself—fear.

Thank you all for your prayers.

Love,
Andy Schrier

REFERENCES

Holy Bible, New International Version. 1984. Grand Rapids: Zondervan House.

Holy Bible: The Message (the Bible in contemparary language). 2005. Colorado Springs, CO: NavPress.

Morris, Lelia, N. Nearer, still nearer, close to my heart. "Nearer, Still Nearer." Public Domain.

Spafford, Horatio G. When peace like a river attendeth my way. "It is Well with My Soul." Public Domain.

Wilcox, David. Let me dive into the water. "Farthest Shore." Big Horizon. CD. 1994.

VACANT FEARS
Where is my God right NOW?

I thought I'd find Him in plateaus of peace
only to find a torrent of anxiety
throwing me back into a gulf so deep
I cannot think or cry or sleep.
Instead, I'm helpless;
I quake with fear
and hope the storm will pass me by
and leave me somehow stronger here.

I don't always find God in the pleasant eye,
nor in the gale of the raging storm,
But when He takes me safe beyond
to yonder solid rock for just a while.
And as I catch—my breath—I smile:
and laugh at myself for vacant fears.